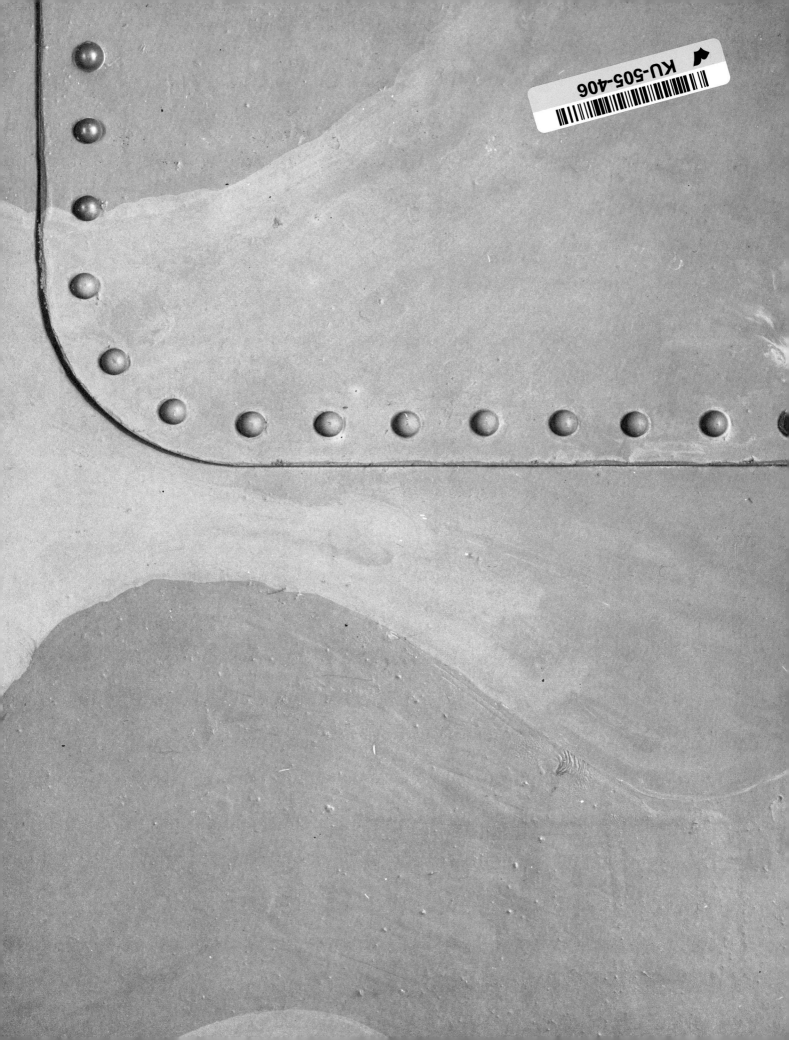

STRATEGY
& TACTICS OF
WAR

Marshall Cavendish

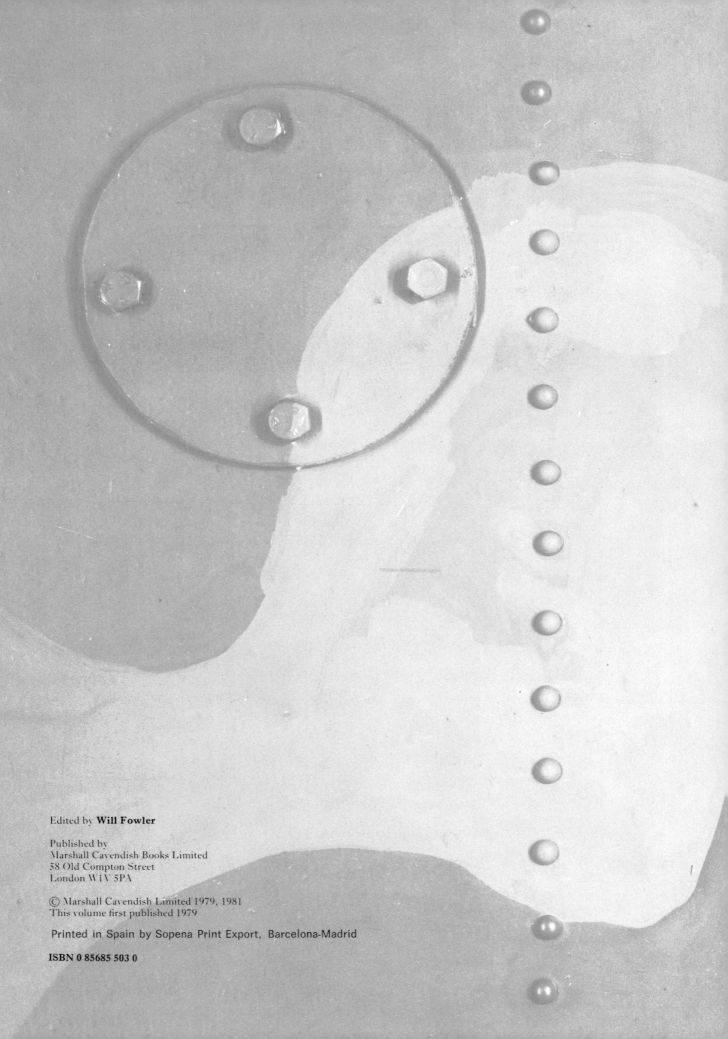

Edited by **Will Fowler**

Published by
Marshall Cavendish Books Limited
58 Old Compton Street
London W1V 5PA

© Marshall Cavendish Limited 1979, 1981
This volume first published 1979

Printed in Spain by Sopena Print Export, Barcelona-Madrid

ISBN 0 85685 503 0

CONTENTS

PICTURE CREDITS

LAND WARFARE

Men and Terrain

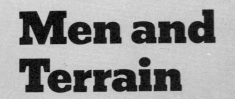

General Ulysses S. Grant in his headquarters during
the American Civil War.

Napoleon at the Battle of Austerlitz (1805) which
he regarded as his greatest victory. Unusually for
him, it was a defensive battle in which he allowed
the Austro-Russian army to attack his right wing
so that he could launch a devastating riposte in
the centre.

Strategy in war is primarily concerned with the formulation of policy. This involves the selection of war aims, the establishment, maintenance or dropping of alliances on a political level, and the application of resources to achieve military objectives. The tactics of a war, on the other hand, are the methods of fighting and manoeuvre employed to secure the immediate objective that is in itself part of the strategic plan. In land fighting, tactics are normally associated with regimental (and below) level tasks, although this can depend on circumstances. The dividing line between strategy and tactics can become extremely blurred.

The strategy of war has, on the whole, not changed radically through the ages, but tactics, with their greater dependence on methods and means have. Glubb Pasha, the British officer who commanded the Arab Legion noted that: While weapons and tactics may change, terrain and men do not. It could, of course, be argued that terrain can and does change and that man himself has altered over the ages, but one cannot really quarrel with the statement: that ground over which action is fought and the motives, fears and hopes of the combatants have remained essentially unchanged, although weapons and their tactical and strategic deployment have altered as a result of human ingenuity. Indeed, advances in civilization could cynically be identified with man's growing capacity to kill ever increasing numbers of people by single, less intensive efforts, and primitiveness with man's inability to kill except at very close range or in hand-to-hand conflict.

The physical nature of war has altered radically within the last 150 years, for technological advances in weaponry have produced massive changes not only in the concept of the battlefield itself, but have also led to a widening of the conflict to include the civilian population on a scale never before realized. A soldier who had fought with Caesar in Gaul, for instance, would have had very little difficulty in recognizing his counterpart in Napoleon's Grand Armée; each fought shoulder-to-shoulder with his comrades in a close-quarter battle. His commanders, too, differed little in their approach, with their reliance on infantry, cavalry and supporting arms. Transplant those soldiers to World War I, however, and neither they nor their commanders would have recognized the battlefield, nor indeed what the commanders were attempting. By World War II, battlefield dispersal had become even more marked, although both Caesar and Napoleon may have been more confident with the strategic direction.

Traditionally armies were organized into four basic groups: infantry, cavalry, artillery and the supporting arms, particularly the commissariat. The three 'teeth arms' – infantry, cavalry, artillery – had their own part to play, but in battle also attempted to operate together to attain victory. The backbone was the infantry, soldiers operating on foot with their own personal weapons, a firearm and bayonet. Their role was the defeat of the enemy infantry by superior firepower or close quarter action, the conquest and occupation of ground. In addition, they gave close support to the artillery and relied on the guns to destroy physically or morally the enemy infantry, artillery and defensive positions (e.g. fortresses). The cavalry existed to fulfil three basic tasks: to reconnoitre and locate the enemy and pass accurate information back to the commander, to provide a screen behind which the main part of the army could advance or retreat without harrassment by the enemy and, finally, to provide shock on the battlefield in the form of the charge. Secondary functions included the picking off of enemy stragglers and the scouring the battlefield of a defeated enemy.

The ability of the three teeth arms to carry out their traditional roles, however, has undergone considerable change during the last century or so, even though the basic definitions remain unaltered.

The ability of commanders to realize a tactical objective has been greatly hampered by developments, particularly in weaponry, that in themselves have ultimately produced strategic stalemate. Whereas, traditionally, commanders attempted in battle either to split an enemy front in the centre, or to turn either or both flanks, or to encircle an enemy and hence achieve the annihilation of all or a part of its army, by the latter part of the nineteenth century, their ability to do so was largely prevented by technological developments. Tactical success could not be turned into decisive strategic success because the cost of that tactical success was too great in lives and time for its rapid exploitation. This happened mainly because offensive strategic development could be offset by a more rapid defensive deployment by an enemy using exactly the same means and tactics. The climax of this situation came about during the First World War and the deadlock of that war necessitated a fresh tactical approach that restored strategic and tactical mobility.

Historians have generally seen the evolution of modern warfare as stemming from the great political and technological changes brought about by the

4

A Union 12-pounder field gun battery preparing to fire during the American Civil War. This was the last war in which muzzle-loading smoothbore artillery predominated on both sides.

French Revolution and Napoleonic Wars (1792–1815), and the Industrial Revolution of the nineteenth century. Certainly the French wars introduced into conflict an element of totality – of national as distinct from dynastic struggle, of victory as opposed to marginal territorial gains – that had been absent from Europe since the end of the wars of religion. The wars in defence of the Revolution had necessitated popular participation in the form of the *levee en masse* to withstand the seasoned professional armies of monarchical Europe. The French wars drained all countries and after Waterloo most countries would have preferred to revert to small professional armies but for certain developments. After her defeat in 1806 Prussia had introduced conscription, the obligation of compulsory military service for men between 17 and 50 years of age. By this means the concept of a standing army based upon conscription in time of peace was introduced.

And ultimately the other major countries of mainland Europe followed Prussia's example.

The consequences of such changes were bound to be profound. With larger armies the demand placed upon society itself – financial, industrial, moral – proportionately increased; politically wars became less manageable in that the mobilization of reserves (the essential prerequisite of a nation in arms) inevitably lessened the chances of avoiding wars and also made less likely the prospect of halting, limiting or ending a war once it had begun because of the emotionalism and sacrifice inherent in a national recourse to arms. In their turn larger armies implied a more ponderous tactical deployment plus the prospect of prolonging wars since the availability of reserves could hold off threatened breakthroughs and deny an enemy any decisive initial success. Such was the influence of the growth in the size of armies, made possible by the synthesis of two

conditions: the first the political will on the part of states to bear the cost and second the development of railways.

Rail was first used for troop transportation in a Prussian exercise in 1846; but the first operational use took place in Italy during the Franco-Austrian war of 1859. Railways simplified the problems of strategic manoeuvrability, supply and the evacuation of wounded, but they were also inflexible and imposed rigidity on their users. While troops arrived at their destination in good condition they were tied to their railhead for supplies and their mobility in the field remained the same as it had been since time began – the speed of animal or human legs. The greater number of troops available meant greater congestion and greater problems of command and control. Thus railways were double edged in effect: they conferred greater strategic mobility (to both sides) but hampered political con-siderations (by the need to mobilize) and reduced strategic and tactical mobility by putting forces into the field too large to be effectively wielded and tactically slower than an enemy's strategic deployment capability. Moreover, if the growing ability to concentrate man-power in a given area more quickly than hitherto was lessening tactical mobility, technological developments, particularly in the fields of chemistry and metallurgy, were adding to the problem. And both problems were compounded by an understandable human failure to appreciate to the full the impact of these changes.

Traditionally the imprecision of weapons dictated the need for close-range fighting between massed infantry (backed by artillery and supported by cavalry) since volume of fire was more important than individual marksmanship. Because of the cumbersome nature of their weapons, the infantry had to load and fire while standing. New weapons, however, altered this situation.

Breech loading, rapid-firing rifles for both infantry and artillery opened effective killing ranges, to the immediate embarrassment of a boot-to-boot cavalry charge. The 50-100m (50-100 yard) ranges of smooth-bore muskets increased fivefold by mid-century, while rapid-firing rifles meant a greater volume of fire could be delivered from a soldier in the prone position. In Prussian hands such rifles proved their worth in Denmark (1864) and Austria (1866) while the French in the Chassepot procured a superior weapon that only their strategic and tactical incompetence negated in the Franco-Prussian war of 1870–71. (Repeating rifles, fed by a magazine, were introduced during the American Civil War though they took some twenty years for general adoption in Europe.) Likewise, in artillery, steel replaced bronze and iron, breech-loading rifles smooth-bore muzzle-loaders, with the result that the ranges of Napoleon's time quadrupled. Moreover quickly firing guns mounted on recoil-absorbing carriages enabled gunners to dispense with re-adjustment after firing, while improved explosives and propellants enabled employment of smaller calibres that by definition retained mobility for the artillery.

These developments among others opened battlefield ranges and upset the balance between the three teeth arms. Infantry firepower could shatter a cavalry charge long before the cavalry could close to effective range and an infantry assault could be similarly broken up by artillery before it closed the target. But infantry, entrenched or behind earthworks, had a large degree of protection against artillery. The American Civil War amply demonstrated that entrenched infantry, backed by artillery, could inflict debilitating losses on an attacker – irrespective of colour of uniform. The power of the defence had for the moment outstripped that of the offence. The lessons that might have been drawn went largely unheeded in Europe, in part because three of the most important wars – in the United States, in South Africa and in Manchuria – were far away and could be dismissed as having little relevance to Europe. Von Moltke the Elder, the Chief of the German General Staff, contemptuously dismissed the notion that American events had lessons for Europe; the British were simply not considered as a military factor; and Manchuria and the Russian experience could be put down to extreme local factors. Certain concessions to reality were made however: the Russian experience in 1877 outside Constantinople showed the necessity of digging in under fire because of

the heavy losses incurred in frontal assault on even field fortifications: infantry tactics necessitated a thinning of an advancing wave into an extended skirmishing line with the fire fight being won at ranges between 400 and 600m (400 and 600 yards). Infantry advanced by waves in depth until fire supremacy had been achieved before the final bayonet assault was launched from ranges of about 100m (100 yards). The British cavalry for a short time after South Africa carried a carbine (a short barrelled rifle) but subsequently reverted to lance and sabre as did other armies who experimented with machine guns to add to the power of their recce forces. But for the most part the lessons were missed: the Polish banker Ivan Bloch, predicted in 1911 that a future major war would be a terrible war of attrition in

Right: The Maxim gun was the first effective machine-gun to be used in action. It is seen here with a British crew during the Boer War in South Africa. Of all weapons in the 20th century the machine-gun has had the greatest impact on land and air warfare. Below: An 18-pounder with its British crew during the First World War.

which defence would predominate. Such a war would be a lingering trial of strength, involving all the physical and moral resources of the combatants, only to be resolved when the strain proved too great for one of the sides. Most people tended to dismiss such observations. The reality of war was distant in Europe by the turn of the century: nationalist propaganda, in all countries, in stressing what were regarded as national traits, came to place moral factors as the supreme consideration in the pursuit of victory. Elan and the imposition of moral authority, a heady and romantic concoction assumed a greater importance than detailed consideration of the effectiveness of defensive machine guns. The process of disillusionment was to take four bloody years to complete.

Trench Deadlock

The trenches in World War I: a British sergeant peers over the parapet while his comrades 'stand down'.

Even before World War I began, it was apparent that the rate of technological advance was exceeding man's ability to understand it – and nowhere was that more starkly illustrated than in the military. The men who led the armies of all the combatants in World War I had been fashioned by a quite different era and they were unable to cope with a total war which produced such tactical innovations as trench warfare, the use of aircraft and the introduction of the tank – all of which destroyed the traditional concept of battle procedure. In fairness to them, it must be said that matters were simply beyond their competence and they had to deal with problems for which their experience and training had not equipped them, though in all honesty, it must be admitted that few displayed much imagination in tackling them. Nevertheless, they were the best available at the time and in certain theatres – Mesopotamia, Palestine, the Balkans – some acquitted themselves well; even on the Eastern Front certain Russian generals, such as Brusilov, and Conrad of Austro-Hungary displayed abilities that were not attended by commensurate success. But these, in the end, were not the decisive fronts. It was the Western Front, a line which ran through Belgium, France and Germany from the English Channel to Switzerland, that was so vital it is still virtually synonymous with World War I. A picture that is painted of shattered trees, shell-holes filled with scum-covered, cordite-reeking water, being drunk to the dregs by decomposing corpses, a murdered strip of nature hundreds of miles long that engulfed the greatest hopes of Europe: World War I evokes deadlock, stalemate. This is not false but neither is it wholly accurate. In the opening weeks of the war, in the last eight months of the war in the West, on fronts other than in the West (particularly in Russia and the Balkans) there was movement, much movement, that seemed to be discounted or ignored.

In 1918 the Central Powers (Austro-Hungary, Germany, Turkey and Bulgaria) were defeated by the Allies (primarily France, Belgium, Britain and the USA) when the former became convinced that despite their sacrifices in four years of war they could not secure through a military victory gains that could justify their losses. By the time this conviction became general the vaunted German offensives of the spring and summer, designed to secure victory, had been held and thrown back. The German Army, while still intact and on foreign soil at nearly every point, was in retreat in the West and facing defeat if not in 1918 then certainly in 1919. The Central Powers had been held together by hopes of German victory: they were broken, morally, when that victory proved elusive. They were beaten not because of superior Allied strategy or tactics but because their means of waging war, physical and psychological, had been exhausted. War had become siege warfare conducted by nations: it had become total and in doing so the military effort had become only a part of the strength – albeit possibly the most important single ingredient – that could not survive when hope had gone and these other ingredients, financial, industrial, economic, agricultural, psychological had been bankrupted. By the time of the armistice, stark famine stalked central Europe; epidemics raged; domestic heating was virtually non-existant. The Central Powers broke as a result of the cumulative strain from two sources that brought the Allies their victory: the superior geographical position of the Allies isolated them from the outside world, thus severing the trade in food and raw materials that could have sustained them, and secondly, the increasing industrial and human resources the Allies could bring to bear on the battlefield. In the end Britain and France almost broke before the Germans; but for the Americans they might have. But for all that, victory went to the side with the greater pool of killable manpower and superior economic resources.

That such a debilitating struggle had to be endured – that the Allies could not win more economically and the Germans not win at all – was the result of strategic failure and tactical stalemate on both sides. Neither side, either in its opening strategic deployment and manoeuvre or in its subsequent tactical undertakings, could impose its will on the enemy. The essential problem – at least for the Allies – was tactical for most of the war. Once trench warfare established itself, the superiority of defence over attack, as Bloch foresaw, meant that even though a defender's front might be broken, the attacker – hampered by losses, exhaustion and the problem of moving supplies and reinforcements into a breach – could not prevent the defence resealing the break in the front by the timely disposal of reserves, brought up by rail. This was the essential problem that all commanders, irrespective of nationality, faced in the war: the momentum of an assault based on human capability could not be sustained in the face of the strategic mobility conferred by railways on the defender.

That such a situation had arisen was the result of the

failure of both sides to achieve a decisive outcome in the opening weeks of the war. In part, these failures stemmed from human frailty and incompetence, in part from the lack of realism on the part of the war plans themselves, in part from insuperable tactical problems and in part from the impracticability of forcing a result given the growth of armies and a nation's durability.

Under the terms of the Schlieffen Plan (the German plan of campaign for a war against both France and Russia), the Germans stood on the defence in the East and on their left flank in the West, while four armies struck through Belgium, Luxembourg and Northern France to try to encircle and then annihilate the French field armies in eastern France against the anvil formed by their left flank. This was to be achieved in six weeks – the time between the start and completion of Russian mobilization – with the German Army then entraining to deal with the Tsarist threat. The French plan for the invasion and clearing of German-occupied Alsace-Lorraine was torn to shreds; the Russian plan for the invasion and clearing of Eastern Prussia similarly fell to pieces; and the Austro-Hungarians scarcely had any worthwhile plans. But it was the failure of the Schlieffen Plan that really decided the nature of the war. As the Germans marched into France, barely delayed by the greatest fortress system in Europe at Liège that was destroyed by howitzers, they were checked by Anglo-French thrusts on their right flank from Paris and from the front at the Marne. A steadier nerve might have saved the day had the Germans tried to envelope the Marne thrust between their Ist and IInd Armies, but in fact they were pushed

back to the Aisne – a line of exhaustion for all three armies. The Schlieffen Plan failed mainly because it was too ambitious. It set for its soldiers (many of whom were reserves) the task of marching and fighting some 600 miles in a line of advance that took them across a whole series of river barriers running across the line of march and then, at the end of a tenuous line of communication served only by horse-drawn transport and exposed to attack on their unguarded flanks, fight a battle against an enemy not necessarily shaken by previous defeat. Moreover the Germans had no answer to the problem of Paris since they lacked the strength and time to take it; nor did they have an answer to the French advantage of lateral and radial railways to redeploy to meet an invasion limited by the speed and endurance of feet.

Thus the front stabilized along the Aisne and the south when the French Ist and IInd Armies managed to hold to the Verdun-Toul and Epinal-Belfort fortress lines after their disastrous defeat in Lorraine. (This attack, characterized by colour and bravery rather than any appreciation of military reality, had seen the French infantry in blue jackets and red trousers and the cavalry in breast plates and plumes attacking en masse behind bands and flags as if nothing had happened in 99 years.) As the front stabilized and neither side achieved a rupture of the enemy line, both sought the traditional strategic and tactical recourse – the turning of the open flank to the north in an effort to envelope the enemy flank. But with both sides attempting this simultaneously outflanking proved elusive and the sea was reached before either side gained the initiative. Once on the sea the front line solidified.

On the Eastern Front devastating success attended the initial Russian assault on the ramshackle Austro-Hungarian armies around Lemberg, but a premature move against the German positions was launched in East Prussia. This was attempted in order to clear the right flank preparatory to a thrust from Russian Poland towards Berlin but the attack by two armies designed to encircle the German army in the region was very badly scouted and even more ineptly co-ordinated. By masterly improvisation the Germans were able to use their central position and excellent rail system in the area to deal with the separated and diverging Russian armies in turn. The Russian Army was annihilated at Tannenberg, the French Army routed at the Masurian Lakes. But in the east, given the great distances and space and the lack of any major strategic objectives for which the Russians would have to fight or against which they could be trapped, the Germans lacked the means of securing a speedy and decisive success. Despite the demands of the Western Front the Germans in time were able to push the Russians out of the industrialized Baltic coast, Poland and Western Russia, inflicting unheard of losses on the Russian Army until in 1917 the Imperial structure collapsed. Russian victories over Turkey and Austria-Hungary (nations even less industrialized than herself) availed her nothing in her conflict with her industrial superior, Germany. Her overall lack of industry and loss of many of the great centres she had, the disruption of her railways and food distribution centres, her lack of ports, her weak social system ensured that with defeat Russia slithered into revolutionary chaos (as did Austria-Hungary and, to a lesser extent, Turkey). By this time, however, the

Left: A British 18-pounder, unsuitable for trench warfare and no protection against the first armoured attacks. Right: A German officer stands by his dramatically painted tank, his chain mail mask is a protection against shell splinters. Below: A German tank. The Germans were slower to adopt the armoured fighting vehicle in the First World War, but made up for this during the Second.

German opportunity for victory had passed. Strategically, she had never fully committed herself to forcing the issue by concentrating either in the West or the East, although with the enfeeblement of Russia she was able to redeploy to the West. But by that time the ultimate defeat had been secured, by her exhaustion, the arrival of the Americans and the tenacity of the British defence, when the Germans launched their offensive in the spring of 1918.

Strategy, for the British and the French, was largely determined by two considerations: Firstly, there was the belief that Germany could only be beaten by defeating her armies in the field; secondly, there was the inescapable reality of the German Army deep inside France itself. When fighting on one's own territory military logic cannot have the final say. Thus while attempts to outflank Germany were considered and implemented by the strategic use of exterior lines of communication in such theatres as the Dardanelles, Salonika, Palestine and Mesopotamia, the Western allies of necessity always found in the Western Front the main theatre for their offensive operations. Having an enemy on home territory the French (and their allies) had to attack. The Germans, for the most part, stood on the defence in the West, making only a minor

An Austrian howitzer in travelling position. These guns destroyed the Belgian forts with their heavy shells at the beginning of the First World War.

attack at Ypres in 1915, a major assault that quickly mushroomed uncontrollably at Verdun in 1916 and the final spring/summer assaults of 1918.

At the end of 1914 neither side fully appreciated the permanency of trench warfare. Wishful thinking convinced many that, with the spring, extra artillery, infantry and determination, the front could be breached and fluid fighting restored. Mobility on any scale did not come to the Western Front until 1918 when the British found themselves in retreat. Although many attempts were made to secure a permanent breach, none succeeded. The initial tactical response to the deadlock tended to be attempts by artillery to blast a way through the enemy position. Given the power of infantry firepower in defence, the attackers sought to provide greater artillery support for the infantry; for the British in particular, battles were seen as progressive advances under a series of detailed artillery fire plans that would either smash through or progressively weaken the enemy to the point when collapse would occur under the strain of the next attack. At Neuve Chapelle in 1915 the British attack opened with a short but intensive artillery assault, but on too narrow a front for an adequate breach to be effected. While initial objectives and the mastery of the first German trenches were being achieved liaison between infantry and artillery collapsed. The artillery was not therefore able to switch to fresh targets effectively, and command of units engaged by commanders virtually ceased to exist. The technology and techniques of the day were not adequate to cope with control of battle.

The second such assault at Aubers in May 1915 was even less successful even though artillery was more plentiful and used in a creeping barrage ahead of the advancing infantry.

During the course of the war British attacks opened by artillery bombardments increased in intensity and duration though after August 1918 they reverted, with success, to short duration bombardment. The extreme length of duration – deemed necessary to cut barbed wire defences and knock out known machine gun positions – in fact proved counter-productive. High explosive cratered the ground, making advance more difficult; at Ypres in 1917 advance was all but impossible because the fire destroyed the drainage system of the low lying area. Such bombardments also telegraphed intentions to the enemy, enabling him to deploy his reinforcements close enough to prevent a breach or to counter-attack but out of range of the initial assault. Moreover, the Germans evolved a defensive system in depth. Thick barbed wire defences were deployed in some areas while breast works in places 10m (30 feet) deep were equipped with underground shelters where troops could escape the worst of the artillery bombardment. On accosions these shelters could house a full battalion and be used as jumping off points for the assault. The Germans also thinned out their forces in the front line with the major part of their strength in the second or third trench lines: wherever possible these lines were sited on the reverse slope of a hill away from direct artillery observation.

Such defensive arrangements all but negated any tactical innovation, and certainly invalidated any attempt simply to blast a way through by artillery assault. Even the creeping barrage – designed to keep down the heads of the defenders until the infantry reached their position and to prevent the forward

deployment of the reserves by the defence – could not secure an economical advantage, while the damage to terrain by shell fire has already been noted. There was another type of shell that had the supreme advantage that it left the ground largely intact, at the same time having a wider area effect of quite long duration: the gas shell. Properly used – en masse and with ingredients against which the defender had no protection – gas might have produced tactical success leading to strategic success, but the German use of chlorine at Ypres in 1915 and phosgene at Verdun failed because of their faulty tactical employment. The frontages on which the chemicals were used were too narrow and at Verdun the Germans failed to risk all on phosgene and instead, after knocking out most of the French artillery, reverted to high explosives, thereby allowing the French to recover in time to meet the assault. Attacking troops, moreover, showed some understandable reluctance to move too closely into infected areas. From being a potentially war-winning weapon gas was relegated to being an additional endurance for the already over-laden infantry.

Infantry, weapons and tactics also altered considerably during the course of the war. Just as the shovel proved as essential as the rifle to the infantryman, trench warfare demanded the use of grenades, revolvers, pistols and nailed clubs for restricted close quarter fighting. Such fighting demanded – and produced – light weapons with high rates of fire (machine pistol) and weapons capable of clearing strong points (the flame thrower). Tactically it was left to the Germans to provide innovations. In the opening assault at Verdun in February 1916 the Germans employed infiltration tactics whereby assaulting infantry dispensed with any notion of an advancing skirmishing line and, operating in small groups utilizing cover and shell holes, infil-

trated a defensive position. As later refined in the 1918 assaults these tactics, based on covering fire to pin the enemy while the attacking force moved to the flank to carry out the destruction of the target, sought to exploit gaps in the defence. Attacking units were trained not to tackle points of resistance but to try to break through to the enemy artillery, leaving unreduced positions in their rear for the attention of follow-up units. Emphasis was placed on speed and momentum and such formations – known as storm troops – were equipped with grenades, light machine guns, light trench mortars and flame-throwers. The follow-up units (battle units) were more heavily equipped in that they had sections of artillery and trench mortars, plus engineers and supply troops. Their task was to reduce the points the initial wave left and to hold ground against the inevitable counter-attack, but they were also expected to take over the advance on storm troop exhaustion and to exploit enemy weaknesses. If the battle units failed to reduce the positions, these were to be left to heavier units with larger artillery following in the wake. The whole emphasis of these tactics was on speed and exploitation – trying to fight in the gaps where the enemy was not: and with reserves being fed into the points of least resistance, rather than the most stubborn.

The employment of these tactics – backed by meticulous artillery preparation to ensure surprise – by the Germans in their assault of March 1918 met with some local success. The British Fifth Army was all but destroyed on the Somme and a maximum penetration achieved; on May 27 the Germans advanced from their start lines on the Chemin des Dames. But tactical success was dearly bought: in the northern sector of the Fifth Army where mist did not hamper defence, ingenuity and bravery availed the attackers nothing. Caught in the open the infantry were cut down as

Right: A British soldier on guard in a captured German trench. His comrade is asleep wrapped in a ground sheet cape. Below: The terror of the trenches, a German sniper with an NCO spotting with binoculars, looks for a suitable target. Sniping needed patience and a ruthless temperament.

effectively as had they been in column: infantry itself could not provide a break through. Exhaustion, too narrow frontages of break through, the inevitability of a flanking machine gun pegging back the wings of the assault, the problem of getting the reserves to the right place at the right time to exploit a situation efficiently were insuperable tactical barriers. Strategically, there were other factors. However fast the storm troopers moved it was still with the speed of feet: defenders could move (strategically) by rail. They could throw down units in front of the advance to buy time to secure a rear defence line with fresh, unshaken troops. Any advance, moreover, left an numerically and psychologically weakened force holding a longer front and a tract of wrecked ground, across which it had to be supplied.

The only possible way a breach could have been opened and maintained would have been through some form of mechanized weapon. Such a weapon could have been an aircraft of sufficient endurance and bomb load to wreak havoc with a defender's communications and thereby exhaust and disorganize reserves. Alternatively, a land weapon of sufficient mechanical reliability, range and speed to take it through a defended zone into open country could also have provided the key. Technology of the day could not provide such reliable machines,

but it did provide the machines themselves, and their performance could only improve.

In its initial employment the tank was not cast in a role of deep penetration. It was used to crush barbed wire defences and assist the infantry in overcoming the enemy defence lines. At Cambrai (November 1917), after tanks had floundered on the Somme (1916) for want of numbers and at Ypres (1917) similarly, in the mud, the British Tank Corps drew up elaborate tactics to ensure infantry/armour co-ordination in order to open and maintain a breach. The attack was difficult

An infantry assault in World War I; a British officer leads his men 'over the top' from their front line trenches.

because the sector of attack was one of the strongest defensive positions in the German line and the trenches were too wide for the tanks to cross. The latter problem was overcome by deploying sections of three tanks each topped by a large fascine of brushwood. The lead tank was to crush the barbed wire and on reaching the enemy line move to the left and shoot up the enemy infantry; the left tank of the 'main body' was to move to the trench, drop its fascine and then cross, moving left to assist the process of trench clearing; the remaining tank was to cross the fascine and moved to the second trench line, drop its fascine and thus allow the original lead tank to move to the third line, fascine still unused. Thus it was hoped that a systematic clearing of trenches could be achieved without many infantry losses. Infantry were deployed, a platoon to each tank, following close behind in single file. One platoon was committed to marking routes through the wire, another the clearing of points of resistance, the last the holding of captured trenches. Behind this force came specialized tanks, some with supplies, others with grappling hooks intended to tear open the wire defences and thus allow cavalry egress because the cavalry was, hopefully, the means of deep penetration.

Cambrai did not succeed in making and sustaining the breach and indeed the battle, which began very well for the British, petered out indecisively. Responsibility for this largely rests on certain of the commanders involved but there is no ignoring the fact that the tanks were not adequate enough to make the break. At Cambrai 474 tanks were committed: 195 were intact at the end of the day though only 65 had been lost to enemy action. At Amiens on August 8, 1918 only 145 tanks were available for action after one day of fighting from an initial strength of 508. Most tanks were out of action because of mechanical problems: crews, too, were utterly exhausted by action in temperatures of 40°C (100°F) and badly affected by cordite and petrol (gasolene) fumes. Had more tanks been available in either of these actions for the second day, a breakthrough may have been achieved. The cavalry amply demonstrated its inability to exploit a breach but there was the prospect of light tanks and armoured cars filling this role. At Amiens 'Whippets' (light tanks capable of 13 kms/hr) and armoured cars more capable of getting into the German defences and savaging

supply columns headquarters and reserves were employed. This was a foretaste of what could happen once numbers and reliability could be assured, speeds raised and communications improved – but in World War I technology could not reach such levels.

Nevertheless, while the strategic and tactical deadlock of the war had necessitated a fresh tactical approach but had failed to provide one, the developments had provided the ingredients for mobile war in future. The tank, new infantry tactics and improved artillery techniques indicated immediate evolvement toward new concepts in land warfare. In addition Verdun (February-December 1916), showed that an army could be supplied solely by road transport if a railway was not available; the Battle of the Marne (1914) showed that an army could be moved strategically by motor transport if necessary. Admittedly in 1914 the distances involved were not great and at Verdun the front was mainly fixed, but the points were not invalidated for these reasons. Given the primitiveness and paucity of motor transport, the French achievements on these occasions were little short of miraculous. Moreover, aircraft emerged as a promising method of interdiction – the severing of the enemy's communications with a threatened area. In this role they could act as long-range artillery, the effectiveness of which was bound to grow as bomb loads increased. Larger loads also opened the possibility of using aircraft to supply units in the advance to growing effect; the British in fact dropped supplies by air to their forces on the Somme in August 1918. And before that they had already used aircraft for a similar purpose when, in one of the most imaginative (and underhand) coups of the war, prior to the start of the third battle for Gaza in 1917, they had dropped cigarettes and safe passes to the British lines on the Turkish positions. The cigarettes contained opium, a fact believed to be not unrelated to the relatively light losses incurred in the attack. The whole of the elaborate deception and security measures effected in this battle proved devastatingly effective and a stark contrast to most operations on the Western Front.

The legacy of World War I provided all the combatants with food for thought. All were agreed that a future war could never be fought in the manner of 1914–1918.

Triumph and Defeat

U.S Marines hunch behind a Browning water cooled machine-gun during the invasion of a Japanese held island in the Second World War.

In the search for a fresh tactical concept that could restore battlefield mobility after World War I, the British took the lead and retained it until the mid-thirties. Even before the end of the war one of the leading personalities in the Tank Corps, Major J. F. C. Fuller, produced a plan of campaign (usually simply called Plan 1919) that, when modified and circulated, caused intense debate. Fuller envisaged an attack on a ninety-mile front – against an enemy forewarned in order to bring more of his forces into the battle area for the purpose of ensuring their destruction. The plan was to use concentrations of medium tanks to sweep through the defensive zones to attack headquarters in the primary defensive zone and thereafter to fan out to attack other headquarters and areas of concentration and communication. The aim was to destroy the nervous system of the enemy, to deny him the means of tactical response. In this, the contribution of air power in a systematic interdiction role against supply and road centres was vital. For the land side of the operation Fuller envisaged some 2400 medium tanks for the assault. With the defender slipping into chaos as a result of his flanks being pierced and the medium tanks wrecking his lines of command and control, frontal assault by some 2592 heavy tanks, motorized infantry and artillery would be pushed through into the second tactical zone, thus accentuating the disintegration of the defence and leaving the enemy open to defeat.

Leaving aside the twin points that Germany sued for peace and thus avoided the fate Fuller had planned for her, and that the medium tanks did not fulfill their design specifications, Plan 1919 was imaginative and contentious. Equally when Fuller suggested that a new division could have twelve infantry battalions, each with a tank company, four battalions of horse-drawn and two companies of mechanized medium artillery and a mixed brigade of two cavalry and one armoured battalions, there were many traditionalists who opposed him. The greatest deterrent to adoption of his ideas, however, was the cut-back in the armed services after the war, of money and with it initiative and enthusiasm. It was not until 1927 that experiments were conducted with armoured forces on the scale and in the manner foreseen by Fuller. By that time, however, he had made a convert of an influential military correspondent, Captain B. H. Liddell Hart. The latter had devised a concept of infantry attack along a whole front to seek out the enemy weak spots and then erupt through them in 'an expanding torrent.' Fuller convinced Liddell Hart that infantry could not overcome tanks and that only tanks could provide the speed necessary for such a concept to have any chance of success. Liddell Hart was a far more tactful exponent of this concept than the prickly, abrasive Fuller though it was Fuller's stock that stood the higher among such people as de Gaulle in France and Guderian in Germany – two of many strategists outside Britain who carefully followed British writings and developments at this time.

The experiments of 1927 proved quite satisfactory for the armoured formations, but the forces established for such trials suffered from continual disbanding and re-establishing until 1934 when the tanks were set up on a permanent basis. By that time, moreover, British tanks led the world in communicating through radio sets, and the 1931 trials introduced for the first time a tank formation being effectively and immediately controlled by a single man, via radio. This was of vital importance since it would allow a very rapid reaction to events, such as a swift shift of force and direction of attack, and thus would fully utilize assets of mobility and shock both to exploit and to counter-attack.

Such developments tended to pass the French by. For France, security meant safety against defeat, not the prevention of war. She was secure against defeat through her alliances – with Belgium, Poland, Czechoslovakia and Russia and her understandings with Rumania and Yugoslavia – and through her overwhelming superiority over Germany by virtue of the numerical size and reputation of her army, particularly the infantry. Politically and strategically, however, she could never resolve the question of whether her alliances and understandings were sources of aid or commitments to be honoured. The ambiguity became apparent in the thirties as Hitler increasingly demonstrated that France's alliance system worked just as long as there were no threats to it. Strategy cannot be divorced from political will and in the twenties and thirties the French were victims of sapped and ever weakening determination. The full extent of her cripplingly high losses in World War I were increasingly felt, and she came to be dominated by two considerations: firstly, military theory stressed that the decisive arm in battle was the infantry, with the result that tank development and experimentation were geared to infantry tactics in the World War I manner. (As a result French tank evolution, though technically

sophisticated and novel in many ways, tended to be far slower and more limited than in other countries.) Secondly, France was hypnotized by the way in which the great Verdun fortresses had resisted months of attack and had held the German assault in 1916. In the thirties, convinced of the power of defence over attack and determined not to expose their manpower to the conditions of World War I ever again, the French applied themselves to building a system of permanent defences against which the Germans could batter themselves into exhaustion. The result was the Maginot Line a masterpiece of military engineering as far as it went – which was not far enough. The Line consisted of subterranean positions where units could live, exercise, feed, be hospitalized and fight in air-conditioned surroundings. Ground approaches to the Line from the enemy side were covered with obstacles and bunkers with uninterrupted fields of fire. These positions backed by massive gun emplacements and observation posts and the individual positions, were sited in order to assure mutual support from similar flanking emplacements. Though the Maginot Line was emulated (and in some places even surpassed) by the Czechs in the Sudetanland and the Soviets in the area between the Baltic and the Pripet Marshes, neither the Czechs nor the Soviets came to regard their defensive positions in the same manner as the French. The true aim of fortresses, the provision of time for the defender and the release of large formations for other under-takings, came to be relegated by the French to minor considerations when set against the feeling of security engendered by the line itself. In building the Maginot Line the French implicitly abandoned her eastern allies and any pretence of offensive action, even though the French Army manual of 1939 laid stress upon offensive action. This, however, could not undo the years of complacency and in any case envisaged an offensive strictly along World War I lines, namely a slow, deliberate advance by armour and infantry in mutual support under overwhelming artillery cover.

The Soviet Union, one might have imagined, would have been in the vanguard of change, given the nature of her revolutionary government, but in fact while she did experiment in the inter-war period her military doctrines were ultimately old-fashioned and conventional. Soviet strategic problems in the defence of the USSR against a western attack were immense. The Pripet Marshes split any attacking force but also divided the defending Red Army into two quite

separate wings. Since these were served by different rail systems, covered different but equally important areas – Moscow and Leningrad in the north, the Ukraine and Donetz in the south – and since there was no means of rapid or easy movement between the two sectors, there was little real opportunity for close co-operation between the two wings of the defence. For the most part Soviet strategic plans involved a light defensive stance in the north – backed after 1936 by the Stalin Line which, however, was never continuous – and deployment in strength in the south, ready, if all went well, for offensive operations into the Balkans. The whole problem was made worse by the huge frontages: almost by definition the great distances involved meant that they could not be strong everywhere and that the fronts had to have gaps. The Soviets did envisage aggressive action and by 1941 had thirty-nine tank divisions, but these were not grouped together but diluted in support of the infantry though separate from the latter who had their own tank and artillery units. The Soviet posture was thus that of the traditional Russian steamroller, updated with modern equipment. There was much evidence to support such deployment. In Spain, the Soviets had supported the Republic and had seen balanced forces of infantry, armour and artillery exert consistent pressure on defensive positions to the point that the defence in all cases broke – most notably at Bilbao and on the Ebro. In actions when tanks operated without direct infantry and artillery support – particularly in exploitation – little success had been achieved. In the bloody encounter with the Japanese in August 1939 at Khalkin Ghol in Mongolia it was the same tactical combination – plus a lack of squeamishness about casualties – that brought the Red Army victory, just as it did in the 1939–40 Winter War against Finland. While such tactics proved adequate in these circumstances they proved totally inadequate in the encounter with the one nation that based an offensive doctrine on the developments in armoured warfare that had taken place after World War I. That country was Germany.

German doctrine, strategically, was characterized by

ruthless and vehement action conducted at great pace against an enemy's command and communications system. It aimed, through overwhelming concentration of force, particularly armour, to penetrate an enemy front and then to encircle and annihilate a surrounded enemy before he had time either to withdraw or mount a counter-attack. This form of warfare, called after its German name *Blitzkrieg* (lightning war), was based on the writings of Fuller and Liddell Hart but it had been left to a small group of enthusiasts in the German Army and the demonic genius of Hitler to overcome the prejudices and reservations of most of the German Army for its general adoption. *Blitzkrieg* envisaged a broad frontal attack in order that the enemy front should be gripped, thereby ensuring that contact could not be broken in order to launch counter-moves. With the enemy's attention held, the main blow(s) would fall on a relatively narrow frontage by concentrated armour and motorized forces. The leading German armour exponent, Heinz Guderian, stressed the need for a division to be built around the tank, not around the infantry: the division in the breakthrough had to move

at the pace of the fastest with the infantry keeping up, not with the tanks held back by lagging foot-soldiers. To this end he conceived a medium battle tank that possessed 'armour sufficient to protect it against the mass of enemy anti-tank weapons, a higher speed and greater cruising range than the infantry escort tank, and an armament of machine guns and cannon up to 75mm.' The tanks were to break through and to be immediately supported by motorized infantry whose task was manyfold – to mop up remaining enemy positions within the attacking area, to harden the flanks of the breakthrough in order to provide 'hard-shoulders' that could defeat a counter-attack and to move forward to exploit the success of the tanks. The motorized forces included specialist engineers – for bridging, demolition and, of course, for use of flame-throwers – but were also backed by mobile anti-tank guns and artillery. Some of these were towed by vehicles but the ideal form was tracked self-propelled guns. In practice the Germans had to use a combination of medium and heavy anti-tank guns, and tanks them-selves, to defend vulnerable flanks and as a defensive

The German PzKw IV which was the workhorse of the armoured divisions. Early marks were in action in 1939 and 1940 and it was still fighting at the end of the war.

screen to take the impact of an enemy armoured attack. The most famous of the guns used in this role was the celebrated 88mm gun, originally designed as an anti-aircraft weapon.

The problem of shaking an enemy defensive position, physically and morally, had been the traditional role of the artillery. But as has been recounted, heavy artillery assault sacrificed surprise in timing and direction of attack, as well as impeding progress through breaking up the ground. The solution to this problem lay in the tactical use of air power against an enemy field force and position. In addition air power was used to paralyze the enemy's field forces by concentrating on his airfields and aircraft (in order to secure air supremacy), his road and rail centres, concentration of reserves and identified headquarters. The object was to prevent or to delay the enemy's redeployment of reserves to the threatened sector of the front, forcing the enemy to feed in his forces piecemeal and in poor order, if they arrived at all. The whole emphasis of action both on the ground and in the air was to delay the intervention of enemy anti-tank guns and tanks in the area of breakthrough except under conditions of utmost favour for the attacker. A further function of air power Guderian envisaged to be the use of parachute forces to secure important objectives – such as bridges – in the path of an armoured advance.

When Guderian was formulating his ideas (which he expounded in his book *Achtung – Panzer*) Germany did not have the means even to attempt such notions. Hitler and technology, however, were at hand to provide the opportunity. Guderian secured command of one of Germany's first three panzer regiments and became Chief of Armoured Troops on the General Staff. Under his guidance the panzer divisions were formed that, after the 'dry-runs' in the occupations of Austria and Czechoslovakia, tore the gallant but hopelessly equipped Poles to pieces in September 1939. The same panzer divisions, operating en masse to secure the very maximum advantage from their fire power and shock effect, ripped apart the French Army in May 1940 and brought about the collapse of the Belgian, British, Dutch and French armies in a six week campaign. In 1941 they were to overrun Yugoslavia and Greece before being lured eastwards to the unconquered steppes of the only country left in Europe not already subdued but capable of posing a serious threat – the Soviet Union.

By the time of the German attack on the USSR one major change had taken place in the panzer arm that was symptomatic of the progressive disease in the German Army – the increasing of units by the dilution of their strength. The Germans literally doubled the number of panzer divisions for their attack on the Soviet Union but this was achieved only by halving the strength of divisions. The new divisions contained between 150 and 200 tanks but with the extra staffs and back-up needed for indigenous units. In 1941 a panzer division had one panzer regiment with only two battalions (six divisions had three battalions in their panzer regiment): the battalions had one medium and two light companies. The divisions had two motorized

The 8.8-cm Flak was one of the great guns of the Second World War. It had been designed as an anti-aircraft gun, but its high velocity and flat trajectory made it a very effective anti-tank gun.

regiments, each of two battalions, a motor cycle regiment (mainly for reconnaissance) and a motorized artillery regiment of four battalions, one of which was an anti-aircraft battalion, equipped with the 88mm gun. As long as the Luftwaffe enjoyed air supremacy this weapon was usually deployed in an anti-tank role.

Nevertheless despite the reduction in strength the panzer divisions smashed their way into and through the Soviet defensive positions with little difficulty; it was only in the vast distances of the steppes that total victory eluded them. The Soviets had the space in which to retreat and bring up fresh units, trading space for time. France and Britain in 1940 had not had this space and had had to fight where they stood.

Moreoever they had lost not because they had fewer and poorer tanks than the Germans – indeed, on the contrary, the Western democracies had more tanks and they were in many ways superior to those deployed by the Germans. In the battles of 1940 and in the early engagements in the Soviet Union in 1941, the enemies of Germany lost because they were wedded to an inferior tactical doctrine and because they lacked the brilliance, elan and superior training of the Germans.

Blitzkrieg

A German soldier attacks an observation position during training on captured stretches of the Maginot Line.

Rommel, 'the Desert Fox', during an impromptu briefing in the chill of a morning in North Africa. Rommel demonstrated that even with limited resources, tactical flare and nerve could take an army from defeat to near triumph. His faults were a desire to lead from the front and, like a Napoleonic general, be seen where the main action was being fought.

The Second World War contained two separate wars – one fought on land in and around Europe, the other on sea around mainland Asia and the western and central Pacific oceans. In the end the Axis powers of Germany, Italy and Japan were defeated by the combined efforts of the world's great industrial and financial power (the USA), the world's most populous state (China), the world's great land power (the USSR), and the world's great Empire (Britain), plus a whole host of lesser countries. What is so astonishing is not the final defeat of the Axis powers (who were supported only by Finland, Hungary, Rumania, Bulgaria, Thailand and a motley collection of quisling states) but that they came so close to achieving victory – a glance at a map of Axis conquests in June 1942 reveals staggering success. Yet behind the conquests, the Germans and Japanese lacked the manpower, industry, transport and oil needed to bring their efforts to a victorious climax. As long as the Allies could evade defeat – and the British just managed to do this during 1940–43, the Soviet Union came to within measurable distance of utter ruin both in 1941 and 1942 – the superior economic, financial and industrial resources of the Allies were bound to bring victory in the end. For the Allies the war·was one of attrition and the cost was enormous. The great killing matches of World War I on the Western Front were repeated on an even greater scale, not by the British, French and Americans but in Europe on the Russian Front, in the Far East in China, and at sea. The Soviets lost some 22 million people;

the Chinese some 14 millions. The cost in treasure was equally prodigal and the ruination of Europe and many areas of the Far East was virtually total.

The major factor in the extent of German and Japanese success lay in the twin facts that as aggressors they possessed the strategic initiative and that their gains prior to the outbreak of general war (1939 in Europe and 1941 in the Far East) had left them in positions of decided physical and moral superiority. The Allies had to fight for the strategic initiative and, in the case of Germany, it was not until 1943 that such initiative was wrested from her. And it was not until that same year that the high watermark of Japanese conquest began to ebb decisively.

German strategy in World War II was dominated by a desire not to become engaged in a long drawn-out campaign of the kind that had so drained her in blood and morale in 1918. Hitler, just as he had in the cases of Austria and Czechoslovakia, rejected the notion of a two-front war and sought instead to wage short wars, economical in manpower and minimal in disruption of the economy. He tried to tackle his enemies singly, picking them off one by one. He did not anticipate that Britain and France would declare war in 1939 over Poland because he thought that the non-aggression pact with the Soviet Union would lead the democracies to accept the *fait accompli* tamely. The destruction of Poland was no great problem for the Germans. She was indefensible in any strategic sense since she was surrounded on three sides by Germany: it was from East Prussia in the north and from Silesia and occupied Czechoslovakia in the south that the panzer columns erupted into Poland, the two arms of the pincer aiming to sweep behind Warsaw to achieve the encirclement and annihilation of the Polish field armies. (The aim of every German *blitzkrieg* attack was not a city but the enemy field forces.) In the case of Poland the battle was scarcely a contest. Totally outclassed in the air, the Poles were exposed to pulverizing air attack from the start. JU-87 Stuka dive-bomber aircraft, operating as precision artillery, pounded defensive positions and fortifications. Polish cavalry charged tanks with a predictability matched only by their commitment and bravery. The campaign was sharp, quick and brutal while the French, as Hitler had foreseen, undertook no offensive action to aid their hapless ally. Indeed the French, given their estimate that the Poles could offer a six-month resistance to the Germans, were as surprised by the ease of the German victory as were some of the Germans themselves.

The turn of the Western Allies was to follow in May 1940, though only after Denmark and Norway had been invaded in a daring and imaginative use of sea power. Though operating in the face of superior force, the combination of audacity and first blow brought the Germans an immediate advantage that ultimately proved decisive. In fact the Germans, who took severe naval losses in the Norwegian campaign, came perilously close to defeat and were saved more by the fumblings and mistakes of the democracies than by their own efforts. At this stage of the war the Western democracies were relatively pacific; they were not seeking to secure the strategic initiative. Granted that the prospects of alliance with the Soviet Union were non-existent and that the smaller states of eastern Europe were not prepared to embrace the western cause, the British and French were still prepared to stand on the defence, waiting for their strength to be built up. In May 1940 the British Army in France numbered ten divisions; in September 1940 it was to have been brought up to thirty-nine divisions. Only when the British and French had drawn on the full strength of their empires were they prepared to contemplate the offensive; until such time they were prepared to wait upon events.

Hitler could not afford to wait. He could not afford to let the balance of power shift remorselessly against him. In 1940 his armies were equal in size to the combined armies of the four major western European states, though Germany had the built-in advantage of unity of command and none of the lack of standardization that plagued the democracies. Only in the air did the Germans possess superiority of numbers and quality (3200 to 1800): in tanks they were outnumbered by about 2500 to 3000 and their artillery had 7710 pieces against the French total of 11,700. Time would only add to this imbalance. The Germans were therefore forced to take the initiative. In formulating their plan of attack they gauged Anglo-French reactions exactly. By attacking all along the Western Front and invading Belgium, Luxembourg and the Netherlands with a force of just over twenty-nine divisions (three of which were armoured, two being earmarked for subsequent transfer), they estimated that the Anglo-French field armies along the Franco-Belgian border would be lured into Belgium and southern Holland and there pinned by the two invading German armies. The main German thrust – in the form of a three army (forty-five divisions) assault – was to fall in the centre with the seven armoured divisions concentrated for a blow on a forty-five mile front through the Ardennes to the Meuse between Dinant and Sedan. The main blow was to fall on Sedan, the very pivot of the Anglo-French manoeuvre into the Low Countries, and was to be delivered, appropriately enough, by Guderian's XIX Panzer Corps. The nineteen German divisions in the south were not intended to demonstrate the strength of the Maginot Line.

Strategically the plan was nearly perfect, aiming as it did to smash a decisive breach in the Allied line in the very centre, thereby allowing the encirclement of the trapped field armies. It was audacious in that a breakthrough to the Channel from Sedan – a place evocative enough for both Germany and France – left an exposed flank of some 200 miles across the front of the French Army. It was brilliant in the calculated risk of passing the bulk of the armour through a narrow congested area poorly served by roads and with good defensive positions. The weakness of the plan lay in its objectives once the breakthrough at Sedan had been made. There was no provision for exploitation of success either with regard to the occupation of France or the reduction of Britain. But the plan itself worked. The French Army was ripped into two on the Meuse within five days; the Channel was reached on May 25 – fifteen days after the battle began. The British Army plus some 100,000 French were able to escape from Dunkirk – largely because of German strategic timidity in forcing the panzers on in an area that had such an ominous reputation from World War I – but there was no escape for the others. The Dutch surrendered late in May, as did the Belgians. France was forced to sue for an armistice by June 22 (effective on the 25th). German losses amounted to 27,000 killed, 110,000 wounded and some 18,000 missing. Allied losses were estimated at 2.3 millions of whom about 1.9 million were prisoners.

On the European mainland Germany had no rival, given her understanding with the USSR, but her ally, Italy, brought about a crisis in the Balkans (already an area of conflicting interests between Germany and the Soviets) as a result of her ill-considered assault on Greece in October 1940. The Italian debacle produced a German intervention in the spring of 1941, with the result that Yugoslavia was annihilated in a nine-day campaign and Greece overrun. Following the occupation of Greece the Germans attempted a unique operation – strategic conquest by air in the form of a parachute invasion of Crete. The operation involved the

seizure and holding of an airhead on the island and the rapid reinforcement of the parachutists by sea and by air. This was very different from the type of operation that the Germans' single parachute division had been used to. In the Netherlands in 1940 and on the Corinth Canal in April 1941 they had been used as Guderian had wished, in front of an armoured advance. The battle for Crete was very finely balanced. Jumping from the slow and vulnerable JU-52s, the Germans took losses in the air and there was much confusion on the ground but they were able to take and hold Maleme, as much by good fortune and British error as their own efforts, and this proved decisive. The relentlessness of the Luftwaffe (the British had no air cover worth the mention), and the persistence of the German elite parachute and mountain troops, decided the issue. Nevertheless German losses were severe and they were never again able to launch such an operation.

For Hitler, however, Greece, Crete and indeed the whole of the Mediterranean area were diversions from the decisive theatre. But he could not ignore either the political or military realities of the Italian alliance and Italy's disastrous operations in North Africa, 1940–41. Such was the Italian situation that Germany had to intervene. Similarly, though on the reverse side of the coin, the British in fighting in North Africa had no strategic choice. Expelled from mainland Europe and

with no allies and no possibility of regaining a foothold on the continent, they had to fight where they were in land contact with the enemy, and only in Africa was there such contact. The indefensible Italian possessions in East Africa were quickly conquered; thus the British were involved in operation in the North African desert for the very good reason that there were no other areas where they could fight. Initially, they prospered against an Italian Army that was hopelessly ill-equipped, poorly officered and of very low morale. Few Italians enthused about the German alliance; even fewer were prepared to die for Mussolini. In December 1940 a 30,000 strong British force under the command of Major General Richard O'Connor began a raid against Italian forward positions at Sidi Barrani inside Egypt. Tactically the operation was characterized by sheer audacity (since the Italian armies in Egypt and Libya totalled 250,000 men) and the maximum use of security and surprise. The approach to contact involved night marches and lying up in the open between, and slightly in front of, the Italian positions. The attack was directed against the Italian centre, using exactly the same tactics as *blitzkrieg* – armour with motorized infantry, and mobile artillery acting with close air support. The Italians, taken by surprise, broke and in doing so lost any hope of rescuing something from the debacle. They were forced into one of the most difficult of military

Left: German troops in Russia. The vast distances and poor roads, as well as an inexhaustible supply of men, made the Russians an enemy who could not be defeated in three months like some smaller, western European armies. Below: British gunners with a howitzer in North Africa. The Desert war was one uncomplicated by civilians, towns and partisans and became the nearest thing to a 'gentleman's war'.

operations, to stand while in retreat and in contact with an aggressive enemy. They found no place to turn and fight, such was the relentless fury of British harrassment. As the Italians retreated through Derna they sought safety along the coast road, but O'Connor divided his dwindling forces and sent part of them on the landside of the Jebel Akhdar to reach Beda Fomm just before they arrived. Encirclement was complete, and at an overall cost of less than 2000 casualties the British destroyed ten Italian divisions, took 170,000 prisoners and captured 400 tanks and 850 guns – one of the most remarkable feats of arms in history. Total strategic success was denied the British, however, by ignorance of basic strategic reality on the part of Churchill. With the Italian Army in tatters it might have been possible for the whole of Libya to have been cleared had all the British forces been kept concentrated. As the Italians began to fall apart, Churchill directed a shift of resources to Greece in what the army commanders on the spot regarded as a hopeless effort: if the Germans attacked Greece no amount of British help could have saved the Greeks. Thus the British lost

out on both fronts, unable to deny the Germans in the Balkans, unable to clear the North African coast. While strategy must serve political ends (and it would have been difficult to let Greece to go the wall without some gesture of support) the strategic deployment of troops must be in accordance with reality and what may be possible.

Nine days after Beda Fomm was fought two German battalions arrived in Tripoli. They were the leading elements of what was to become the Afrika Korps under Lieutenant General (later Field Marshal) Erwin Rommel. With the arrival of the Germans the war in North Africa was to last another twenty-seven months, though the issue was more or less resolved in October-November 1942. Rommel was undoubtedly a tactical genius and in conditions of fluid fighting more than a match for any British general pitted against him. But few campaigns bring home the importance of logistics, time and space, and of the inter-meshing of land, air and sea operations and their strategic effect than does the North African campaign. Every bullet, every item of clothing, food and supply, every litre of petrol (gasolene)

had to be brought to the theatre of operations since there were no sources of supply in the desert itself. The Axis forces in North Africa were supplied across the Mediterranean: the British either around the Cape or across the continent itself via the west coast, Chad, Sudan and Egypt. The amount of Axis supply was directly related to the scale of British naval activity from Malta but if the Germans held Libya (in addition to Crete) the supply of Malta could be made virtually prohibitive. But unless Malta was supplied there was little hope of breaking the German grip in Libya. In trying to clear the coastal area of the enemy both sides amply demonstrated the validity of the concept of 'the diminishing force of the offensive,' the weakening of an offensive effort as the toll of exhaustion and the drag of logistics began to make themselves felt. At the same time, while the attacker was moving away from his supplies on ever lengthening lines of communications, the defender was falling back on his support, growing in strength while the attacker weakened. So while there were considerable tactical successes for both sides there was no decisive strategic success in the theatre until 1943.

Tactically the war in the desert was dominated by the need for speed and surprise since there was no cover. In all his operations Rommel attempted to get around an open flank and into the British defensive system with his armour. Perhaps his most classic performance was at Gazala in May-June 1942, which ended with the capture of Tobruk. The battle had been extremely confused, with Rommel at one stage virtually out of supplies and trapped against the British minefields inside the British defensive zone. The British, however, had been unable to concentrate their armour and had fed it in piecemeal in the battles of May 28/29. The overall result was that they suffered a shattering defeat, while the Germans penetrated deeply into Egypt until halted outside a place called El Alamein. Rommel had begun Gazala with 560 German and Italian tanks; he reached Alamein with 55, and only 29 of the 88-mm guns that had repeatedly caught the British armour in the open at Gazala. At the end of a very long line of communications, and with a desperate shortage of petrol (gasolene), Rommel had to face a revitalized British Army drawing on supply dumps only sixty miles away. The British forces, moreover, were receiving new tanks and guns on a scale never experienced before: the fall of Tobruk had led the Americans to despatch 300 tanks and a hundred 105mm self-propelled guns immediately. To add to his problems, Rommel faced a continuous front at Alamein since there was no open flank. The British front rested on the sea in the north and the Qattara Depression in the south. An initial attempt to rush the position failed, as did a subsequent, more deliberate effort; then the battle died. The Germans were too weak to take the initiative but for political reasons could not retreat; the British were too weak and unready to take the initiative. The inescapable laws of supply and exhaustion imposed their will on the battlefield. It was not until October that the British moved. By then they had built up a 5:2 superiority in tanks, 2:1 in men and a definite edge in the air. The stage was set for a battle that was not characteristic of those fought in the desert during World War II, a battle of attrition, with the British attempting to force their way through the German positions in the north by clearing two corridors through the minefields in the hope of having enough battleworthy armour at the end to exploit the breach. They relied entirely on numbers, weight of firepower and sheer doggedness in order to wear down an inferior enemy. Ultimately they were successful in breaking into and through the Axis positions but were not able to encircle and annihilate the enemy, and the greater part of the German forces was able to escape. But the price of the British success was high – 13,500 dead with some 500 tanks and 100 guns out of action – but not high in comparison with the losses inflicted on the Axis. It is worth noting, however, that for twice the number of British dead at Alamein the Germans had conquered France.

The problems of supply and shortage of manpower in the face of an aggressive and numerically superior enemy were, by November 1942, causing the Germans acute embarrassment not only in North Africa but in Russia. At first the campaign in the east had gone well for the Germans, but never well enough since imprecision of objectives (the failure of strategic direction) and the problems of maintenance and supply imposed fateful delays on the German advance of 1941. The invasion itself, Operation Barbarossa, began on June 22, 1941 with a three-front assault (four if the Finns are included). The main weight of the attack was to the north of the Pripet Marshes with two separate and diverging objectives – Leningrad and the clearing of the Baltic coast on the one hand, Moscow on the other. The thrust on Moscow – for many of the planners the only worthwhile target since it was the seat of government, an armaments centre and at the hub of the

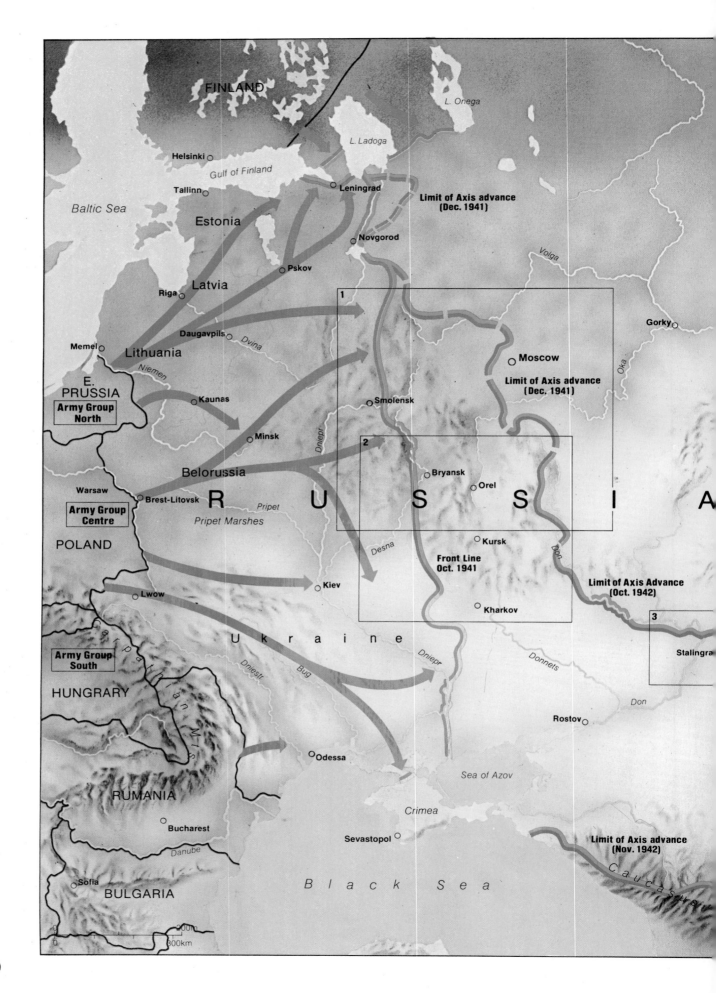

FINLAND

L. Onega

Helsinki

L. Ladoga

Gulf of Finland

Tallinn

Leningrad

Baltic Sea

Estonia

**Limit of Axis advance
(Dec. 1941)**

Novgorod

Volga

Pskov

Latvia

Gorky

Riga

1

Daugavpils

Dvina

Moscow

Memel

Lithuania

**Limit of Axis advance
(Dec. 1941)**

Niemen

Kaunas

Smolensk

E.
PRUSSIA

Oka

Army Group
North

Minsk

Dniepr

2

Bryansk

Belorussia

Orel

R   U   S   S   I   A

Warsaw

Brest-Litovsk

Pripet

Army Group
Centre

Pripet Marshes

Desna

Kursk

POLAND

**Front Line
Oct. 1941**

Don

Lwow

Kharkov

**Limit of Axis Advance
(Oct. 1942)**

Kiev

Army Group
South

U   k   r   a   i   n   e

Dniepr

3

HUNGRARY

Dniestr

Bug

Donnets

Stalingra

Rostov

Odessa

Don

Sea of Azov

RUMANIA

Crimea

Bucharest

Sevastopol

Danube

**Limit of Axis advance
(Nov. 1942)**

Sofia

B   l   a   c   k   S   e   a

Caucasus

BULGARIA

300m
300km

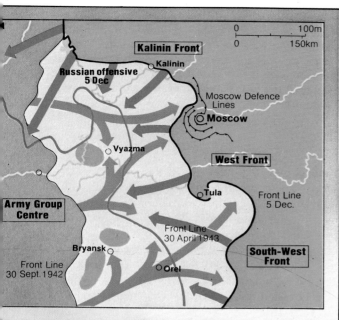

Kalinin Front
Kalinin
Russian offensive
5 Dec
Moscow Defence
Lines
Moscow
Vyazma
West Front
Army Group
Centre
Tula
Front Line
5 Dec.
Front Line
30 April 1943
Bryansk
South-West
Front
Front Line
30 Sept. 1942
Orel
0   100m
0   150km

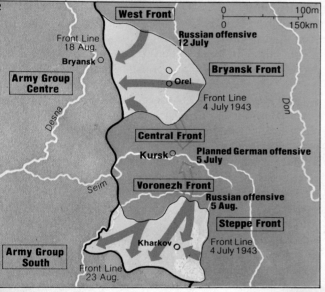

West Front
Front Line
18 Aug.
Russian offensive
12 July
Bryansk
Army Group
Centre
Bryansk Front
Orel
Front Line
4 July 1943
Desna
Central Front
Seim
Kursk
Planned German offensive
5 July
Voronezh Front
Russian offensive
5 Aug.
Steppe Front
Kharkov
Front Line
4 July 1943
Army Group
South
Front Line
23 Aug.
Don
0   100m
0   150km

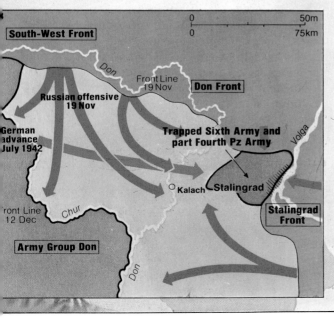

South-West Front
Don
Front Line
19 Nov
Don Front
Russian offensive
19 Nov
German
advance
July 1942
Trapped Sixth Army and
part Fourth Pz Army
Kalach
Stalingrad
Volga
Front Line
12 Dec
Chir
Stalingrad
Front
Army Group Don
Don
0   50m
0   75km

The German invasion of Soviet Russia reached the suburbs of Moscow and the banks of the Volga, but foundered in huge spoiling battles like the winter offensive at Moscow and the protracted battle of Stalingrad. The huge tank battle at Kursk finally guaranteed that Germany would lose the war. From 1943 onwards she fought a long withdrawal across Russia, Poland and the Balkans until Russian troops burst into Germany.

whole of the Soviet rail system – was made dependent on the outcome of the secondary battle, the clearing of the coast and control of Leningrad. To the south of the Pripet Marshes, German forces in and around Lublin were to attack towards Kiev with the object of trapping Soviet forces in the west and south Ukraine. The immediate tactical aim of the Germans was the entrapment of the Soviet Armies in front of the Dvina and Dneipr river line in order to prevent their retreat into the interior. Certainly Soviet deployment forward into these areas made them particularly vulnerable, but the notion of trying to catch them there begged a very important question: that before the rivers there were no cities of major importance that could act as centres of deployment for reserves being brought to the front. The German dilemma was therefore whether to rush the panzers forward on very thin axes of advance with their flanks wide open or very vulnerable, or to hold them back. If the panzers were held back they could assist the infantry (over 80 per cent of the Germany Army) in the reduction of the pockets of resistance that had been encircled by the panzers' initial thrust; but if they were held back, the panzers would not be able to move against the hinterland and would leave unthreatened for the moment the distant mobilization centres. If the panzers were moved forward then they faced the obvious problems of supply and maintenance on lengthening and difficult lines of communication, with enemy pockets still in their rear. Events were to show that the German infantry needed the armour to reduce pockets whose resistance seemed to be inversely related to their chances of success. But the real problem that developed in the summer of 1941 was twofold: exhaustion (particularly of machines in the dust and heat) and the intoxication of success. Exhaustion is obvious; the intoxicating belief that they had already won the war, led to the proliferation of effort on secondary targets at the expense of the main object. As the Soviet Armies scattered, the central thrust was weakened in order to help events along in the Ukraine, where the diverted help was not needed; the German success in the south drew them ever eastwards, far beyond initial objectives and supply capabilities. With all the delays during the summer caused by allocation of priorities and re-equipment, the final thrust on Moscow itself from the start line of Smolensk/ the river Desna began in late September 1941, the two armoured pincers on the flanks aiming for Vyazma and Bryansk in an effort to clear the way to the Soviet

German gunners and infantry trade shots with pockets of Soviet troops during street fighting in Russia. Fighting in built-up areas is a long, bloody and very tiring operation which absorbs large numbers of men and requires careful control and planning. At Stalingrad the battle absorbed the best of the German VIth Army.

capital. The Germans took their initial objectives very quickly and the route to Moscow seemed wide open. The Soviets were on the horns of a dilemma. From Vyazma the Germans could advance on several axes – either directly upon Moscow or to the north or the south of the city. The Soviets had, moreover, very little left with which to fight: German intelligence estimated Soviet losses to date at about 2½ million men, 20,000 tanks and a similar number of guns. On the other hand, the Germans had their problems; re-supply was breaking down and their losses were heavy. By December, rail supply was only about one quarter of what was needed, and some divisions were little more than regiments. The autumn rains and mud slowed the advance, in some places stopped it altogether. The shortening days limited the hours of conflict and advance and severely curtailed the activities of the Luftwaffe. Moreover, the Soviets, favoured by the miles of forests before Moscow that slowed the rate of advance and limited the room for German manoeuvre and confident of the coming of a winter whose fury no European army had ever survived, had two priceless assets: a general of genius, Georgi Zhukov, and the last of the reserves, the twenty-five infantry divisions and nine tank brigades of the Far East, moved from that area when it became obvious that the Japanese did not intend to move against the USSR but to the south.

Zhukov's strategic objective was the retention of Moscow, the loss of which would have led to the isolation and almost certain collapse of both flanks. This had to be achieved by keeping what remained of his armies intact until the onset of winter; resistance had to be effective to keep the Germans at bay, but mobile enough to keep out of range of the encircling German armoured pincers. To fight this battle Zhukov had very few good troops, and those that he did have, he wished to hold back until the whole of the German effort was spent. So he used his worker battalions and *ad hoc* army units to meet the initial attack and his one and only tank brigade against Guderian's IInd Panzer Army, advancing from Orel to slow this assault while thinning the other fronts in order to build up armour reserves on the flanks while holding in the centre. The final German thrust on Moscow broke through to Dmitrov and Ryazan, but the ferocity of Soviet resistance, the extreme cold and German exhaustion enabled the flanks to hold, while on December 6 the Siberians, for the most part uncommitted up until this stage, went over to the offensive in the centre. In tem-

peratures which fell to −63°C Soviet tactics, massed armoured and infantry attacks along predictable axes of advance, mauled the Germans badly. Moscow was saved by this counter-attack and the Germans never again tried the direct approach on the capital. With Leningrad besieged, and the front in that area stabilized after the Soviet failure to relieve the city, attention switched to the south.

One of the little known facts to emerge from World War II is that the Germans secured more industrial and agricultural produce from the Soviet Union between 1939 and 1941 than they did from their period of occupation of parts of the USSR between 1941 and 1944. For Hitler in 1942 – having added the USA to his list of enemies – strategy dictated that Germany had to force a decision in 1942 and that he had to secure the Ukraine, the Donbas and the oil of the Caucasus. Without the natural resources of these areas Germany could not hope to win the war; with the defeat of the Soviet Union the task facing the Allies would have been virtually impossible. Germany was forced to attack in the south in 1942.

For the Germans the 1942 campaign started well. Although they had taken reverses in the winter, including the loss of Rostov, the Soviet spring offensive around Kharkov resulted in the destruction of the Soviet forces committed to the attack and the leaving of the eastern Ukraine wide open to a German advance. At Kharkov, the Soviets needed close co-ordination between their forces to avoid defeat because for this attack they had no margin of superiority over the Germans. They attempted to batter their way through the German positions north of Kharkov and were able to tear a gap some seventy miles wide in the German front, but their inexperience in moving forward across razed countryside away from supply dumps, led to confusion. As German resistance stiffened on the flanks of the breach and the Soviets pushed deeper into the German positions, their chances of escaping from the inevitable counter-attack diminished. Because of the stupidity of Stalin the offensive was maintained long after any hope for success had passed and the prospects for annihilation had become almost certain. At the end of May the Germans sealed the breach and encircled the Soviets, the latter losing 200,000 prisoners and 1000 tanks. In its own way the battle around Kharkov was one of the most effective battles of riposte fought in the war.

The subsequent German offensive that sought to

exploit this situation started well, quickly securing a firm flank in the capture of Voronezh. The thrust of the advance, however, was both southwards towards Armavir, Maikop, Grozny and Baku (1st Panzer Army) and eastwards (4th Panzer and 6th Armies) towards the Volga, the initial aim being to secure the flank for the southwards move but with the long-term objective of moving up the Volga towards Kazan, thus outflanking Moscow from the east. Via a string of impressive victories, this offensive led the Germans to utter defeat at Stalingrad. That city was merely the stop point for the attack, the location on the Volga on which the flank should be pinned. But the Germans failed to take the city in its first rush (August 19) and both sides began to feed in their reserves. But whereas the Soviets fed in reserves on the basis of the minimum necessary, the Germans began to feed men in on the basis of the maximum possible in a desperate effort to break Soviet will. Thus, while the Soviets were able to build up most of their reserves on the flanks for the counter-attack, the Germans exposed themselves to a situation whereby their panzers and elite infantry were ground down in street fighting (where their supreme attributes of mobility and firepower were discounted), stationary at the very tip of a stalled advance. The German flanks, moreover, were in the air. They were held by the inadequately equipped Rumanian and Italian armies while the Soviets held many bridgeheads in the bend of the Don. Totally absorbed by the battle for

Stalingrad the Germans ignored these bridgeheads: the Soviets did not and it was from them that the Soviets launched their strikes against the Rumanians on November 19. For the offensives on either side of Stalingrad, the Soviets deployed a million men, over 13,000 guns and 900 tanks formed into 66 rifle divisions, 18 mechanized brigades, 5 tank corps and 14 brigades, 3 cavalry corps and 127 artillery regiments. Given the shortage of artillery the opening barrage had to last as long as eighty minutes and the shortage of ground troops generally meant that the attack lacked depth, with the armour held back for the exploitation of a breach made primarily by infantry. On the northern flank, how-ever, the tanks had to pass through the infantry in order to make the breach themselves. But the breaches were made and despite the problems of navigation over the featureless Steppes, and the chaos both on and off the pincers closed at Kalach. The entombed Germans in Stalingrad numbered some 250,000 men, 100 tanks and 2000 guns, a force roughly three times as strong as the Soviets had anticipated. It was not until February 2, 1943 that incessant Soviet pressure, the bitterness of the weather and starvation finally brought about the end of desperate resistance. Until that time the German position in Stalingrad tied down a considerable part of the Soviet forces in the south, thus making it more difficult for them to pursue German forces to the west in the central Ukraine.

In operations involving relatively short distances in

Left: Germans on the defensive in Russia. Pioneers dig in frozen snow in the winter of 1943/44 to lay Teller anti-tank mines. Right:
Soviet sailors man a multi-barrelled Maxim machine-gun on an anti-aircraft mount. Though the Soviet anti-aircraft defences were almost non-existent at the beginning of the Battle of Stalingrad they improved steadily until the beleagured German 6th Army was denied most of its airborne supplies by a ring of heavy and medium anti-aircraft guns.

was being increasingly felt in the European war; and secondly, the Red Army was now such a threat that it had to be brought to battle and defeated. The configuration of the front determined where the Germans should make their effort. From the Baltic to Orel the front was solid, almost World War I style with trenches, permanent emplacements, and minefields. To the south lay the Kursk salient that overhung the German positions in the Ukraine. Here the Germans hoped to bring to battle the bulk of Soviet armour and to defeat it. Here, too, the Soviets were prepared to give battle in the calculation that in such an encounter the Germans would have to come to them. The Soviets trusted that their tenacity in defence plus weight of shot would prove decisive. To this end, in the defence of the salient the Soviets ultimately deployed about 1,337,000 troops, 20,220 artillery pieces and 3306 tanks plus an extra tank army in reserve. The defence system was some 110 miles deep across the neck of the salient and consisted largely of groups of five 76.2mm AT guns sited in batteries, mutually supporting, and backed by mortars, engineers and infantry. Extensive minefields were laid – on average about 5000 mines to the mile – in order to channel the German thrusts onto the batteries where weight of broadside rather than individual shots would hopefully deal with the tanks. In immediate support were tanks, hull down, with medium artillery, and behind these more tanks either to help in the defence or, more hopefully, held for the counter-attack once the Germans were halted and exhausted. Tactically the Germans relied more or less on the *blitzkrieg* technique with the new Tiger tanks in the van, the lighter tanks on the flanks and in the rear. But in the north they attempted to punch a series of separate holes through the Soviet defences in order to feed tanks through the breach, just as the British had done at Alamein, but in this case without the assured superiority of numbers and equipment that Montgomery had enjoyed.

The battle was predictable (at least in retrospect) in that as in World War I the attackers broke into but not through the defences, and the counter-attack eliminated all the attackers' gains. German losses in men and tanks – possibly as high as 1200 tanks – were so high that the Soviets were able to push on for the rest of the summer, beyond the Dneipr, liberating Kiev and Poltava in the process. In this, as in all subsequent Soviet offensives, thrusts were noted for their strategic and organizational flexibility if not their

the offensive and with only severely weakened opposition in the way, the Red Army at Stalingrad showed that it could penetrate a front and then encircle and annihilate an enemy. But a more ambitious offensive in the Kharkov direction in February/March 1943 produced the same result as the offensive of May 1942, the Germans demonstrating their strategic and tactical superiority over the Soviets at this stage of the war. As the Soviets pushed to the south west in the face of light resistance, the Germans thinned their front and gave ground, building up fresh panzer forces on the flanks ready for the counter-attack. The Germans were confident once again that the further the Soviets advanced the greater the ultimate German victory, but German infantry scarcity meant that when the trap was sprung much of the Soviet force was able to evade the pincers and escape. The Soviet offensive, however, which had threatened to destroy the whole of the German position in the central and eastern Ukraine, was brought to nothing and the front stabilized roughly along the line from which the Germans had started in May 1942.

There were, however, two vital differences from the situation in May 1942. Firstly, crises were brewing for the Germans in the Mediterranean with the surrender of Axis forces in Tunisia, while the power of the USA

tactical finesse. Their tactics in the offensive were characterized by heavy artillery concentration and a broad frontage of attack with either a mixed infantry or tank assault in double echelon, pressing hard on an initial reconnaissance. (Various attempts were made to launch three- or four-echelon attacks to give depth but these were abandoned because, inevitably, they reduced to unacceptably low levels the weight of firepower in the assault.) The Soviets aimed to make one or two breaches and, thinning the front but still holding the enemy along it, transfer the overwhelming part of the attacking force into the breach(es) for exploitation. Soviet tactical practice in the initial tank assault was interesting for reasons that even now may still be applicable. In the early days of the war tank divisions were quite literally used until they took 100 per cent casualties. Later they were more carefully used, in that exhausted divisions were pulled out when roughly at brigade strength and then used as shock divisions, having been strengthened by some infantry and tank reinforcements and with a full division's allocation of artillery. These divisions operated on very narrow frontages: in one case only 700m (700 yards) wide. In the event of a breakthrough being achieved, the division then lost its artillery support. Moreover,

committing tanks to an initial assault was invariably very costly, yet towards the end of the war the Soviets frequently resorted to massed tank attacks at the start of operations, possibly because they were prepared to suffer high losses that might be incurred anyway and probably also because their overwhelming superiority of numbers allowed them to be somewhat prodigal. These attacks had little infantry support but many repair and maintenance parties. Only about one in three tanks knocked out were unfit for repair and the Soviets worked on a system of the momentum (and overall strength) of an attack being maintained by the repair and relief crews. This did lead to the situation whereby the Soviets could lose two to three times as many tanks as they had at the start and still have some left at the end of the battle.

German defensive tactics in the face of mounting Soviet power was to try to make the initial assault hit air by withdrawal immediately before the attack. This needed good field intelligence, which was generally available. Armour was held back to deal with breakthroughs with the main killing zones covered by light, medium and heavy anti-tank weapons. Though very effective such tactics could never do more than delay or exact a heavy toll on the attacker; they could never

Patton in a new war meets Montgomery also fighting
– the two generals were rivals for the honours of
clearing France and breaking into Germany. Below:
American troops in street fighting in Tangemunde. A
BAR gunner takes aim round a corner to cover his
comrade as he moves up the street.

give the Germans any hope of regaining the strategic initiative.

Anglo-American strategy in the European context was determined not by what they wanted to do but by two things – the outcome of the war at sea (fundamentally resolved in summer 1943) and the availability of troops, shipping and landing craft, none of which were plentiful before 1943. The lack of landing ships plus the fact that North Africa was already a major theatre of war led the first Anglo-American efforts to be in the Mediterranean against Sicily and Italy. This was portrayed as attempting to penetrate the 'soft underbelly' of Europe and was subsequently justified in political terms – concern over the Balkans, influence on Turkey, etc. In reality there was no option. Though a cross-Channel assault would have been desirable, such an action was impossible before 1944.

Caution and prudence dominated Anglo-American tactics: great care was taken to minimize losses and to avoid the likelihood of defeat. The latter was particularly in evidence during seaborne landings when defeat on the beaches could result not simply in the defeat of that particular invasion but the ruining of future prospects, with incalculable results. Thus Patton's more imaginative plan for invading Sicily by landings around both Palermo and Syracuse was set aside in favour of Montgomery's more cautious one to concentrate all forces around Cape Passero – within the range of air cover, with undivided fire support from the sea and with the land forces enjoying a greater concentration of firepower than they would have had had they been split. At Normandy the same process was repeated with the landing beaches concentrated along a narrow front and (with one exception) within two river lines, the bridges over which were the targets of airborne assault. Much ingenuity went into solving the tactical problems of forcing an advance across open beaches into open country, the British particularly being well supplied with specialist tanks from the

79th Armoured Division. Amphibious tanks led the assault to the water's edge from where they engaged enemy strong points; they were followed by flail tanks to beat a way through the minefields and then by tanks with bridging equipment or fascines to climb sea walls and cross anti-tank ditches. Flame-throwing tanks were used to reduce points of resistance, and in order to prevent tanks and wheeled vehicles being stranded in soft sand a modified Churchill tank chassis laid a 9' 11" wide canvas cover in front of itself as a road.

The fighting on the beaches was generally successful in all cases with unexceptional losses but, except for the almost unopposed American landings in southern France, the Allies found great difficulty in moving off the beaches into open country. In Sicily, at Anzio and Normandy the Allies found themselves sealed in by very effective German resistance. To break out they, particularly the British, had to fight battles of attrition – heavily relying on naval gunfire and tactical air power – to 'write-down' German armour that was qualitatively far superior to their own. At Normandy, Montgomery used narrow frontal attacks, armour heavy, to grip the German armour in Operations Epsom and Goodwood, while the Americans, faced by less powerful forces, used their heavy strategic bombers to blast a path through the German defences in Operation Cobra.

Strategically the Allied advance from Normandy across France to the German border was dogged by problems of logistics and personality. The broad front approach favoured by Eisenhower had the advantage of keeping the pressure on the Germans across the whole of the front and keeping them off-balance; the narrow front approach – favoured by Montgomery as long as it was not his forces that were held back – had the advantage of possibly delivering a knock-out blow by concentrating a maximum effort to take advantage of Germany's parlous state. The weakness of this argument was that in order to concentrate for a single attack all the other fronts would have to be closed down, though this was going to be inevitable at some stage or another given the problem of supply. In the end a narrow front attack was adopted in Operation Market Garden, the crossing of the Rhine by a land advance via bridges captured and held by airborne troops. The weakness of this particular operation was the predictability of the axes of advance once the parachute force had landed, a minimal use of the great assets of numbers and mobility since the land operation

Above: platoons have deployed off a road and a despatch rider has arrived with others.

Below: the platoon is dug in and while one man stands down his comrade remains on guard.

Nagasaki in October 1945. The Atomic bombs ushered in a new era in warfare in which many people believed that old lessons and experience were valueless. However, smaller, localized wars since 1945 have showed that terrain and men remain the same and war presents similar challenges.

was by definition a long narrow penetration with the firepower of the assault limited to its lead elements and, finally, poor intelligence and planning. The attack also suffered from the insoluble problem that the armour was forced to use roads raised above the level of the surrounding countryside, thus leaving the tanks silhouetted and vulnerable to German anti-tank guns. The operation failed and it can be argued that the effort spent in Market Garden could have been far more profitably employed in clearing the Germans from their positions on the banks of the Wester Schelde, thereby opening the sea route into the port of Antwerp that had been captured intact. Had this happened the Allied offensive into Germany might well have taken place far earlier.

Supply in this case was vital, as it was in the Pacific theatre. The war here was primarily a sea and land war to which land warfare, though intense on occasions and vitally important, was subordinate. The story of the Pacific war illustrates as few campaigns could, the immense flexibility of sea power and results that can be achieved by the combination of military and sea power. Japan was beaten to her knees even before Hiroshima in a war decided in the Pacific to which events in Burma, China and Manchuria were totally subordinate. Yet the blasting of Hiroshima and Nagasaki marked not an end but a new beginning. The surrender of Germany, Italy and Japan, and the devastation of Europe and vast areas of the Far East were witness to the fact that the old order had passed beyond recall. Already divisions among the Allies were obvious and the world was being divided ideologically between the superpowers, both of whom sought allegiance and support from the defeated and the neutral. In the areas they occupied the superpowers were to tolerate only mirror images of their own societies. The great colonial empires were in turmoil, particularly in Asia, but even in areas that had not been directly affected by war, change was in the air as nationalist aspirations began to surface. With these changes went the development of new and more powerful weapons of destruction that were to change the face of warfare itself.

War in The Third World

Mao Tse-tung in the early days of his guerrilla war.
He is the father of all post-war insurgencies.

Mao delivers a speech at Kangta, the Chinese people's anti-Japanese Military and Political College. His writings and propaganda are now widely translated and though heavy reading give an insight into the planning, patience and ruthless energy that motivated the Chinese Communist revolution. Other revolutionaries have used his name and some of his ideas in their own battles.

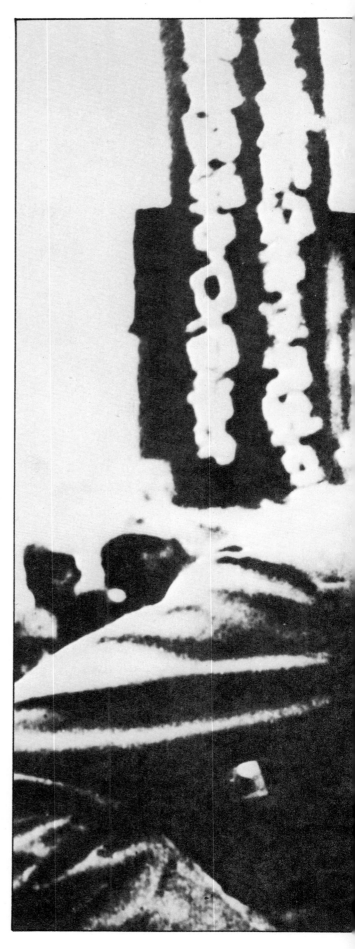

The techniques and tactics of guerrilla warfare are probably the oldest forms of warfare known to man, but the uses to which these forms have been put, and the context in which they have operated during the last thirty years, do bestow upon guerrilla warfare elements of novelty. In the past, guerrilla warfare was employed as one of the means by which nations fought one another (the Spanish and Russians against Napoleon; the French in 1871 against the Germans) but since 1945 it has become a method used to conduct and resolve internal political disputes. Since 1945 there has been an increasing employment of revolutionary guerrilla warfare – the application of guerrilla warfare method to revolutionary objectives, particularly in the context of national liberation in colonies. Given the Soviet view of 'peaceful co-existence,' (the destruction of Western capitalist society by any method short of war), wars of national liberation will remain despite the absence of colonial regimes, the target being governments of countries that oppose communism.

The concepts of revolutionary guerrilla warfare are a synthesis of the writings of various political and military writers and of the practical experience, writings and example of various individuals, most notably the leader of the largest such campaign ever fought, Mao Tsetung. Mao drew from his hard-learned experiences in China, the writings of such military analysts as Sun Tze, Clausewitz, T. E. Lawrence, and his interpretation of Marxist-Leninism, a concept of warfare that was simple and straightforward, explaining it to and impressing it upon his colleagues. In effect, he provided a do-it-yourself guide that through a dogged and unwavering dedication to his model, he finally made work in 1949. By success he invited emulation and just as the Russian pattern of revolution became the established method of revolution after its 1917 success, so the Maoist pattern became the established norm after 1949.

Mao Tse-tung developed a strategy based on guerrilla warfare that allowed an under-industrialized and primitive society, lacking modern arms and equipment, to adopt a militant political philosophy based on armed struggle. From this fundamental premise, Mao developed a military doctrine that enabled a backward society such as China to adopt a political posture and form a resistance even when confronted with the militarily superior forces of a highly industrialized state – hence its continued relevance. Naturally within this context Mao measured

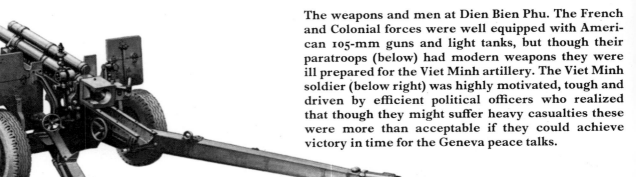

The weapons and men at Dien Bien Phu. The French and Colonial forces were well equipped with American 105-mm guns and light tanks, but though their paratroops (below) had modern weapons they were ill prepared for the Viet Minh artillery. The Viet Minh soldier (below right) was highly motivated, tough and driven by efficient political officers who realized that though they might suffer heavy casualties these were more than acceptable if they could achieve victory in time for the Geneva peace talks.

military potential by standards very different from Western, even Soviet, norms. In the West military effectiveness is chiefly equated with weapons systems, logistics and trained manpower; Mao, faced by an absence of these three commodities, claimed that revolutionary military effectiveness had to be measured in political terms. Accepting war as a form of politics and that revolutionary warfare was nothing if not political, Mao argued that military factors must always be subordinate to ideological phenomena. Thus he relegated purely military considerations to the background, or, more accurately, made them dependent upon political factors. A careful reading of *Protracted Warfare* and *Strategy in the Guerrilla War Against the Japanese Invaders* reveals that to Mao the decisive factors in war are will (the political morale of society), time (which will exhaust the superior resources of the sophisticated society) and space (essential for the exploitation of time and will).

Thus to summarize Mao's writings, the revolutionary's only chance of defeating a superior enemy lies in his ability to raise the population. Once this is achieved, space and manpower provide time. Time was the equalizing factor between the sides since (writing of Japan) '. . . in spite of . . . industrial progress . . . her manpower, her raw materials and her financial resources are all inadequate and insufficient to maintain her in protracted war or to meet the situation presented by a war prosecuted over a vast area.' Mao appreciated the need for an industrialized society to force the issue quickly: his intention in guerrilla warfare was to avoid a decision, ensuring an enemy's tactical success could not be translated into strategic victory. He thereby prolonged war to a point where it became politically

and economically unacceptable to the enemy. This is the basis of communist faith in ultimate victory in war, irrespective of the duration of the struggle.

Mao saw his strategy as a series of three merging phases, the first of which was the mobilization and organization of the people in order to maintain the eventual military effort. In this first phase the aim was to establish safe bases, free from outside interference, in which the population could be brought under control and during which military preparations could be commenced. In this phase fighting was subordinate to indoctrination, control and organization. The building up of local home guard units, intelligence networks and the training of regular units were the priority. Emphasis was placed on political objectives that would be sympathetically received by the population and upon the correct treatment of the population by the army. Mao had seen a ruthless policy of coercion by the communists backfire disastrously in the twenties while in the thirties the effect of the casual and deliberate barbarity of the Japanese was obvious to anyone with eyes. By sound and fair administration, reforms, mildness of taxation, popular support could be obtained; by use of mass organizations and popular slogans, society could be orchestrated. Thus regimented, society and the revolutionary soldier were linked inescapably together: what was in reality a piecemeal process of national reconstruction allowed the creation of the water (friendly civilian attitudes) in which the fish (the revolutionary soldier) could operate. During the second phase, the military preparations were put in hand in the form of guerrilla action in the attempt to disperse, immobilize and break down the resolve of the enemy, while at the same time building

up experience, improving organization and securing arms. This in itself was a self-generating process in that it brought under control new areas and more people for political mobilization. In northern China between 1937 and 1945 communist forces expanded from a single base area to control fourteen major zones inside Japanese-held territory. The final phase of protracted war was conventional or positional warfare. Guerrilla warfare in itself could not achieve victory but could only pave the way for it. Victory had to be secured by regular formations exploiting the favourable conditions achieved by the first two phases, in the last phase, the roused countryside moving in to engulf the towns. From this basic framework two subsequent points emerge. Firstly, the flexibility of the model in that the whole process was reversible on meeting a check and the cycle then recommenced. Secondly, the final phase could be curtailed by negotiations but only for the purpose of securing a surrender: in other phases they could be used to secure a respite. Negotiations were a means to an end: there was no element of good faith in such undertakings.

Mao's concepts worked well enough in China though it must be noted that his success owed as much to the failings, incompetence and divisions of the opposition as to the strength and potency of communist insurgency. In other areas, they did not do so well, as in Malaya where a combination of governmental resolution, severity, enlightened administration and the provision of security combined to stem the communists. In Malaya, a lack of space in which to manoeuvre in order to avoid defeat while not losing touch with (and some degree of control over) the population was a grave handicap for the insurgents. In order to survive as government counter-measures began to exact their

toll, the communists had to move away from the battle area – the Chinese shantytowns that lined the jungle fringe – and move into the *ulu*. Counter-insurgent tactics in this phase of the struggle were the basic ambush and intense, long patrolling: the aim was to control the jungle around settled areas to a depth of five hours marching time. In time this proved very successful as the jungle craft of the security forces improved and outstripped that of the insurgents. Nevertheless it was the accumulation of pressure that led to the communists breaking off the struggle in the settled areas, and here the British relied on a variety of measures that were retained after independence in 1957. Foremost among them was the resettlement and concentration of the population under close and increasingly effective police surveillance. Material inducements to the population (tactically raising the level of the campaign from a competition in coercion to one of government in which the communists, given their resources, could not compete), the liberalization of the naturalization laws and a tightening denial programme of all types of supply, particularly food, were the chief measures by which the government secured firstly control and then the support of the population. Added to these, was a streamlining and extremely close co-ordination of administration, police and military efforts of which the police were arguably the most important. Gradually recovering from a very shaky start and growing in effectiveness with an influx of new weapons, communications and, above all, manpower (particularly Chinese) it was the police, operating within the security gradually built up by the army around the villages, who identified and eliminated the communists within the battle zone. This was achieved by the systematic clearing of the country area by area, concentrating on the

weakest communist areas first before moving on the more badly affected areas later.

Nevertheless insurgent failure in Malaya – and in such places as the Philippines – could be attributed to exceptional local factors such as Malaya's isolation, the fact that the insurgency was almost exclusively based on one racial group, the missed opportunities of 1945–49 that gave the government both warning and time in which to act effectively to deny the communists victory. The 1948–60 failure can also be explained away as being only the first round in a struggle which is still going on, the final outcome of which is by no means clear. In any event the Maoist concepts were put into practice in various places, most notably in nearby Indo-China where Truong Van Chinh, better known as Ho Chi Minh, closely followed Mao's ideas and whose book *The Resistance Will Win* became the revolutionary gospel of the Viet Minh in the war against the French, 1946–54. Certain modifications were provided after 1950 by the appearance of *The War of Liberation and the People's Army* by Ho Chi Minh's chief lieutenant, V. N. Giap.

Giap accepted virtually all of Mao's ideas but modified the final stage in which he considered four conditions were necessary before a final offensive could be undertaken. He believed that insurgent forces had to achieve a marked psychological ascendancy over the enemy and to have confidence in their ability to win in conditions of conventional fighting while there was a declining offensive spirit in the enemy camp. Further, possibly because he was operating in a colony, Giap believed that an essential requirement had to be a favourable international situation or climate of opinion. Both against the French and the Americans, the communists had more than one eye on the psychological

impact of military actions and, indeed, both campaigns were characterized by the insidious confidence-sapping psychological offensive against the enemy homeland and population. In both instances, the wavering of determination in the effort of the counter-insurgents took place before defeat in the field occurred. Moreoever, to the practice of revolutionary guerrilla warfare, Giap contributed the deliberate and systematic use of terrorism against the population, not simply to coerce the people and totally commit the perpetrators but to undermine the society against which he was pitted. Using terrorism in the late fifties and early sixties, the Hanoi-controlled Viet Cong as a matter of policy exterminated the village leaders and government officials of South Vietnam in order to destroy the stability of the society they sought to undermine. The consequence of such actions was that in many areas of South Vietnam, government except by the Viet Cong ceased to exist and, unlike the British in Malaya who had to maintain and then expand a threatened but existing political infrastructure, the South Vietnamese and Americans actually had to try to create one in the midst of a losing war and in conditions of utter loss of confidence on the part of the population in Saigon's authority. The idea of using terrorism was not new, of course, but Giap raised it to a level of intensity hitherto unknown.

The notion of using selective terrorism to undermine society was taken up in the late sixties by a Brazilian, Carlos Marighela. His ideas were to become increasingly important (and relevant) after the failure of numerous rural insurgency attempts throughout Latin America in the aftermath of Castro's successful campaign in Cuba (1956–59). In part the mainland failures resulted directly from Cuba in two respects. Firstly, Castro's success and subsequent drift into the communist camp alerted Latin American governments to the danger of insurgency: Cuba sacrificed by her success the priceless advantage of surprise. Moreover, Castro's links with Moscow squeezed the middle ground – the area of genuine doubt, uncertainty, confusion and tolerance essential for democracy as much as for its enemies – by forcing a choice between two monoliths, communism and the *status quo*. Such a choice crushed much potential support. Secondly, certain lessons were drawn from Cuba, most notably by Castro and Guevara, that became revolutionary dogma in Latin America in the sixties. These lessons were three in number. Firstly, that the security forces were not invincible and could be

beaten; secondly, that the countryside was the natural area of operations for the revolutionaries; thirdly, and most contentiously, Guevara argued that military action could produce the revolutionary situation necessary for insurgent success. This was in direct contradiction to Lenin's concepts of preparation while waiting for the profound crisis in society of which the communists hoped to take advantage. It was also a total rejection of Mao's emphasis on a long period of indoctrination of the population as the basis of military operations. Guevara argued that a small, mobile, hard-hitting nucleus of professional revolutionaries (called the *foco*) could, by military action, provoke the crisis and hence the momentum for success by tactical victories in the field – a bandwagon effect whereby success fed upon success, the credibility of the government being eroded by failure while insurgent victories brought an influx of recruits, supply and political sympathy.

Guevara's incompetent and disastrous Bolivian campaign in 1967 was sufficient comment on the validity of his ideas. The countryside, particularly in the Andean states, was simply not ripe for revolutionary insurgency. In no Latin American country in the sixties did rural insurgency survive to pose a major threat and only in five instances did campaigns even get beyond the preliminary stages. American training, personnel and equipment, reform programmes, the problems of movement, and poor fieldcraft, of the insurgents, the apathy of rural populations and the effectiveness of the security forces conspired to crush the revolutionary movements. But as the survivors of these attempts drifted back to the towns there dawned the slow realization of the revolutionary potential of the towns themselves, hitherto overlooked and in the case of Guevara, decried. In the sixties Latin America became more than 50 per cent urban for the first time. This in itself meant that rural insurgency was less relevant than it had been. In these rising and sprawling cities the pool of under- and unemployed, the young, the squatter population in the shanty towns beckoned as an immense reservoir of potential disaffection. The towns themselves were concentrations of power – and vulnerable targets – with easy access to the population

The Vietnam war: Men of an American airborne division on patrol through secondary jungle. Behind the point man the patrol commander has positioned his grenade-launcher ready to engage the enemy should the patrol trigger an ambush. Contacts with the Viet Cong were often accidental and led to small, but steadily mounting casualties throughout the war.

via the media. And the towns afforded cover, security and easy routes to and from targets. These were the points realized by the Tupamaros guerrillas in Uruguay and by Marighela. It was from the practical example of the former and the writings of the latter (*Handbook of Urban Guerrilla Warfare*) that there emerged the concept of urban-based insurgency which led to a global upsurge in this form of conflict in the early seventies.

Marighela concurred in Guevara's belief in the *foco* concept but differed in his approach. He believed that a revolutionary elite could precipitate revolution through armed struggle but he believed in an urban *foco* as the means of achieving this. The aim of urban revolutionary warfare was twofold. Firstly to draw the security forces into the towns and thereby weaken their grip on the countryside, thus allowing the insurgents to establish themselves in rural areas. Marighela believed that rural and urban insurgency had to complement each other, otherwise they would be defeated singly. Together they would unbalance the security forces and prevent their concentration, thus allowing the insurgency groups

room to manoeuvre. Secondly, urban guerrilla warfare tried to demoralize society by forcing the security forces into repression, thus polarizing society by revealing the repressive but impotent nature of the state to a disenchanted population. By a combination of criminal technique and astute manipulation of the media and of popular grievances, urban guerrilla warfare hoped to create a revolutionary groundswell by alienating people from authority. In short, urban guerrilla warfare was a sort of nationwide protection racket that tried to humiliate authority and lead to such a crisis of confidence that the population would turn to the insurgents for protection and as the only means of ending the struggle.

The darling of the academic revolutionary, Che Guevara, took the foci theory of revolutionary war to Bolivia and failed. The theory as expounded by Regis Debray required the revolutionary to plant himself in a country and win the people over by armed propaganda – it worked in Cuba, but failed in Bolivia where Guevara was killed. Inset: Fidel Castro the leader of the Cuban revolutionaries with the hunting rifle that was his personal weapon.

Marighela was killed in a clash with the Brazilian police in November 1969 but, unlike Guevara, this could not be considered as a comment on his ideas. But there were obvious weaknesses in the concept. Most notable was the fact that a government need not necessarily be forced into repression prior to an insurgent action of a kind that could alienate the population from the insurgents – a backlash in reverse. This in fact has happened in Turkey, in West Germany and, even before Marighela formulated his ideas, in Venezuela in the early sixties. Moreover, if there was a backlash against the insurgents it could result in a mild and tolerant government that hesitated to use repression being replaced by one that had no such scruples. In Uruguay the Tupamaros themselves were destroyed by exactly this process. A further difficulty, besides the obvious problem of liaison between rural and urban insurgent groups, was the expansion from small four- or five-strong groups whose survival depended on their security and elusiveness, into large scale organizations capable of taking the initiative and securing victory in the event of a weakening of authority. The strength of Marighela's concept was that it provided a do-it-yourself guide to aspiring guerrillas on the mechanics of urban insurgency. The *Handbook* outlined techniques, not political claims and strategy. This ensured imitation, particularly given the ease of communication of both people and ideas. The basic ideas of urban guerrilla warfare applied in Northern Ireland have tied down a considerable part of the British Army for a period longer than the duration of World War II.

The tactics used in Northern Ireland have been essentially those outlined by Marighela: raids and assaults (particularly on commercial, police and military establishments and on the methods of communication of the security forces), occupation of targets such as radio stations and factories (for propaganda effect), the basic ambush, the formation of street disturbances (often to draw the security forces into a killing zone), murder (euphemistically termed execution), kidnapping, sabotage and general, indiscriminate terrorism. While individual actions may vary in aim and be mounted for specific purposes – such as the liberating of hospitalized or imprisoned colleagues, securing weapons, eliminating police agents, etc. – the whole emphasis of action is placed on its psychological impact and value. Every action has to be geared to its morale value, a place on the evening television news, the next morning's newspaper headlines. Every action must

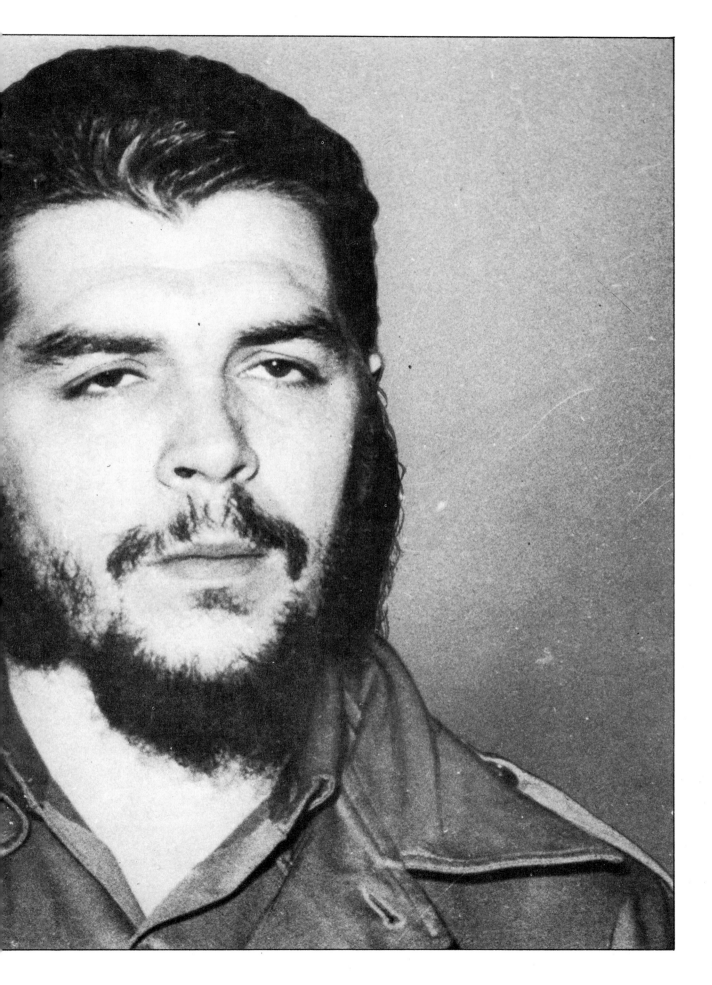

A British soldier takes a tumble during stone
throwing and provocation in the streets of Ulster.

be seen in this context. Two good examples of the way in which urban insurgents may attempt to seize the psychological advantage over the security forces can be indicated by the activities of the IRA. Prior to the meetings in September 1971 of the British, Irish and Northern Irish prime ministers, IRA bombings and shootings were stepped up to unprecedented intensity – diminishing the value of the talks themselves and forcing the meeting to react to events, rather than debate actions that could impose upon events. Similarly the bombings in central London on March 8, 1973 were deliberately designed to distract attention (particularly international attention) from the fact that that day Ulster voted by 591,820 votes to 6463 to stay in the United Kingdom. In both cases the presentation of photogenic violence tended to offset the political initiative of the governments concerned. This is not to argue that the physical damage that may be achieved in such actions is not without great importance in its own right; obviously it is. It is interesting to note that the original IRA campaign of 1919 opened with attacks on 119 Income Tax offices, actions bound to be popular with people but also striking directly at the heart of state power which lies in its ability to tax. Three hundred and fifteen abandoned police barracks were also attacked, seemingly a somewhat quixotic gesture until it is realized that any counter-offensive by the army and police in 1919 or 1920 could only have been based on their re-occupation of deserted stations. In the present campaign in Northern Ireland, a huge amount of damage has been caused, in part resulting from the calculation that the cost of the campaign can be made too high for the British.

Such have been some of the tactics used by urban terrorists. The primary objective has been to secure control over the population and to divide society against itself. It may be that the greatest weakness of urban guerrilla warfare is that it cannot polarize a society unless it is already divided. But it may also be that the second objective, the weakening of resolve on the part of authority, may also be beyond the reach of the insurgents since such operations will in future be bound to be undertaken in metropolitan homelands, not in far distant colonies or dependencies from which one can retreat.

The fact that they were fighting on what they considered to be home soil and that there was no place to which to withdraw in part may explain the vehemence of the French reaction to events in Algeria, 1954–62. France committed 500,000 men to the Algerian war and in military terms won the conflict. France isolated Algeria from external sources of succour by the creation of massive barriers along her frontiers and by intensive patrolling of the coasts. She resettled the population and garrisoned the country in strength, the size of garrisons being determined by the size and importance of the location. In the countryside the French used aggressive light units in scouting operations characterized by an unprecedented use of helicopters. At one stage, 600 helicopters were deployed and they quickly showed their advantage over other aircraft in being able either to airdrop or land forces in a closely compact group with none of the problems of re-organization after a jump. These tactics were employed in order to gain contact with enemy formations and to harrass them relentlessly to destruction. This task was mainly left to the elite formations in the French Army, such as the Legion, Paras, Marines and Chasseurs. Though extremely costly in money and prodigal in manpower, such tactics worked: by 1961 the military side of the insurgency was spent. But in making this effort the French dissipated the political advantage which was vital to success overall.

For the counter-insurgent the provision of security, material benefits and good government for the population is not enough: the population has to be induced to give its free consent to the government – and in Algeria this was not given. In fact it was withdrawn. In part this was the result of the unbridgeable divide in Algeria on racial and religious lines, in part by the fact that because of the international situation and the presence outside Algeria of considerable insurgent forces, intact and undefeated, there could be no inducement for the population to support the French

effort. But in large part the alienation of Algerian society stemmed from the methods used by the French. Though the insurgents used barbarous methods to terrorize the population – the lopping off of ears, noses, lips, mutilation generally and macabre methods of inflicting death – the French counter-measures, particularly in Algiers, totally polarized society. On the French figures, one in eight prisoners taken in for questioning in Algiers in the first six months of 1957 failed to survive interrogation. Torture became widespread: the war a competition in terror. Not only was this self-defeating in terms of the Moslem population, it was inimical to the interests of the French state itself. French society, disillusioned by losses and effort not simply in Algeria but before that in Indo-China, would not countenance the use of such methods on the part of a democratic and civilized society. Nor would it, in the last resort, admit the claim by extremist elements in the French Army to the effect that the total effort needed in Algeria determined the Army's involvement in and, if necessary, domination over, domestic politics, if the government of the day seemed to fail in its duty (as interpreted by them). Most of the French Army rejected such a notion but it was sufficiently widely held to help bring down the IVth Republic in 1958. The doctrine of *La Guerre Revolutionnaire* seemed to reverse Clausewitz's dictum that war is an instrument of policy, and to assert that politics exist to serve a total war effort. As it was, the success of French tactics made such a concept a very potent force until de Gaulle secured the ascendancy of the French state over the army by purging many army units and, finally, by granting independence to Algeria.

For counter-insurgents the only known method of combatting insurgency, rural and urban, lies in the basic methods that worked so well in Malaya, even though in fighting that campaign the counter-insurgents possessed many advantages that others have not enjoyed. The basis of political success in Malaya was intensive policing and extremely high quality Special Branch action, of military success the superiority of the security forces in minor tactics – intensive patrolling, marksmanship, ambush and anti-ambush drills. Essential to victory in Malaya was the close co-ordination of army and police actions within the framework of civilian control and the rule of law. One must recognize, however, that in certain cases the priority must be on orthodox military actions, such as in a situation where insurgent forces operate in strength in conventional fighting (such as the situation in South Vietnam when the Americans began to deploy in strength in 1965). But in the final analysis, granted that revolutionary warfare is total war, the military effort is secondary and the essential characteristics are political; in this situation the military can handle no more than part of the conflict. The essential struggle is for the control and loyalty of the population and in this economic, social, educational, health and welfare programmes and the evolution of meaningful political programmes are more important in the long run than the security situation, although these ideas cannot take root in a society where security is under stress.

The Superpowers Line Up

Soviet soldiers double down a range in Hungary
during a live firing exercise in the early spring of 1967.

The dropping of atomic bombs on Japan in August 1945 was a testimonial to American industrial and technological might. On all the seas ran the writ of the American Navy; in the air her aircraft were in numbers and quality infinitely superior to those of any other nation; on the ground her armies were numerous, lavish in equipment and experience. The only power that could be realistically contrasted to her was the USSR but she was markedly inferior industrially, economically and financially. Moreover, American superiority over the Soviet Union in two other fields was most notable. Firstly, the USA had a monopoly, and then decisive superiority, in nuclear weapons; secondly, she was geographically superior in that while both countries had an extension of power and influence during the course of the war, the American expansion had been to a point where she (or her allies) surrounded the USSR and possessed the means of taking a future fight to the Soviet homeland while remaining invulnerable herself. These considerations dominated strategy for nearly two decades.

With peace came American demobilization, but as the Cold War assumed its shape in the form of disputes over Germany, communist backing of the Greek Civil War, the Czechoslovakian coup, the Korean war, it fell upon the Americans to assume the leadership of democracy since they alone possessed the resources and the capacity for leadership needed to resist the aggressive nature of Soviet dictatorship. The Europeans were manifestly incapable of defending themselves since Britain and France had colonial commitments and the West Germans were disarmed. The formation of NATO in 1949 and the formulation of the Lisbon goals in the 1950s were unable to rectify this weakness. For the first years NATO was utterly dependent on the American nuclear umbrella for protection. American strategy was relatively straightforward, and was based on deterrence whereby they undertook immediate nuclear retaliation against the Soviet homeland in the event of Soviet aggression. The aim of American policy was to ensure such damage to the Soviet state through the razing of her cities that any political objective sought by the Soviets could count for very little if anything when set against the devastation of the homeland. And such was American power and certainty of intent that this strategy was very effective.

Initially the strategy of American deterrence was placed on air power – the simplest, cheapest and for a long time the only means of delivering a nuclear weapon on its target. But technology, just as it had produced the nuclear bomb, was working to produce other means of delivery of such bombs and, moreover, that technology was not the monopoly of the Americans any more; the Soviets were working along the same lines, though at later dates. These two factors led to an evolution in the strategy of nuclear deterrence. Although the US/NATO basic strategy did not change, the means by which the strategy was to be implemented underwent fundamental alteration. Because of the danger of placing total reliance on a single weapons system (the aircraft carried nuclear weapon) the search began for alternative means of delivery. These alternatives have become embodied in the triad system which is a combination of aircraft (both large strategic bombers and carrier-borne aircraft with gravity bombs and stand-off missiles), strategic missiles from submarines, and missiles fired from land bases, either mobile or especially protected in hardened silos. The missiles themselves evolved from single warhead weapons into missiles carrying different numbers of warheads, some pre-set to land in a group around a target, others capable of independent targetting. These developments ensured a multiplicity of weapons and a diversity of delivery that meant that an enemy could not hope to launch a surprise attack that would eliminate all the nuclear weapons of his opponent. The ability to withstand such a strike against one's own nuclear forces and still retain sufficient power to inflict unacceptable damage on the aggressor – termed a 'second-strike capability' – is a vital pre-requisite of deterrence strategy. In this process the role of land-based nuclear forces remains vital, even though the main element of the triad system remains with the submarine-launched ballistic missiles.

Because of these developments, and because the development of a Soviet nuclear deterrent seemed in the late fifties and early sixties to bring to an end American nuclear invulnerability, there was a movement away from the concept of deterrence based on massive retaliation. Given the power of the nuclear arsenals there was always the possibility that the reliance on nuclear weapons would make the Americans, muscle-bound by forcing a choice between surrender or suicide, gain only posthumous revenge. Thus one had in the early sixties the evolution of the idea of flexible response as the deterrence strategy for NATO. In this, the Americans envisaged NATO attempting to fight conventionally in the event of Soviet aggression in order to try to find

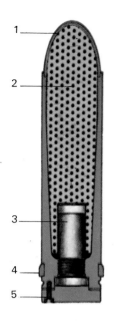

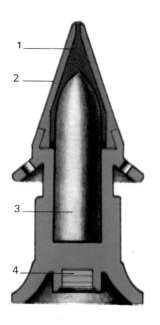

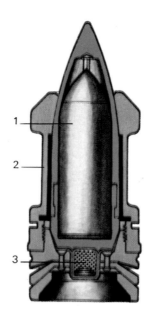

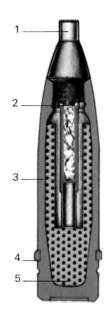

HESH
1. Outer nose casing of
    aluminium or copper
2. RDX plastic explosive
3. Base fuse
4. Driving band
5. Fixing screws

German APCR
For Tapered Bore
1. Phenolic plastic filling
2. Aluminium alloy ballistic cap
3. Tungsten carbide core
4. Tracer composition

APDS
1. Armour-piercing core of
    tungsten carbide
2. Plastic or light mangesium
    alloy sleeve or sabot
3. High-explosive charge

High Explosive
1. Nose cap
2. Fuse assembly
3. Outer casing
4. Driving band
5. High explosive filling

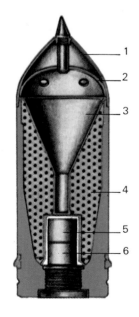

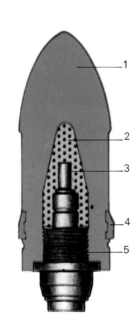

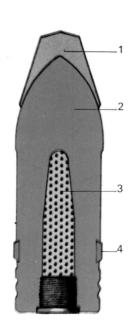

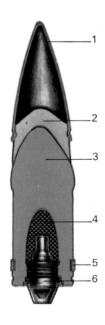

HEAT
1. Nose cap
2. Diaphragm
3. Steel liner
4. PEN/D1 charge
5. Exploder charge
6. Tracer

Armour Piercing
1. Solid shot
2. High explosive charge
3. Detonator
4. Driving band
5. Fuse assembly

Armour-Piercing Capped
(Improving AP shell)
1. Nose cap
2. Casing
3. High explosive charge
4. Driving band

APC + Ballistic Cap
1. Windshield
2. Cap
3. Body
4. High explosive charge
5. Driving band
6. Brass fuse and tracer

Scorpions of the 17th/21st Lancers and the 14th/20th King's Hussars during Exercise 'Glory Hawk' – the first major Scorpion exercise to be held in Germany.

ways of resolving the conflict without recourse to nuclear release on a strategic level. Given that both of the superpowers in the sixties were edging their way towards a situation of mutually assured destruction in the event of nuclear exchange – and the destruction of everything on earth at the same time – this change was essential.

The problem for NATO was that such a policy, while perfectly sensible for the Americans, spelt ruin for the Europeans. The buying of time by fighting conventionally would have to be achieved in fighting in Europe – on the territory of NATO. This was likely to be extremely destructive indeed. For the Europeans only a policy of massive deterrence made sense. Moreover, if such a policy of flexible response was to be put into effect, it could only be achieved at the cost of a considerable increase in the size of conventional forces. In the event of massive retaliation, conventional forces were limited in that their main role was designed to demonstrate a willingness to defend by the presence of some strength on the ground, rather than to be seen as a means of prolonged or successful defence. Therefore more ground forces needed to be deployed, but the immediate tactical problem was the manner in which these should be used. The basic choice was for forces to be deployed forward or to the rear. The advantage of a deployment to the rear was that while an initial assault would hit air, the defender would be able to discover the main line(s) of enemy effort before battle was joined, and if necessary, redeploy before contact. Such tactics would also have the advantage of forcing the enemy to come on to chosen ground and to have tired himself and his supplies in the process. In fighting this type of battle the enemy could be channelled into 'killing zones' which he would have to pass through in order to continue the advance and could be attacked there by armour, artillery or infantry (or any combination of the three) or by tactical nuclear weapons. Politically, however, the notion of a rear defence – possibly involving defence on a distant but major natural feature – was not really acceptable to a country that was the scene of such intended action. For the 'host' country defence must involve the forward defence of territory, not ceding voluntarily ground that in any case could be used as negotiation counters should conflict be limited or contained. The tactical disadvantage of such deployment, on the other hand, is the exposure to the full shock of the initial assault and the possibility of mistaking the main axes of advance by the enemy. An initial strategic

deployment forward could prove impossible to rectify if it was proved to be wrong.

For the USSR conventional forces have played a very different role than those in the west. An ability to over-run western Europe by virtue of superior conventional strength was the essence of Soviet deterrence strategy when she lacked nuclear weapons and when she was decidedly inferior in such weapons to the United States. The value of these conventional forces, however, has greatly risen as a result of the Soviet achievement of nuclear parity with the United States (or if not parity then something approaching it): the continued Soviet build-up of strength on land, sea and in the air can only be seen in the light of this situation. While it is true that obsolescence of design, the demands of new technology and the peculiar defence requirements of a country so vast as the Soviet Union can be used to explain away the immense growth in armed strength in the last decade, the present stance of Soviet forces, ground troops included, can only be seen in the strategic context whereby the communist bloc seeks to secure such a strategic superiority over the West that the latter would be denied any means of effective response in some future crisis. At the last congress of the CPSU Foreign Minister Gromyko made just this point.

In the purely military sense, by reason of its political ideology, the strategy of the Soviet Army is committed to the offensive, the chief characteristics of this stance being the emphasis on speed and mass. Speed is of the essence since Marxist ideology dictates the ultimate victory of the economically more powerful combatant. Given the marked industrial inferiority of the communist bloc to the West the Soviets must be committed to a rapid campaign of conquest before the resources of the West can be fully mobilized. Mass, the other characteristic, has long been the hallmark of Soviet operations but in the last few years there have been qualitative and quantitative increases in Soviet formations that give new dimensions to the meaning of mass, certainly within the context of the Central Front in Europe. As a result of the Soviet invasion of Czechoslovakia in 1968, the number of Soviet divisions in eastern Europe (excluding the Soviet Union) rose from twenty-six to thirty-one: since 1973–74 the firepower of these divisions has risen by about 20 per cent. The increase in firepower largely stems from the fact that the anticipated (or desired) speed of advance envisaged by the Soviets in the early sixties led to the introduction of self-propelled artillery since towed guns could not be

The new NATO FH70 during troop trials on Salisbury Plain. The gun developed jointly by the Germans, Italians and British has its own power unit for local redeployment. A German crew (far right) move the gun, while Italian gunners ready the ammunition and check the alignment. Cooperation on arms development not only saves money and speeds construction, but also ensures standardization throughout NATO.

relied upon for rapid and adequate fire support in fluid situations. Unfortunately for the Soviets no self-propelled guns were available to meet this requirement, and this led to the employment of old tanks, the T54/55, being used in this role. As self-propelled artillery they were allocated as an independent unit within Motor Rifle Divisions; these independent units have not been phased out with the subsequent introduction of the self-propelled artillery.

Soviet ground forces are formed into three types, depending on the predominant arm: the Motor Rifle Division, the Tank Division and the Parachute Division. All are, in fact, all-arms formations with indigenous infantry, armour, artillery and specialist troops with supporting arms and lines of communication formations. The airborne forces are the elite of the Army and consist of seven divisions. These can be used either in small formations for reconnaissance and sabotage or in larger formations, size depending on the state of the air battle and the nature of the objective. In the latter role they are likely to be employed in the seizure of bridges and river crossing sites by parachute

or helicopter-borne landings. The brunt of the land fighting, however, would obviously fall on the Tank Divisions (sixteen in Eastern Europe and forty-nine overall) and on the Motor Rifle Divisions (fifteen and 110 respectively). Both types of division are formed on a 3:1 ratio, with the Motor Rifle Division having its independent tank battalion left over from its SP artillery role. At all levels from division to battalion, the units have their own organic combat support arms which overall contributed to a massive concentration of firepower, particularly of the artillery. Overall a Tank Division deploys 325 tanks and about 9300 men: a Motor Rifle Division 266 tanks and 11,600 men. The artillery support differs between the divisions in that the Tank Divisions rely on their own guns for anti-tank protection whereas the Motor Rifle troops are given a battalion of anti-tank artillery. Overall the divisions are organized into either Tank or Combined Arms Armies on a 3:1 basis, though occasionally there may be more than four divisions in an Army. The Armies are then organized into fronts.

Basic Soviet practice has not changed substantially

since the war though their capacity to wage deep offensive warfare has naturally increased with the rapid mechanization of the Soviet Army. Emphasis is placed on mobility, the concentration of force at a given place in the attack, surprise, aggressive action and a desire to close with the enemy and retain contact until his destruction is complete. In order to ensure both width and depth to an attack, stress is laid on extensive operations (witness the 1944 offensive), and close co-ordination between units with air support. The aim of such operations is either the encirclement and hence annihilation of the enemy forces or the deep penetration of the enemy positions in order to destroy his supplies, reinforcements and capacity to fight. To achieve such objectives the Soviets aim to make a decisive breakthrough by concentration of decisive numerical and material superiority at a point of their choosing (usually taken off the map). This would entail a division formed into all-arms battle groups (armour predominating) on a front no more than five miles wide with either one, but preferably two, axes of advance. In all likelihood a division would be given only one axis of attack on a frontage of no more than two miles. Given the fact that an army frontage would be between twenty and thirty miles and that a division in the assault would be between thirty and sixty miles in depth in order to avoid bunching and hence nuclear attack, the flanks would in effect be left open. Reconnaissance elements would be used not simply in front of the leading elements but on these flanks and between the divisions that comprise an Army. In the assault the Soviets would normally attack in two echelons with the first echelon being the more powerful. This would contain a majority of the armour and be supported by all the artillery. The task of the first echelon would be to break through the enemy front with the second echelon passing through the (probably exhausted and possibly shattered) first echelons in order to exploit the breach and maintain the momentum of the advance. By the same token second echelon divisions would pass through the first wave in order to press on to objectives, or to make a breach if this proved beyond the capacity of the leading divisions.

The concentration of manpower and vehicles (over 2500 in a Motor Rifle Division) is obviously very hazardous and complicated, especially in the tactical switch from line of column advance to a rapid lateral deployment for an attack once contact is made. To this end the advance is led by a divisional recce element some thirty miles ahead of the regimental recce

elements that would be some five miles in front of the vanguard. The vanguard would usually be a motor rifle company and a tank platoon. In a sense all three have a similar role in that they are intended to locate, assess and report the enemy's positions and, where possible, to overcome them and continue the advance. This would enable the division to avoid having to waste time in deploying for a set piece assault. In the assault, the leading regimental battlegroup would deploy into battalion battlegroups, two forward, one in reserve, with the artillery in close support some three miles from the enemy positions. The task of the artillery is to provide covering fire during the deployment into companies and hence into platoons as the actual assault is taking place. (This deployment naturally is intended to take place beyond the effective range of infantry weapons.) The assault is intended to be carried through at speed, ideally with APCs and not with dismounted infantry; when the infantry are forced to put in an attack on foot the APCs are intended to provide covering heavy machine-gun fire.

Set piece battles are not favoured by Soviet forces, particularly since they could involve attacks on strong positions (including hull-down tanks) and would need time and superiority of numbers which a commander would not necessarily have at his disposal. More favoured is what is known as 'the encounter battle' which involves an open action by a Soviet formation against an enemy moving for the counter-attack. In essence it is a 'fire and manoeuvre' situation on a large scale but it is favoured by the Soviets because in this case the enemy would be robbed of his natural defensive advantages and Soviet superiority of numbers could be employed to maximum effect. The encounter battle envisages a major flanking movement after reconnaissance elements and the vanguard, acting as the pivot for the deployment, have blocked the course of an enemy advance and pinned him, hopefully at the same time discovering the size and direction of advance of the enemy. Depending on the ground deployment, the main attacking force would go to the flank while the enemy was held in his position and prevented from preparing defensive positions. The flanking movement is intended to envelope the enemy position until, under artillery cover, the attack is pressed home in regimental strength. Because of the danger of the flanking movement itself being taken in its flank, the Soviets envisage using defensive arrangements – such as the deployment of AT guns, ATGW helicopters and minefields – to hold their position from attack. The obvious problem of such an attack is the one inherent in any battle – success cannot be guaranteed and the role of attacker and victim can be reversed.

Perhaps the most frequently practised Soviet exercise is one of the more difficult operations in war – the forcing of a river obstacle in the presence of an enemy. Since any advance by Soviet forces into western Europe would result in their encountering a major water obstacle, it can be seen why this is of great concern. In theory they regard such attacks as routine, considering that they should be carried out from the line of advance without any delays either in forcing the obstacle or in breaking out of an established bridgehead. Accordingly they have equipped themselves with extensive and efficient amphibious and engineering equipment. All but one of their APCs – and that an obsolete one – are amphibious, as is the PT 76 light reconnaissance tank. Soviet MBTs can, given a hard river bottom and shallow banks, snorkel while their bridging and ferrying equipment has proved useful for the Indians in the war for Bangladesh, and for the Egyptians in the 1973 war with Israel. Nevertheless there may well be a difference between intention and reality since fitting snorkels is a time-consuming process and some delay in reconnaissance, organization of the crossing and in re-organization after it is only to be expected.

The problems of mounting a river assault are numerous, not least the prospect of having to select crossing sites without the advantage of previous reconnaissance. There is also the problem of mounting attacks on a relatively narrow front but not bunched so closely that a nuclear attack would be invited. Emphasis is placed on opportunist crossings by reconnaissance groups, which would attempt to seize and hold unprotected crossing points. But for a deliberate assault engineer reconnaissance would be necessary some time before the arrival of the main body. In a divisional assault the forward unit – usually a motor rifle battalion battlegroup – would be moved forward in order to clear the approaches to the river, take positions on the far bank and, if possible, prevent an enemy counter-attack or withdrawal. The division itself would cross in two echelons, the stronger part being the second to cross. That they reverse their normal procedure of advancing with the stronger part of their forces forward suggests that a river crossing may not be so routine after all, but the reason for holding the major part of strength back for the second wave is the belief that the second echelon would be able to maintain the momentum of the advance by passing through the first wave without having to re-organize. In the first echelon assault, the leading regiment would normally commit two or three battalions, each with all three companies deployed forward in line, ideally all entering the water together. On reaching the far bank the infantry dismount from their APCs in order to secure immediate objectives. Once the leading battalions have secured the far bank – and the leading regiments could have immediate objectives as far as six miles beyond the river itself – the second echelon is moved forward with GSP ferries and bridging equipment in order to take over the armour. Tanks are not committed in the first echelon. The time reckoned to elapse between the first assault and the tanks crossing is about thirty minutes. To aid the process, airborne forces could be used either to secure the crossing before the arrival of the division or during the actual assault. Close air support generally is envisaged for the assault and for the period of the immediate re-organization in the bridgehead when the leading motor rifle units would be lacking their armour and artillery support. General artillery support would be available, up to and including nuclear release, if the objective was considered sufficiently important. It could be that for a river assault crossing, the Soviets would use their rocket artillery against enemy positions and that chemical weapons would be used extensively, since these would give area saturation. Smoke would be used extensively to cover the attack during all initial stages.

The set-piece battle, the encounter battle and river assault are the basic stock-in-trade tactics of the Soviet Army: simple, direct and not very elaborate or sophisticated, they play directly to the strengths of the military machine. In outline the methods to which the Soviets are committed tend towards the expanding torrent concept on a totally mechanized scale and up-dated to incorporate new weapons. A major source of weakness may lie in supply and maintenance, both of which are rather poor and here the Soviets could encounter severe problems. The Arab-Israeli war of 1973 revealed the high rates of ammunition and equipment expenditure on the modern battlefield. They were somewhat hidden in the 1967 war by the early impact of Israeli air power and the disorganization of the Arabs. In 1967 the Israelis crushed the Egyptians, Jordanians and Syrians with contemptuous ease. In the euphoria of victory the Israelis and many outside observers tended

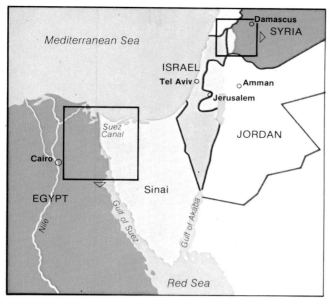

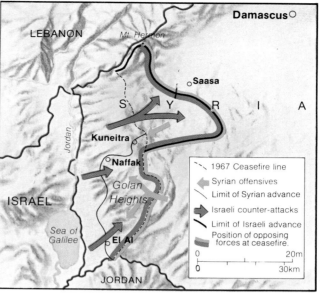

Map 2 legend (Golan Heights)

- --- 1967 Ceasefire line
- Syrian offensives
- Limit of Syrian advance
- Israeli counter-attacks
- Limit of Israeli advance
- Position of opposing forces at ceasefire.

0 — 20m
0 — 30km

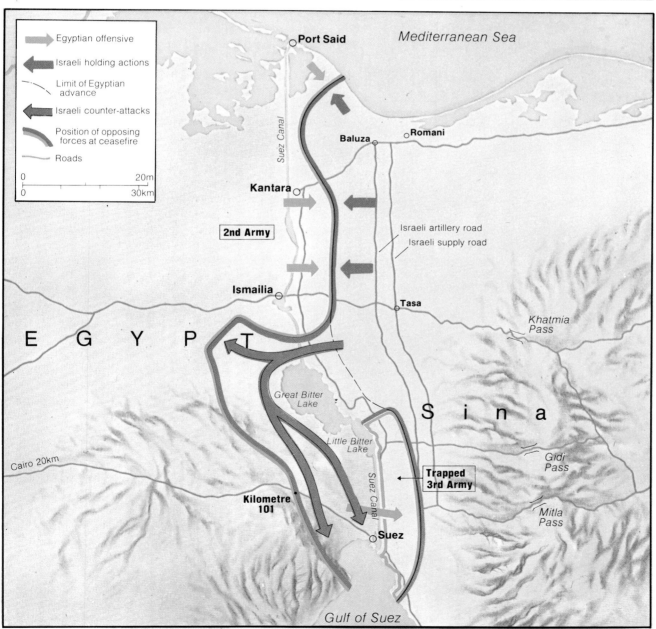

Map 3 legend (Sinai / Suez Canal)

- Egyptian offensive
- Israeli holding actions
- --- Limit of Egyptian advance
- Israeli counter-attacks
- Position of opposing forces at ceasefire
- Roads

0 — 20m
0 — 30km

Mediterranean Sea

Port Said

Suez Canal

Romani

Baluza

Kantara

2nd Army

Israeli artillery road
Israeli supply road

Ismailia

Tasa

E G Y P T

Great Bitter Lake

Khatmia Pass

S i n a

Little Bitter Lake

Suez Canal

Trapped 3rd Army

Gidi Pass

Cairo 20km

Kilometre 101

Mitla Pass

Suez

Gulf of Suez

An Israeli Centurian during the Yom Kippur War. The Middle East wars have enabled experts to evaluate weapons and equipment in action and have demonstrated that many of the lessons of 1940 are still valid thirty years later. Air power allows free movement on land which in turn gives the attacker greater freedom of action to hit his enemy when and where he wants.

to see the outcome of the war as vindication of the tank. Indeed, the performance of Israeli tanks was impressive. Centurion tanks broke open the Egyptian defensive positions at Khan Yunis and Rafa and forced their way through the main part of the Egyptian defences towards El Arish; Israeli armour was largely responsible for the encirclement and annihilation of the Egyptian armour east of the Mitla Pass. Israeli tanks also performed well in the fighting on the West Bank and in the storming of the positions on the Syrian Heights. The 1973 war, however, showed that while the tank was undoubtedly extremely important it was not the pre-eminent weapon that some observers had believed it to be. As the Egyptians swarmed across the canal in their opening assault, the Israelis committed their armour in the same manner as they had in 1967. These counter-attacks were unbalanced, poorly co-ordinated and lacking in infantry, artillery and close air support. The Israeli attack was literally stopped in its tracks, the armoured brigade attacking towards Suez shot to pieces not by tanks or artillery but mainly by new weapons making their debut on the battlefield – new PGWs (precision guided weapons) of the Sagger variety, man-portable ATGWs. Used in profusion the ATGWs were able to inflict unacceptable losses on the Israelis who, because of the deepening crisis developing on the

Syrian Heights, were forced to go on to the defensive in the Sinai and to await reinforcements and re-organization. In the north, however, Israeli tanks showed their value as tank killers. The sheer weight of the Syrian attack, combined with tenacity and great bravery, forced the Israelis to give ground but only at an exorbitant cost in time, losses and physical endurance. Moving forward in orthodox Soviet tactical formations the Syrians moved on to Israeli tank guns, and the Israelis made maximum use of their favourable ground conditions in their defensive fight. Israeli gallantry and losses bought time to bring up the reserves needed to launch the counter-attack as the momentum of the Syrian advance slackened. In the Sinai the increasing problems of the Syrians forced the Egyptians to abandon their initial and very limited objectives and to move into the attack in order to relieve the pressure on their allies. In moving forward the Egyptians lost their cohesiveness and exposed themselves to hull-down Israeli tanks. In the fighting that followed the superior training and experience of probably the best tank forces in the world secured a decisive Israeli victory. In moving forward after the defensive phase, moreover, the Israelis showed that they had absorbed the lessons of the opening exchanges. New tactics were employed involving the all-arms battlegroup, infantry in advance of armour and APCs, the latter providing heavy fire on areas from where PGWs could be or were fired. In effect the infantry were crumbling the front to allow the passage of armour for exploitation: both arms were co-operating in order to secure a fire supremacy over the enemy by relying on a superiority of indiscriminate area firepower to offset the effect of a precision weapon.

By heavy area fire, guidance of precision weapons is made hazardous, lessening the chances of a hit. In part the antidote to more powerful weapons has always been the securing of more of the same weapons. In part the future may show that general saturation fire may offset the value of precision-guided weapons. Be that as it may, the evolution of PGWs may give the infantry a more active role in the NATO killing zone than has hitherto been the case.

SEA WARFARE

Sea Power and its development until 1914

Sea power is the means by which a nation, or a group of nations acting together, attempts to secure and maintain command of the sea so that it can transport its own mercantile and military resources necessary for the prosecution of a war effort. In doing so it naturally attempts to deny such facilities to the enemy. The strategic elements involved in maintaining this power range from building up shipbuilding and ordnance facilities, bases in the homeland and abroad, fishing, mercantile and hydrographic fleets, to the final arbiter of sea power, the fighting ship. On the latter ultimately depends the safe passage of the other ships and the security of the homeland.

Warships are compromise constructions in that they combine defensive protection, propulsion and endurance facilities with offensive power. This has been true throughout history, thus the nature and power of a fighting ship at any given time is dependent on the level of technology at that time. Warships, at least, have always tended to be built around the most powerful weapon in existence, or in support of the ship that carries that weapon. In the present century, however, technology has produced both weapons and means of delivery that have vied with one another to be the decisive weapon at sea; and these weapons have produced specialization of ships and altered strategic and tactical concepts concerning their employment.

At the time of the French Revolutionary and Napoleonic Wars there was only one type of naval vessel: the wooden fighting ship, built around a crude, inaccurate, short-range cannon. The destructive power of such cannons was so small that they needed to be mounted in broadsides and to be used at very short ranges to be of any use at all. This had two effects. Firstly, it meant that the gun decks had to be heavy enough to take the weight of many guns and the sides had to be strong enough to afford some degree of protection for the gun crews. The weights implied in such considerations meant that the ships had to rely on wind and tide for movement since independent movement by means of oars was out of the question. Secondly, in the field of tactics, the nature of the ship determined that it had to fight in broadside action since it lacked any means of forward or rear offensive power (or any substance). This meant that a force seeking action had to secure the advantage of wind conditions in order to bring an enemy to bay. If an enemy was inferior but had the better of the weather conditions there was very little a superior enemy could do to force action since he had no superiority in speed with which to close the range. The sailing ships of all nations were roughly the same (hence the rough equality of speed), since the prevailing level of technology – knowledge of ship-building techniques, skill in sail and rope making, the forging of cannon and shot – was roughly the same in Europe and North America. It was continually evolving and advancing (albeit very slowly), yet in essence the ships of the latter sixteenth, seventeenth, eighteenth and early nineteenth centuries were similar in construction, performance, skill of crews and in their dependence on the elements for movement.

The purpose of sea power was primarily defensive. The over-riding aim was the defence of the integrity of the homeland against invasion and raids against which military forces would otherwise have to be deployed. In the case of Britain, an island kingdom off the coast of a Europe littered with states that possessed armies larger than her own, this was the whole of the *raison d'etre* of the navy: other countries, being continental, needed navies for exactly the same reason but were not so absolutely dependent on sea power for national survival as the British. In the search for security against naval attack certain strategic interests could be of immense importance (for instance, for Britain the prevention of the Low Countries being occupied by a hostile major power because of the proximity of those areas to the east coast of England), the normal tactic employed was the close blockade of enemy ports by an equal or superior fleet. In the era of the sailing ship such a policy was always possible for the British because such ships had immense endurance – as long as discipline and fresh water lasted – and did not have to return to port for refuelling. Moreover, if winds drove the British from their stations (off the French and/or Spanish ports since these were Britain's natural enemies) those same south-westerly winds confined the enemy to their ports. In addition, the British were more favoured with suitable ports than were the French and Spanish on their Atlantic coastlines. Geography and meteorology therefore conferred on Britain immense benefits in naval warfare with her normal enemies in the days of sailing ships. It was to do so again in the changed circumstances of the twentieth century in the struggle to realize the second objective of sea power – the defence of trade.

A glance at a world map of 1914 quickly reveals the two most salient features of the British Empire, namely its immensity and its essentially maritime nature.

Largely, but by no means wholly, built up in the era of the sailing ship, the British Empire had been acquired by sea power. Nearly every point of constriction was held by Britain, virtually every point where communications were forced through a narrow sea passage was held by the British; every point where narrowness of sea passage had marked out a battlefield for the great powers was controlled by the Royal Navy. Wind and currents had determined the location of these positions in the days of sailing ships, coal bunkers in the age of steam. By 1914, by dint of efforts in past wars, Gibraltar, Malta, Port Said, Suez, Aden, the Persian Gulf, Colombo, Singapore, Hong Kong, Mombasa, Cape Town, Freetown, the Falklands, the West Indies, New Zealand – all were under the British flag. From these positions, and from her home ports, Britain controlled the major part of the world's trade; from these positions she could immediately bring pressure to bear against any other country; in these places could be assembled the means of protecting merchant ships – the convoy system of merchantmen sailing together under armed escort provided by the Royal Navy.

Thus the functions of sea power were essentially twofold in their historic evolution: the security against invasion and the defence of trade. In the days before railways and motor transport, these were of immense importance, proportionately even more so than they are today. The reverse of these functions, however, was also of great importance: command of the seas allowed the holder to pick the time and place for an invasion, expedition or raid that formed part of his intention to make an enemy conform to his will; command of the seas also allowed the commerce of an enemy to be seized; *lack* of command of the seas (on the latter point) was an encouragement to a country to furnish commerce raiders to seek out lone enemy merchantmen in

Left: Sail plan and elevation of an eighteenth century line of battleship. Such warships could stay at sea for years, given food and ammunition. Below right: Cutaway of a three-decker's gun decks with cannon run out, at full recoil and secured.

order to bring supplies to home ports.

There remained two further functions of sea power, applicable in times of peace and war. Firstly, the existence of a fleet intact was a powerful instrument of diplomacy, a bargaining chip at the conference table, the means of extracting concessions, of reaching accommodations that would be beyond recall if the fleet did not exist. In time of war such a fleet could also tie down the resources of an enemy that were urgently needed for such operations as a colonial expedition or defence against commerce raiders. Secondly, fighting ships could 'show the flag,' as an instrument of diplomacy, a symbol of power, intent and capability: in the nineteenth century this was a role virtually synonymous with the Royal Navy.

The ships that carried out these functions, as noted earlier, were of a single nature – wooden sailing ships with broadsides of cannons. These ships divided into two basic types: the line of battle ship and the frigate; the basic distinction being in the number of gun decks carried. A line of battle ship was, by definition, a ship that could take its place in a battle line against the heaviest enemy ships; such ships carried upwards of three gun decks. Frigates, much nimbler but not necessarily faster, usually carried a single deck of guns and were used as scouts, message carriers and commerce protection. In carrying out their appointed roles both were hampered by problems of communication – gun smoke, rigging and light winds made visual signalling difficult, and admirals had many problems in controlling their fleets once in action. It was also hard to take advantage of sudden opportunities that arose in the course of a conflict. Overall this had the effect of stifling initiative, since the simplest solution was to adopt a line ahead formation in action, ships taking on their opposite numbers in the enemy line. Such theories were first laid down in England in 1653 as *Fighting Instructions* and elaborated later in 1673. These became, with some modifications, holy writ for the Royal Navy in the seventeenth and eighteenth centuries. Admirals could depart from the line of battle formation only at their peril and there was no encouragement to break the enemy line in order to provoke a melee or secure an annihilating advantage over part of the enemy fleet. Only in the case of an enemy in flight could the sanctity of the battle line be broken in the General Chase. Blind adherence to these ideas frequently resulted in indecisive battles, and Professor Lewis in *The History of the British Navy* has pointed

out that between 1692 and 1782 fifteen orthodox 'line' battles resulted in not one enemy ship being sunk or captured, whereas six 'chases' resulted in overwhelming British victories. The tactical sterility of the line tactics, which caused battles to be decided by geographical position and strategic deployment rather than initiative, did result in improved signalling techniques being introduced by Howe and Kampenfelt, but eventually the whole concept was challenged theoretically by writers such as de Morogues, Clerk and de Grenier and practically by admirals such as Nelson. It remains a fact, however, that no matter how frequently the line tactics showed their futility in war, they were always reimposed in peace time. This was certainly the case after the Napoleonic Wars, but there was one very important development at this time which almost guaranteed change: the Industrial Revolution in its application to sea warfare.

In the fifty years after Trafalgar the homogenity of ship design that had been carefully evolved over the previous two hundred years disintegrated under the impact of a rapidly advancing technology in which there were no guide lines and no pools of accumulated knowledge on which to draw. Ships underwent profound change. Independent movement was restored by the introduction of first paddle and then screw propul-

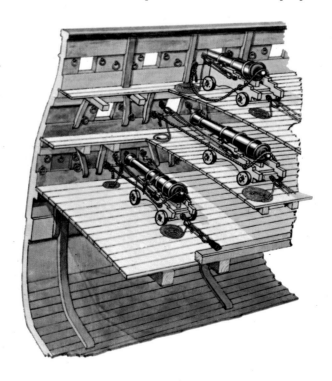

sion; guns became heavier, rifled and fired shells. The new shells necessitated protection other than wood and led initially to ships being sheathed wholly or in part by iron and then to ships made entirely of iron. Broadsides were suppressed as were sails and masts. Guns began to be mounted on revolving turntables to enable them to be trained over wide arcs of fire, and they were enclosed by turrets to protect the crews. By 1870 the ships of different navies varied vastly in design, capability and sea worthiness.

Moreover, not only were ships being changed by the evolution of gunnery but, under the impact of metallurgical and chemical developments, new weapons were emerging as potential rivals to the gun. These weapons aimed at striking an enemy ship at its most vulnerable point below the water line. The search for such weapons (other than the ram) can be traced back over three centuries but it was not until the nineteenth that technology enabled them to be developed. The

first of the new weapons was the mine (initially called the torpedo), and its invention is generally credited to Samuel Colt, although work on such a weapon was taking place in various places at the same time. Colt invented a mine – a metal-enclosed explosive charge – that could be detonated by electric current operated from an observation post on land. Subsequently, contact mines were developed that exploded when in collision with a ship. Early mines were naturally primitive but the passage of time permitted more effective explosives to be used, more efficient initiation to be adopted and the development of a reliable method of laying mines at a proscribed depth. (The latter was achieved by laying mines from a specialized craft with an attached anchor, cable and hydrostat that fixed the mine at the required depth.)

Mines had immense strategic and tactical effects. They were used extensively during the Crimean war (1854–56) but caused no losses (the first ship to be lost to mines was the *USS Cairo* in 1862, in the Battle of the Yazoo River). Thereafter their increasing effectiveness meant that a policy of close blockade of an enemy coast became increasingly unrealistic, for mines, a cheap mass produced weapon needing no maintenance and little manpower to use, were ideal defensive weapons for coastal and harbour protection, denying the room to manoeuvre for an aggressive fleet. Offensively, moreover, the mine could be used to try to restrict an enemy in his harbours.

The second of the new weapons was the 'locomotive torpedo' – an underwater weapon with its own means of propulsion which differentiated it from other forms of torpedoes that demanded death wishes on the part of their users. (The *USS Housatonic*, in 1864, was the first major surface ship to be sunk by underwater attack when a Confederate hand-cranked submarine detonated a charge under her: the submarine perished in the attempt, such were the dangers of early types of torpedo.) The 'locomotive torpedo' was pioneered by an Austrian, Luppis, and a Scot, Whitehead, in Fiume. It was erratic in its direction and depth-keeping capabilities, but could only improve. After the late seventies contra-rotating propellers, the horizontal rudder and the gyroscope conspired together to enhance its potency; by the 1890s a torpedo with a 300-lb warhead had a 1000 yard range at 30 knots (or 4000 yards at 19 knots) and could be fired from below the waterline of a moving ship.

The development of such a weapon had to have

A German naval mine. 1 Glass tube containing a bichromate solution. If the glass was broken the solution met a zinc carbon plate. 2 Electric current ran through a fuse wire to a detonator. 3 Firing the main charge 4. The mine was secured by a cable which was anchored to a weight that rested on the sea bed.

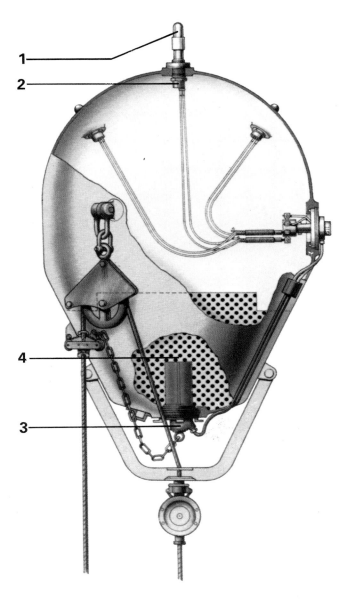

1
2
4
3

they could be used offensively, even with the primitive torpedoes then available. Nevertheless, the restrictions on the use of such craft could only be overcome by building larger and faster craft. The British built the *Lightning*, so named because of her 19 knots speed capacity. By the turn of the century torpedo boats were rising in displacement, speed and armament, and there was a need for a ship that could take on such boats before they could get into a position to attack the battle line. The British, since they had a strong battle fleet, tended to build 'destroyers' with a good turn of speed and quite heavy gun armaments: many other navies, especially the German Navy, tended to build smaller but faster boats with stronger torpedo armament since they were more interested in the offensive than defensive possibilities.

The second means of delivering torpedo attack was the submarine, developed around the turn of the century. The previously insurmountable problems encountered in building submarines had been overcome by technology. Steel provided a suitable material for construction; the horizontal rudder (hopefully) controlled the dive; and the internal combustion engine and accumulator battery provide a safe and reliable means of propulsion. By 1900 six navies had ten submarines among them, the British, alert to the danger that this vessel could be to their naval supremacy, quickly taking the lead in this field. It was the British who incorporated the conning tower and periscope into the first prototype submarines and led the field in submarine development up until the outbreak of World War I.

The third method of torpedo delivery was from the air, and the first occasion that this was achieved was one week before the outbreak of World War I. It had no immediate strategic or tactical impact, but air power was beginning to make itself felt in small ways on naval thinking before World War I though it was the war itself that gave this new dimension of warfare its main impetus.

The torpedo had one decisive effect on tactical thinking: it forced ranges to open. In the course of the nineteenth century, there was little real appreciation of how battles would be fought and the Nelsonian dictum that a captain could do no wrong if he placed his ship alongside the enemy was still widely held to be applicable. The advent of heavy guns in the sixties and seventies did nothing to change this because their accuracy rate was very low. [In one test in 1871 a

immense repercussions on naval warfare for, by its very existence, it required a new means of delivery and a revision of tactics. Over the years three ways of delivery were developed.

Initially, as early as 1870, special 'torpedo boats' were built but these were small, not particularly seaworthy and lacked range and crew accommodation. Primarily they were intended to be used for harbour defence although, as the Russians showed when two of their craft sank a Turkish guardship at Batum in 1878,

Huascar, **an ironclad monitor built by the British for the Peruvians in 1865. She was powered by sail or steam and had a powerful twin 10-in gun turret and armour protection with a robust ram bow.**

British battleship, at 200 yards, missed another battleship target, both ships being anchored; in the Spanish-American war of 1898 the Americans had to close to under 300 yards against moored opponents in order to achieve hits and then only scored 3 per cent accuracy rate (Manila Bay).] The torpedo, however, forced these ranges to open because battleships dared not get so close in case they were exposed to underwater attack. Torpedoes also forced the heavier ships to carry secondary and tertiary armament to deal with torpedo boats before they came within effective range. Mixed armament of heavy, medium and light guns was therefore needed for a battleship in order to fight heavy ships and defend itself against torpedo attacks. Mixed armament was also considered necessary to provide the heavy volume of fire that was held to be the key to victory, in part a reaction against the monster guns of earlier decades that were slow to handle and low in accuracy. The development of quick-firing guns in the eighties enabled a heavy volume of fire to be put down by a ship, but the increasing range at which actions had to be fought to keep out of the range of torpedoes

Strategically and tactically the *Dreadnought* had a profound effect. Strategically, she was so superior to previous types of battleship in her firepower and speed that she inaugurated a naval race between the powers for superiority in numbers of this type of ship. This eventually became an Anglo-German race, won ultimately by the British but only at a profound cost in relations between the two countries. Tactically, in opening the range of action and demanding accurate gunnery at high speed, the *Dreadnought* required a fresh tactical approach to her handling. The acquisition of more gun power and greater speed could only be an advantage if used to secure an overwhelming concentration of force; but in fact the tactical deployment of most navies remained the line ahead formation, with the battle line being manoeuvred as a single inflexible whole. The aim of such deployment was to secure the most favourable conditions – wind clearing gun and funnel smoke, light and sun – for concentration against the enemy line, ideally with the broadside of the line being concentrated against the enemy vanguard. This was known as 'Crossing the T.' Much thought went into considering ways to ensure the timely deployment of the battleships from their cruising formation – a compact mass covered by attendant craft – into a battle line where the fullest possible weight of fire power could be brought to bear on an enemy. Less thought went into the manner in which the squadrons that made up the fleet could be used in a semi-independent role, thereby encouraging initiative and aggression. Great emphasis was placed on conformity and wooden orthodoxy, with too great a reliance being placed on the commander of the fleet to see, know and order everything.

The problems of the fleet commander were greatly increased by the new developments. He still had to contend with old problems such as smoke, which often made flag signalling impossible (although he was aided by the introduction of radio before the war), but the battlefield had been extended by the restoration of independent movement and any battle was bound to be a fast moving affair. There was an increasing need to know the location and strength of the enemy at all times through detailed reconnaissance and reporting. This was the role of the cruiser. Cruisers had been eclipsed by iron battleships against which they could neither fight nor run away since they lacked metal construction or any superiority in speed. The first iron cruiser was the British *Inconstant*, almost as large as

meant that fire control became increasingly difficult. Different calibre guns and shells meant different flight times of shells to a given range and difficulty in identifying individual fall of shot. In the early twentieth century the principle of centralized fire control was established and with it uniformity of guns, which allowed the accurate firing of salvoes as long as the guns were of the same size. The first ship to incorporate a uniform heavy armament was *HMS Dreadnought* (launched 1906) though the Americans had been the first to announce their intention of building such a ship.

contemporary battleships. There was a temptation for second class naval powers to use heavily protected cruisers in a dual role as cruisers and line ships, but in fact theoretical and metallurgical developments led to a diversification of cruiser evolution into two main themes. On the one hand, the French development of the *Guerre de Course* strategy of commerce raiding by surface ships led to the evolution of heavy cruisers, fast enough to evade battleships but capable of looking after themselves by virtue of their strong gun armament. The French initiated this process with the *Dupuy de Lome* in 1888, a 20-knot ship which made her a little slow in comparison with contemporary cruisers, but armed with 7.6-in and 6.4-in guns. There followed a race between the British and French in heavy cruisers, in which the example of the *Inconstant* was virtually repeated by the *Powerful* and *Terrible* in that they were almost as large and costly as line ships. The development of steel made for better quality cruisers on lower displacements, but even in the first decade of the present century there was a tendency for size, speed, protection and armament to increase again. The culmination of the process was to be seen in the battle-cruisers, initiated by the British at the time of the *Dreadnought*. Almost as large as the *Dreadnought*, they were nearly as powerful in main armament, and much faster, than contemporary battleships. Battlecruisers were specifically designed for the twin purposes of hunting down and destroying commerce raiders and acting as the fast vanguard of the battle fleet, capable of carrying out unaided a reconnaissance in force and of lying in the battle line. The weakness of the battle-cruiser concept, certainly in the British case though less so in the German and Japanese Navies, was that the tactical advantage of high speed – being able to choose range and position in an exchange of fire – was bought at too high a price in defensive power: the battle-cruisers could not take the punishment they themselves could inflict.

The light cruiser, on the other hand, was not intended to take punishment. Its task was to make contact with the enemy and to retain it until fleet contact was obtained: the light cruiser was in other words, the eyes of the fleet. Once battle was joined the reconnaissance role remained, but the light cruisers were supposed to afford protection to the battle line from enemy cruiser and destroyer attacks with torpedoes, and to launch such actions themselves. For the British before 1914 the defensive aspect of this role was the more important.

The destroyers in the Royal Navy had priorities that were essentially defensive though they were exceptional in that they were allocated an offensive role for night operations. On the whole, the Navy tried to avoid night action on the grounds that it was something of a lottery, but while the battle line would decline night action, the destroyers were given the initiative to launch attacks on the enemy line that would be perilous if mounted in daylight. Destroyers were generally exercised before the war in co-operation with the battle line by both the British and the Germans. Both Navies realized that co-ordination of gun and torpedo attacks was more likely to bring results than separate efforts: equally both Navies based their tactics not on individual ship attack but on flotilla attacks, in the belief that the concentration given by a flotilla of destroyers would be harder to avoid. The tactical response of the battle line to such attack was generally agreed to be 'the turn away from the attack' – exposure on a small stern with its disturbed wake of water that was moving away from the torpedo. In this way the battle line could outrun the torpedoes as the latter began to slow down when they approached the end of their runs. This tactic was preferred to the ploy of turning towards the torpedoes and 'combing' them which was considered dangerous because the converging speeds of ship and weapon made evasive action more difficult. The weakness of the safer turn away was that the ship ran the risk of losing contact with the enemy battle line.

Destroyers also carried out an anti-submarine role in forming a screen for the heavy ships when the latter were either in their cruising or their battle formation. The effectiveness of destroyers in such a role was very limited before 1916 since they lacked the means of detecting or attacking a submerged craft other than gunfire or ramming. Despite these limitations, however, they were effective in keeping submarines away from the fleet: indeed between 1914 and 1916 only one instance of the British destroyer screen being penetrated by a German submarine was reported – and that resulted in the ramming of the submarine in question by the *Dreadnought*. Nevertheless, the threat of submarines imposed certain quite severe restrictions on the strategic and tactical handling of battle formations. Strategically, fleets did not dare to enter certain waters: in order to move at all they had to employ continual high speed cruising formation and often zig-zag – all the time cutting down the range of the destroyers, and hence the fleet itself. Submarines themselves could be

used in defence of approaches to ports and coasts – but this was generally recognized to be a weak arrangement that was costly in manpower and resources and not likely to achieve very much. More emphasis was placed on their offensive use, either individually or in an extended line, for both reconnaissance or opportunity attacks on the enemy battle formation. Tactically, in battle an enemy fleet could be drawn across a patrol line into a submarine 'killing zone,' and for this reason the British were somewhat reluctant to follow an enemy that 'stood off' during an engagement. The tactic was more theoretical than real, however, since the low speeds of submarines, both on the surface and while submerged, made close co-ordination very difficult indeed though the threat was real and remained. In these roles the submarine was seen basically as an adjunct to the big gun, rather than as a weapon with an

independent role to play, and before 1914 only a very few people considered the possibility that its chief role could be that of commerce destruction. Since a submarine could not take off crews of merchantmen, it was not seriously entertained that any civilized nation could resort to such an operation since it would involve either killing or setting adrift defenceless merchant sailors.

To summarize the situation prior to 1914 is difficult because of the many different strands involved. Material and tactics were dominated by the big gun and its use in broadside on an extended battle line. The battleship was no longer the absolute ruler of the seas but was under challenge, though the First World War was to show that that challenge was for the moment over-rated. Fear of the new weapons, however, bred caution both in the strategic employment of fleets and tactical handling at sea.

The First World War, triumph of Sea Power

Stores and munitions burn in Anzac Town as the guns of H.M.S. *Cornwallis* cover the Allied withdrawal from Gallipoli.

Before the war a French general made the celebrated remark that the British Navy was not worth a single bayonet. Though he was speaking the truth in that he was concerned with an initial clash of arms on the land frontiers, he failed to recognize the extent to which the capacity of France and Britain to wage war at all rested on sea power and the decisive part it could play in any war not decided in the opening exchanges. Had the Anglo-French armies been crushed in the opening battles – as they were in 1940 – there would have been very little the navies could have done to retrieve the situation: that the armies were not defeated but could not, in their turn, impose their will on the enemy ensured that sea power played an absolutely vital, indeed crucial, part in the Allied victory. It was a role that was unglamourous, even insidious, but it was sea power that ultimately strangled the life and will out of the Central Powers. Official sources placed the number of German civilian deaths between 1914 and 1918 as a direct result of blockade as high as 800,000; certainly it was despair at the prospects of having to endure the winter of 1918-19 after the disasters of the previous one, that played a large part in the German collapse in the autumn of 1918.

In World War I the Allies possessed certain basic advantages over the Central Powers, foremost among them their considerable superiority in numbers of ships of all types, and a well-nigh absolute superiority in geographical position. Through her metropolitan and imperial positions, Britain sat astride the trade routes of

the Central Powers in both the Mediterranean and the Atlantic and was thus in a position to sever virtually all her enemies' trade, with the notable and vital exception of German trade with Sweden.

The British policy of blockade was implemented by three measures: the basing of the fleet in the north of Scotland, the patrolling of the seas between Scotland and Greenland and Scotland and Norway, and the mining and patrolling of the English Channel. The Channel was mined, with gaps left for shipping only between the Kent coast and the Goodwin Sands, thus making it a very easy task for the British to intercept any merchantman passing through the Straits of Dover. In the north the British started the war with eight vintage cruisers, well enough armed to deal with any likely opponent, to patrol the routes to Germany: after November 1914 requisitioned liners were used as armed merchant cruisers to patrol these waters. The latter ships had the great advantage over military cruisers of good turns of speed when necessary and very long endurance: indeed the flagship, the *Alsatian*, once

cruised at thirteen knots for forty days on patrol.

The northern partrol operated search lines with ships ten miles apart, south of the Shetlands and west of Norway in the early stages of the war but gradually evolving ever more complicated patrol patterns that proved remarkably effective in preventing the blockade from being breached. Such patrols could not be 100 per cent effective since night and poor visibility always gave a blockade runner a chance of getting through, but the success of the measures can be gauged from the fact that between December 1914 and June 1915 over 1610 ships were investigated and nearly 400 were detained for further search. In the whole of 1916 over 3000 ships were investigated.

Such a policy was bound to conflict with neutral interests since the shipping trade was very lucrative. If a ship was detained for search the British could seize her if she was carrying war materiel, such as guns or explosives, or if certain goods, such as foodstuffs or raw materials, could be shown to be destined for the armed forces or government of the enemy. Certain

goods, including raw cotton, oil and rubber, were immune under the terms of the 1909 Declaration of London (never ratified by the British). By the beginning of 1915, as the realization dawned that the war might be a long one, the British began to declare certain items that were 'free' or 'conditional contraband' as 'absolute contraband.' They also began to enforce their measures more severely, although this raised problems with countries such as the Netherlands and the USA. It was not until the Americans entered the War in 1917 that the Allies were able to ignore those rights that the US had championed when uninvolved. In the meantime, however, the British had resorted to various ploys to avoid friction with neutral countries: in August 1915, they declared cotton as absolute contraband with no American protest because they had already bought virtually the whole of the American cotton crop; they made bilateral arrangements with the Norwegians, Danes and Dutch (September 1) in order to ensure that those countries did not supply Germany with goods that the British let through to them. They also resorted to the purchase of entire ships' cargoes (above the market value) simply to prevent trouble. By such measures, the British were able to draw the teeth of neutral opposition and to add vehemence to the blockade. After July 1917, the Allies added various foodstuffs and forage to the conditional contraband list, and to the absolute or conditional lists virtually all types of vegetable, animal and natural oil, virtually every significant ore, mineral and chemical, most forms of yarn, and a whole list of industrial materials and equipment. In all 238 items (excluding derivatives and by-products) were on the banned lists. The effect was devastating. As early as 1915, German harvest yields began to fall as a result of the demands for explosives and the lack of nitrate imports. By 1918, cereal production had fallen 40 per cent from its 1912–13 level; potato production by nearly 50 per cent; sugar by 33 per cent. The situation for Germany's allies was even worse. It was not in the armies in the field but in the nation as a whole that the collapse occurred. This was in large part the result of the superiority of Allied seapower.

The policy of blockade from Dover and northern Scotland was one that had been decided upon during May 1912, when the close blockade of the German Bight had been abandoned in British war plans because of the danger from submarines and mines. Only as late as that had Britain adopted the policy of distant blockade, and even then she thought in terms of an observational blockade stretched across the North Sea. Early losses in 1914 forced her to discard an observation line, albeit reluctantly, for this smacked of a defensive mentality that was anathema to many naval officers. The redeeming feature (to the British Navy) of blockade was that its rigours might force the German Navy to come out and fight: the Royal Navy overall was convinced that the German fleet would go the way of previous enemies. Overwhelming decisive victory was what the British public demanded; it was also what the world expected. Here was a major problem for the Admiralty and the Commander-in-Chief of the Grand Fleet, Jellicoe, who had no illusions about the reality of the situation. Jellicoe clearly appreciated that Britain did not have to fight to retain command of the seas: she was in the position that she merely had to avoid defeat in order to keep Germany at bay in a position of inferiority. He also realized, on the other hand, that a naval defeat would have incalculable results – perhaps catastrophic ones among the neutrals – and would leave open to attack the whole of Anglo-French trade upon which depended the survival of the Allies. Such were Jellicoe's strategic considerations. His tactical deliberations were similarly defensive and, being defensive, Jellicoe partially forfeited the likelihood of decisive engagement, since an inferior German fleet was more likely to try to avoid action than accept it.

Jellicoe wanted to bring the Germans to battle under circumstances most favourable to the British. Therefore, in his tactical deliberations he had to consider that, in addition to being limited to a range of 900 miles from his bases (because of the limited endurance of the fleet escorts), he had to avoid an action in the southern North Sea where the threat of mines and torpedoes was at its greatest. Because of this threat Jellicoe made it clear that he intended not to comply with an enemy turnaway when in contact since this could be an attempt to draw the British fleet into a submarine or mine trap. Thus two major strategic decisions – the geographical advantage of the British Isles *vis-a-vis* Germany and the need to avoid defeat – fortified the existing fear of new and largely untried weapons and fatally restricted aggressive tactical deployment.

For the Germans the situation was very different. They had built their navy following the 1898 and 1900 Navy Laws with the deliberate intention of exacting

Friedrich der Grosse a Kaiser Class battleship probably at her surrender in 1918. Coal burning ships produced funnel smoke which could be a liability in action. During the Battle of the Dogger Bank, the British had hoped to secure a position to the east which would have cut off the Germans from the home ports and given the Royal Navy the advantage of the light and a breeze to clear the funnel smoke away.

concessions from the British: this had merely resulted in estranged Anglo-German relations. Now, in time of war, the Navy was powerless to prevent German trade disappearing from the surface of the oceans with no corresponding gains for the Germans outside Europe. The German Pacific Squadron was effectively written off with the outbreak of war; although the imaginative and aggressive handling of this squadron led, in fact, to its having a longer life and a more useful one than might otherwise have been the case. Nevertheless, if the German Navy was very inactive in the first months of the war in the defence of German overseas interests and trade, it did play a vitally important role throughout the war simply as 'a fleet in being' which, undefeated, prevented the dispersal of the enemy battle fleet and light forces for other urgent tasks. Since the British needed to concentrate all their available strength in the North Sea, for it was up to the Germans when, if and in what strength to make a move, the Royal Navy could not allocate much of its strength to secondary theatres. The full effect of sea power could therefore never be fully brought to bear as long as the German fleet remained intact. Moreover, for the Germans the battle fleet existed as a line of defence for limited tactical mobility for light surface ships and as distant support for commerce raiders. As long as the High Sea Fleet remained intact, British minesweepers and minelayers could not move into the German Bight in an effort to confine the Germans to their harbours. If they did the German light forces would have countered them, and any escalation of the scale of action would have resulted in the British battle line being engaged in the southern North Sea very close to Germany and far from its own bases. The Grand Fleet could only afford to take losses in the German Bight if the German battle fleet was already sunk; as long as it remained there was no way that the British could risk a deep penetration in the North Sea. This being so the commerce raiders were left with room to get to sea. The German battle fleet, however, was not simply passive. It, like the Grand Fleet, sought battle but only on its terms and these terms included a preliminary equalization of strength by mine and torpedo warfare – which, in fact, never materialized. Unless the Germans could lessen the odds against them, or catch only part of the Grand Fleet, they were not prepared to seek a stand-up fight. Given this reluctance to stand and fight there was little the Royal Navy could do to force the issue. For the most part the Germans were content to use their main fleets on small scale operations rather than on fleet actions against the British. Such operations included co-operation with the Army in the Baltic against the Russians and the militarily insignificant, but politically and morally beneficial, hit-and-run raids on the English east coast and operations in conjunction with the Army against the Russians in the Baltic.

The operations against the English east coast should have been reasonably safe affairs given the fact that the Grand Fleet base at Scapa Flow was so far away that the Germans might reasonably expect to be halfway home before the British were able to respond. This hope proved unreasonable for the Admiralty intelligence organization was very effective and, with the help of captured code books recovered by the Russians from the wrecked cruiser *Magdeburg*, was able to read German radio orders as rapidly as the intended recipients. Thus, when the Germans made a sortie with a main force of three battlecruisers and one armoured cruiser in January 1915 towards the Dogger Bank, with the intention of disrupting any British

fishing and naval units that might be in the area, the British were able to put five battlecruisers against them. (The Grand Fleet was in close support, though on this occasion it never came into action.) The subsequent action was very confused, with the light cruisers and destroyers, operating in the reconnaissance role, clashed on the flanks of the main forces. When the Germans realized that they had come into contact with a force considerably superior to themselves and that they had no possible support available, they attempted to flee to the south-east. The British would have preferred to have moved around the German rear to secure a position to the east of the Germans, where they would have had the advantage of the light, wind (to clear funnel smoke) and position between the German ships and their bases, but the fear of mines prevented their moving in that direction. The battle that followed was therefore a stern chase with the rear of the German line and the van of the British force taking fearful punishment as ranges closed. In the engagement, British tactical deployment was faulty in that the slowest ship in line was left behind somewhat, thereby lessening the advantage of superiority of numbers, and British fire distribution went horribly astray. With the first two British ships correctly taking the German leading ship (though without accurate observation), the third and fourth British ships took on their opposite numbers, leaving the second German ship untouched. The first three German ships took on the British flagship which, heavily damaged, had to fall out of the line. In doing so, she issued a series of very confusing orders that led to the remaining four battleships breaking off the action and turning instead against the crippled armoured cruiser that had pulled out of the German line some fifteen minutes earlier. Poor signalling by flags (the radio had been shot away), a lack of initiative on the part of subordinates who unquestioningly followed orders in spite of the battle situation, poor gunnery and total confusion robbed the British of what should have been a considerable victory – though most of the lessons that could have been drawn from the battle were lost sight of in the euphoria.

The only fleet action of the war came briefly at Jutland (May 31/June 1 1916) when the pressure of blockade, the indecisive battles at Verdun and the need for the German Navy to do something to justify its existence and raise morale, led the Germans to seek an action that would result in the destruction of part of the Grand Fleet. From the start the Germans never intended to fight an extended action against a superior force, rather they hoped to make a 'demonstration' off the Norwegian or Danish coasts and hopefully lure part of the British forces on to their own battle line, acting in support of the demonstrating (battlecruiser) force. They also aimed to use submarines as reconnaissance forces and for opportunity attacks, in accordance with the strategy of whittling down British superiority of numbers. The British, informed by superb intelligence, were aware that some such operation was in the offing and similarly arranged their forces with the battle-cruisers in the van and battle fleet in support. Overall the British deployed 28 battleships, 9 battlecruisers, 1 seaplane carrier and 112 cruisers and destroyers; the Germans had 16 battleships, 6 pre-dreadnought battle-ships, 5 battlecruisers and 72 cruisers and destroyers.

Initial contact was made between the cruisers of the battlecruiser forces at 2.20 p.m., the British battle-cruisers turning south-south-east to engage the German battlecruisers as the latter turned to fall back on the German battle line. Because of a signals failure the British battlecruisers went into action with only a six to five advantage, because the four fast battleships in support failed to see their orders. Thus with more than half their gunfire unavailable in the opening exchange the British failed to make the most of their advantage, while the problem of the Dogger Bank, namely incorrect fire distribution, repeated itself. In what was known as 'The Run to the South' the British lost the *Indefatigable* and the *Queen Mary;* as the battleships, by cutting corners, came into line, however, an increas-ing toll was taken on the rear of the German line. The climax of this phase of the action came at 4.30 p.m. when, with the range closing, both sides launched massed destroyer attacks on the enemy line. As the destroyers clashed, both sides losing two ships, both of the battle lines turned away in accordance with tactical doctrine, and contact was temporarily lost. As both sides turned to renew contact the British light cruisers in the van of the force found the whole of the German battle line to their front. Their reports to the battlecruiser force enabled the British ships to turn through sixteen points and reverse course in order to draw the Germans on to the Grand Fleet just as they had been drawn on to the German battle line. Because the British turned in succession through a given point rather than together, the last ships in the line (the battleships) took heavy punishment. But in 'The Run to the North' light conditions for once favoured the British and the German battlecruisers were further mauled to the extent that the van was forced to fall back and use torpedo attacks to relieve the pressure. In this melee the German cruisers were severely hammered by the timely intervention of more British battlecruisers acting as the van of the Grand Fleet. This intervention served to protect the deployment of the Grand Fleet into its battle formation, and to mask its presence from German scouting forces whose performance throughout the battle was unimpressive.

Though very badly served in a reconnaissance role by the battlecruisers, and severely handicapped by the inevitable navigational discrepancies, the final deploy-ment of the Grand Fleet from its cruising to battle formation for the first phase of the battle fleet action was masterly, indeed seldom if ever surpassed. Moving east-south-east from the port column, the deployment ensured that the line crossed the German advance and wrapped around its side, thus securing the vital position between enemy and his base; it also enabled the British to have the very best of the deteriorating light, and prevented any masking of guns during the deployment. Moreover, any other movement could well have brought the line into range of torpedo attack while still not fully deployed. Though the Germans tried to fight back as they ran into a seemingly solid horizon of British battleships, the sheer weight of fire forced them to buckle since the van was bereft of most of its power because its batteries were masked.

To extricate themselves, the Germans carried out a sixteen-point turn, reversing the order of their line because the ships turned together, and carrying them away from the British line. This manoeuvre was carried out under cover of smoke and torpedo attack, and the skill with which it was carried out, combined with smoke and indifferent light, led to the British losing contact. Those ships that did see the manoeuvre did not report it to Jellicoe. The Grand Fleet did not immediately turn towards the enemy. Because of the approach of dusk – by this time it was about 6.42 p.m. – and the fear of torpedoes, the British concern was the maintenance of the fleet's strength and position

War and Commerce: Right: A convoy at the close of World War I; grouping ships only gave U-boats one opportunity for attack before they themselves were attacked. Below: The British High Seas Fleet in the North Sea.

between the enemy and his bases, for Jellicoe was confident of a resumption of action in the morning. The British steered south-west and then south *en echelon*, the divisions partially masking one another, when at about 7.10 p.m. they found themselves again crossing the German line. The Germans, having reversed their line by another sixteen-point turn together, tried to slip around the rear of the British line in the last of the light, but blundered into its centre. Once more the Germans came under merciless attack and they were forced to reverse order yet again under cover of smoke, and employ a torpedo attack and a suicidal lunge by the battlecruisers in order to draw fire. This time the British battle line had to turn away quite violently in order to outrun the torpedoes, and in doing so they lost contact and never regained it, though the battlecruisers did exchange fire between 8.23 and 8.40 p.m. – the last occasion in World War I when capital ships of the British and German Navies engaged one another.

With nightfall the tactical position changed: the British intended to decline action; the Germans were determined to break through to their bases at all costs since the alternative was to face annihilation the following morning. For the most part they were successful. The British destroyer screens placed behind the battle line to prevent such a breakthrough simply lacked the power to prevent the German thrust; the destroyers scored some successes but took very heavy losses in a one-sided action in which the Germans had the advantage of knowing the British night challenge. By the next morning the Germans were on the landward side of the Grand Fleet and safe. Overall neither side lost a battleship though the Germans lost a pre-dreadnought: the British lost three battlecruisers to the solitary German loss; three armoured cruisers to the four German light cruisers sunk and eight destroyers to the five German losses. Given the balance of naval forces the overall losses were roughly equal.

Tactically the battle was drawn, the Germans

103

UC-71, one of the submarines deployed by the Germans in World War I. She fought a savage four-hour battle with the 'Q' ship HMS *Dunraven* on August 8, 1917.

getting slightly the better of the losses. Strategically, however, the battle was a decisive British victory in that their control of the surface of the seas remained intact, the blockade unbroken. Indeed never again in the course of the war did the Germans come out to seek a fleet action. It could have been, and perhaps should have been, more total for the British. Material weaknesses (poor quality shells, lack of anti-flash precaution in the magazines, weak armour protection in the battlecruisers), tactical inflexibility, over-caution, downright lack of competence in certain instances, the misuse of intelligence and, above all, lack of knowledge of the enemy's position and strength (in days before radar) combined to rob them of out-right victory. The German tactics in defence, on the other hand, were flexible and superbly conducted though the fact that they placed themselves in very compromising positions on two occasions lessens the claims of tactical genius on the part of their commanders.

Because the Battle of Jutland ended indecisively for the Germans, they were forced to consider other means of trying to wage the war at sea to a successful conclusion. While clashes of light forces continued in the Channel area for most of the remainder of the war, the overwhelming brunt of the German naval effort was switched to the submarine campaign against trade. Germany had, in fact, carried out two restricted submarine campaigns prior to Jutland, but both had been ended when American protests assumed a severity that the Germans heeded. Nevertheless by 1917 with the German strategic position becoming increasingly difficult – deadlock on the Western Front, no prospects of victory in the east, the increasing effectiveness of the blockade and the growing numbness that came from the knowledge that things would get worse – the German Naval Staff estimated that on the basis of previous campaigns, German submarines could sink 600,000 tons of shipping a month. This, they estimated, would force the neutrals into breaking off their trade with Britain and, as a result, would force Britain out of the war. The calculation was that even if the USA entered the war as a result of unrestricted submarine warfare, Britain could be beaten before American intervention became effective. With the British out of the war, the French and Russians posed no real threat.

In the first half of the war German submarines had little difficulty in sinking merchantmen, if they were freed to do so by their orders. Submarines were able simply to patrol or wait on a sea lane knowing full well that sooner or later merchantmen would sail along it. While a submarine would move into the attack under-water, the most favoured method of sinking a ship was either by gunfire or by charges laid by a boarding party: commanders were loathe to use up their small supply of torpedoes against weak and inoffensive merchantmen. There was a problem in that a submarine had to surface to complete such tasks and there was the difficulty of identifying inoffensive merchantmen from those that were not since the British resorted to Q-ships (disguised merchantmen with strong gun armament whose role was to lure a submarine to point blank range by simulated panic and, when the enemy was close, to drop her disguise and destroy the submarine by overwhelming firepower or ramming).

The major British response to the submarine was relentless patrolling of the sea lanes, searching laboriously for elusive enemies that could usually slink away unnoticed since they had the advantage of first sighting. Such patrols operated under grave handicaps. Firstly, before 1916 there was no means of detecting or attacking a submerged submarine and even after that date, when hydrophones and depth charges were introduced, there remained many problems of operation that had to be overcome. Secondly, patrolling did not afford immediate protection to merchantmen since the latter remained undefended for the duration of their passage. In short, because of the British weakness, the only limitation on the number of merchantmen that could be sunk by German submarines was the endurance, weapons and orders of the submarines plus the number of Allied merchant ships sighted.

Such was the bankruptcy of British tactical ideas that in the first three months of the unrestricted submarine campaign, some two million tons of shipping were lost. The nadir of British fortunes came in April 1917 when 430 ships, totalling 843,549 tons were lost, the merchantman : submarine exchange ratio reaching 167 : 1. The U-boats were simply running amok and defeat was inevitable unless the British rapidly came up with some solution. With the Admiralty paralyzed by indecision it was left to the French and then the British prime minister to force an experiment with convoys on a reluctant British Admiralty.

Troop convoy had existed from the very start of the war effort, but although trade convoy had been instituted in previous wars in which the British had been involved, and its effectiveness recognized, its potential was at first ignored in World War I. (Trade convoy had been compulsory in many British wars, in fact, but the Admiralty's insistence on it was dropped in the nineteenth century in the belief that steam propulsion invalidated the concept: it was conveniently forgotten that the principles of war basically remain unchanged despite technical advances.) In fact the value of convoy was twofold. Firstly, a group of merchantmen under escort presented a single concentrated target. This meant that a submarine would have only one chance to sight the ships and only fleeting opportunities to attack some of them; the same number of ships sailing independently along the same course presented single sightings and easy targets. If the submarine failed to sight the convoy at all then the ships were safe. Secondly, in order to attack ships in convoy, the submarine had to come within range of escorts, thus exposing itself to counter-attack. Convoy therefore encouraged both a concentration of force on the part of the defence and an economy of effort since it meant that only the waters immediately around the convoy needed to be searched since it was in these waters that submarines were forced to operate in order to sink merchantmen. Overall, convoy forced submarines to attack strength, not weakness, under conditions increasingly less favourable to themselves.

Because of crippling losses towards the end of 1916 (40 per cent in December alone), the French in 1917 insisted that their coal trade with Britain had to be convoyed: without British coal French industry would have virtually collapsed. As a result of the introduction of convoys between southern England and France in 1917 losses fell abruptly. Under pressure from Lloyd George, the British premier, the Admiralty authorized oceanic convoy on April 26, 1917, the first convoy leaving Gibraltar for the UK on May 10; regular convoys were initiated in July. At the start the convoy

The RN crew and 'merchant' crew of 'Q' ship HMS *Hyderabad*. When 'Q' ships began to operate, U-boats would sink freighters with torpedoes but often surface afterwards. The 'merchant' crew would 'panic' and abandon the ship after contact with a U-boat and leave a skeleton crew (the RN crew) aboard to engage the submarine when she closed in.

system had two weaknesses. Contrary to common sense convoys were dispersed once in the Channel, for ships to sail independently for their home ports; outward-bound ships sailed independently. The basic strategic pattern, therefore, was to give protection right up to the point where it was most needed. It was not until August 1917 that outward convoys were initiated and not until November 1917 that convoy was extended right into selected ports. But gradually all of the most vulnerable routes – the Atlantic, Gibraltar-UK, the Mediterranean and UK coastal waters – were covered by two-way convoy.

Overall the results were startling. During the war the Germans sank nearly 13 million tons of shipping, 7¾ millions of which was British. But of the 16,070 ships that sailed in oceanic convoys only 96 were lost, and 161 were lost of the 67,888 sailings in coastal convoys. Losses among stragglers and independently sailed ships were much heavier but never of the order to give the Germans any chance of victory. Only five ships were lost when in the company of both sea and air escorts. In short convoy drastically cut losses. In November 1917 losses were the lowest they had been since the start of the campaign in February, despite the fact that in October German submarines reached the peak of their strength with seventy vessels at sea. By September 1918 losses had been cut to less than a hundred and in October 1918 only twenty-five Allied merchantmen were lost, though these figures do reflect the restrictions placed on submarine operations while the Germans sought an armistice. Not merely did convoy result in fewer ships being sunk – which meant that Allied shipbuilding could more than replace the losses –

but it enabled the Allies to start sinking U-boats on a large scale. That depth charges had claimed their first victim on March 26, 1916 and that the combination of depth charges and hydrophone made their first kill on July 6, 1916, were effective demonstrations that submarines could be effectively countered. The loss rate among U-boats between August 1917 and January 1918, when the issue was in the balance, was greater than German replacement capacity. At the same time the merchantmen:submarine exchange ratio fell to 10:1. Overall in the course of the war, 178 out of 373 German submarines were lost, most of them after the introduction of convoy.

Thus the strategic and tactical value of convoy was well illustrated by the events of World War I. The German submarine campaign failed not because of the considerable losses endured by the U-boats but as a result of the submarines being unable to maintain the high rate of sinkings that they had achieved between February and April 1917. Through a policy of convoy, ruthless rationing in the UK and the concentration of shipping on the critical US-UK trade route, the British were able to economize on their use of shipping. The Germans were also hampered by Allied counter-measures in the Channel where the mine barriers were considerably strengthened and patrols increased in order to prevent the Germans passing through the Straits of Dover. Instead they were forced to move to and from Germany to the battle zones via the north of Scotland, a time consuming route with few targets to make the passage profitable. By such methods the Allies were able to deny the Germans the strategic victory they sought – and the failure to win on the sea

routes made the German defeat even more certain as American forces began to pour into Europe in the spring of 1918. Nevertheless, despite this failure, the U-boats did serve to tie down the light forces of the Allies on escort duties and, as such, they were unable to take part in any proposal to make more aggressive use of Allied sea power.

In theory, given the possession of superior sea power and the advantage of external lines of communication, the Allies should have been able to use the great flexibility of sea power to impose their will on the enemy by a series of independent seaborne assaults. In practice, the short coastline of Germany and Austro-Hungary, combined with the power of mines and torpedoes, made these countries almost totally invulnerable to seaborne assault. The first few months of the war were characterized by a restless search for a naval offensive on the part of the British Admiralty, partly in the hope that this would force the Germans to come out to give battle, partly in order to force the enemy to conform to British strategic intentions. Various schemes were proposed, most of them nonsensical. There were schemes to seize a German island in the North Sea – or a Dutch island or Danish or Norwegian town, it did not seem to matter too much; there was a proposal to launch a one-way raid up the Elbe to attack Hamburg and the Brunsbuttel and Kiel Canals; there were schemes for landing on the Schleswig-Holstein coast and in the Baltic, though how these operations were to be carried out in the face of German and Danish mines without much in the field of destroyer protection, was not seriously considered at the outset. Subsequently, all were found to have problems so severe that they had

to be dropped: it is hard to resist the conclusion that they should not have been considered in the first place. Leaving aside the contemptibly incompetent landings at Tanga in November 1914, the British carried out only one major attempt to get around the German land flanks by the use of sea power. That was with the brilliantly imaginative and totally unrealistic operation at the Dardanelles.

From the very inception of the campaign, there were three strategic weaknesses in the arguments in favour. Firstly, while admitting that the longest way around is often the shortest way there, the notion of dealing a fatal blow at Germany via Turkey – the knocking away of the props – implied a relationship between Germany and Turkey that did not exist. The central problem in defeating Germany had to be the German Army, not Turkey. Striking at a place where the Germans could not strike back had, as its penalty, striking at a place where the Germans could not be touched. Moreover, the notion that the Balkan states could provide the key to victory by opening up a further front is dubious in that, rather than providing support for the Allies, these countries could easily have become liabilities and obligations to be met. Secondly, the operation was carried out at a time when the British (and French) lacked the strength to maintain an effort on even one front, still less a second at the far end of the Mediterranean. The Dardanelles operation was an attempt to gain a victory on the cheap and in attempting this the Allies expended more effort overall than was ever realistically needed for a thorough and properly prepared operation in the first place. Moreover, even if the operation had been successful, and access gained to south Russian ports, it is hard to see where the ships and supplies that were supposed to keep Russia magically in the war could have come from, granted the fact that most shipping and arms suppliers were committed already to the British and French causes. Thirdly, and lastly, the notion that developed in the winter of 1914-15 that the Navy alone could force the Dardanelles was in flat contradiction to staff appreciations before 1914; all of which stressed that any operation at the Dardanelles was bound to be hazardous and demand a joint Army-Navy effort. In the winter of 1914 a state of euphoria, reckless personal ambition and irresponsibility on the part of Churchill, a large measure of downright ignorance of, and racial contempt for, the Turks, led to the evolution of a plan for a solely naval offensive. Yet any such offensive fell foul to two immediate considerations. Firstly, even if the fleet managed to force its way up the Dardanelles there was no guarantee that this could be turned to a decisive strategic success unless its flanks were cleared: the flanks could only be cleared, and held, by the Army. Secondly, the essence of the problem of forcing the Dardanelles was that mines blocked the passage and were covered by guns. Because of the fast flow of water the primitive minesweepers could not clear the mines because of the unacceptable volume of firepower they had to face. This gunfire could not be suppressed by the remainder of the fleet because the minefields prevented close range action on the part of the ships. The only way to break the vicious circle was to take the guns covering the minefields from the landside – by using the Army to seize the enemy positions. Churchill, intoxicated by the early successes of the Navy against the dilapidated outer defences, pushed forward with the plan for a solely naval attack. The steady crumbling of the defences came to a halt on March 11, 1915 with the Navy unable to make any more progress. There followed an ominous lull in British deliberations while the questions of whether or not to mount an invasion, and in what strength, were discussed, and arrangements put in hand. On March 18 a final effort was made by the Navy with eighteen battleships including the brand new *Queen Elizabeth*, to break through the still intact defences. It was very nearly successful, in that the Turks came close to exhausting their ammunition in fighting off the ships, but in the course of the action three capital ships were lost and three more badly crippled. The naval commander was unwilling to risk more of his ships in a final effort that could have proved

decisive – throughout the operation greater emphasis seems to have been placed on ship preservation than in recognition of the fact that losses could be endured if the strategic objective was gained. In mitigation it must be noted that the cause of the losses was unknown at the time and the weakness of the Turkish situation on land was obviously not realized. With the Army unready to begin operations the attacks had to be called off for the moment and it was not until April 25, 1915 that landings on the Gallipoli peninsula took place. Many things went wrong: some landings took place on the wrong beaches, fire support from ships was insufficient because of the inadequacies of fire control, and toal chaos reigned on V beach where the assaulting infantry were cut down in swathes by intact machine guns. But in spite of this the critically important village of Krithia could have been taken on the 25th, and the commanding height of Achi Baba might well have been taken on several occasions. Had the latter fallen, the outcome may well have been very different but in fact it was held throughout by the Turks. Ultimately, despite heroic efforts on the part of the land forces the British had to admit failure and the peninsula was progressively evacuated with superbly executed withdrawals that were carried out without a single casualty, despite the presence of the enemy.

The Dardanelles operation illustrates the limitations

of sea power and the extent to which it is dependent on proper co-ordination with other services. In the actual details of the operation, the need was shown for specialized headquarters ships for amphibious operations: part of the difficulties encountered on April 25 stemmed from having Army headquarters on board a ship that had its own tasks to complete. The landing underlined the need for proper fire control arrangements and landing craft and, equally, the importance of proper loading and shipping arrangements to ensure that the most important supplies were loaded last and delivered first. In addition, the need for adequate medical facilities was appallingly obvious for those at the Dardanelles would not have done justice to the Crimea.

Nevertheless the Dardanelles on several occasions did come very close to being a decisive British success.

Had more care been taken in the initial stages it might well have been a measure that knocked Turkey out of the war, and might have brought about the situation that some of its proponents assert would have occurred. But this is conjecture. What is certain, is that the Dardanelles notched up an impressive series of 'firsts': for the first time a submarine sank a battleship with torpedoes; the first aerial spotting for guns occurred; and for the first time aircraft sank ships on the open sea with plenty of searoom. Though there were other advances in other theatres – for instance in the Baltic both the Russians and the Germans used aerial mines – the Dardanelles marked the debut of the weapon that was to figure largely in the inter-war tactical and strategic arguments, and that was to dominate war at sea between 1939 and 1945.

Exit the Battleship enter the Carrier

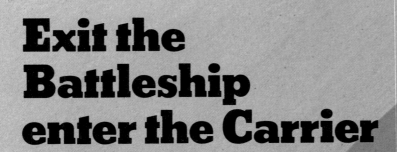

HMS *Hermes* in 1937 passes through the Suez Canal. She was the first ship designed from the keel up as a carrier for the Royal Navy.

It has already been recounted how the long period of Victorian peace, then the revolution in material at the turn of the century, was not conducive to the study of war at sea. Strategy was neglected and tactical thought has been described scathingly as 'a few catchwords and a lot of tradition.' In the period between the two wars strategic and tactical thought was similarly stifled and also distorted – though for very different reasons and never to the extent that it had been prior to 1914.

In part this resulted from three major considerations. Firstly, though there were periodic scares, none of the navies in the immediate post-war era could point to 'the next enemy' against whom preparations had to be made. It was not until the thirties that events began to take shape that clarified the nature of the future conflict and made possible the identification of the likely enemies. Secondly, the inter-war period was dominated by economies in the naval services and international agreements that resulted in the cutting back of naval strengths generally, both of which had the effect of dampening initiative, drive and new ideas. Thirdly, there was a natural tendency to fight the battles of World War I over again – this was particularly true of the British and the Battle of Jutland. In a very real sense the emphasis of British naval thought and training in the inter-war period was devoted to making sure that in future similar opportunities would not be missed. The results were very impressive: in numerous actions during World War II British gunnery and night fighting proved extremely formidable; the elan and initiative of the light forces, so conspicuously lacking at Jutland, exhibited themselves at every opportunity; and in battle there was frequent demonstration of flexibility of

command, partly, it must be added, as a result of the development of radar which, with radio, enabled a commander to know more about the battle area in spite of high speed manoeuvring than had been possible in the past. Naval thought, on the other hand, was distorted by two factors. Firstly, little attention was paid to economic warfare, particularly in the field of trade defence against submarine attack. In the whole of the inter-war period the Royal Navy conducted only one exercise in trade defence. Such complacency stemmed partly from the belief that convoy was the effective answer to submarines and partly in the confidence placed in ASDIC (later called Sonar) as the means of detecting a submerged submarine. (This had been invented towards the end of World War I.) The British, particularly, believed that it was the antidote to the submarine. Secondly, furious arguments raged over the questions of the role and importance of naval aviation, questions inevitably tied up with arguments about the role of air power in general.

In the inter-war period naval thought essentially divided into four major streams on the vexed problem of naval aviation, with many shades of opinion in between. On one extreme were those who believed that air power made the existing battle fleets and most of the surface ships obsolete; on the other those whose belief in gunnery led to their discounting the aircraft as a serious factor in war at sea. Between the two extremes was an area of doubt. Although there could be no doubt that an aircraft could physically sink a battleship – the American general Billy Mitchell had shown that in trials with the *Ostfriesland* in 1921 – there was a school of thought which was of the opinion that,

HMS *Argus* the first real carrier; she was a conversion from a battle cruiser and was ready in 1918, too late to see action. Few theorists realized what an important vessel the carrier would become by the close of World War II. Below left: A Sopwith Pup, the naval version of the famous Camel.

given better protection (particularly in deck and water-line armour), improved damage control arrangements, more and better high angle guns and, if possible, organic air defence, the role of the battleship as the principle weapon at sea could remain unchallenged. Within this school it was felt that air power was very important indeed and that the destructive capability of aircraft was second only to the guns of the fleet – but it was clearly secondary, for to them air power existed to provide air defence for the battle line, to spot for the guns of the fleet. Aircraft, too, could push out the range of reconnaissance several hundreds of miles, effectively reducing the importance of the cruiser in this role. The final major stream of thought reasoned that not only would the range of reconnaissance be pushed out several hundreds of miles, but that there was the distinct possibility, even probability, that any engagement between the battle lines would be preceded by an air battle, the outcome of which might in itself be conclusive. For the most part this school shrank from the

ultimate logic of its line of argument, that indeed the aircraft had made the battle line obsolete, though many officers suspected (or hoped) that this either was or shortly would be the case. Such reasoning inevitably pointed towards a concept of naval warfare in which the battle fleet would be led by a carrier force committed to fighting for air supremacy: it was towards this conclusion that the Japanese and Americans were gingerly feeling their way during the inter-war period.

While the Japanese and the Americans forged ahead in the theory and practice of naval aviation, the British by comparison stagnated – a fact possibly not unrelated to the fact that the Royal Navy lost its own fleet air arm to the Royal Air Force while the American and Japanese Navies retained total control of their own naval aviation. The war-time British lead in ships operating aircraft, and in numbers and types of aircraft, was quickly dissipated. In 1918 they had 1000 aircraft and lighter-than-air machines; a year of peace and demobilization reduced this total to fifty. Although after

1918 the British were the first to build a ship with a continuous free flight deck (the *Argus*), and to have a carrier with an offset island in order to clear smoke from the flight deck (the *Eagle*), it was the Japanese who were the first to complete a purpose-built carrier (the *Hosho*) in 1922, and it was the Pacific powers that attempted to produce specialist aircraft. Whereas the British tended to rely on multi-purpose aircraft that could never perform any task really well, the Japanese and Americans set out to create specialist torpedo, fighter and reconnaissance and, later, dive bomber formations. The result was that over time, Japanese and American aircraft opened up a considerable qualitative gap between themselves and British naval aircraft, this becoming particularly marked during the thirties with the introduction of the monoplane into the American and Japanese Navies. In only two areas did the British continue to possess a lead: they had many more carriers than the other two countries (though this advantage was offset by the greater carrying capacity of the US and Japan), and their carriers had the supreme advantage of heavily armoured flight deck, hangars and magazines.

When rearmament began apace in the second half of the thirties, it was perhaps inevitable that first priority was given to carriers, the battle line (no nation was willing to risk abandoning battleships), cruisers and destroyers. Even the British largely went along with such priorities though it must be noted that the 1939 War Emergency, 1940 and 1941 Programmes placed great emphasis on destroyer escorts, frigates and corvettes. These ships were specifically built for the protection of trade since it was on this front that Britain faced her greatest test. The threat of course came from Germany. In 1937 Germany set out a construction programme for her rejuvenated navy of six battleships, three battlecruisers, four heavy cruisers, seventeen light cruisers, four carriers, numerous destroyers and two hundred and twenty-one submarines. The date when these ships were to be ready was 1948. This fleet was not intended to fight in the classic manner for supremacy at sea: it was aimed primarily at the destruction of British trade – either by the physical sinking of ships or by the prevention of ships even sailing because of the unrestricted presence of German warships on the high seas. Given the fact that forty-eight British warships had to be committed to the destruction of the *Bismarck* in May 1941, and that two of the battleships proposed in 1937 were half as big again as the *Bismarck*, the Germans may well have achieved their objective had

war come later rather than in 1939 when their construction programmes had barely started.

The war certainly came too early for Karl Doenitz, the commander of the German submarine arm. He knew exactly what he wanted since he alone clearly appreciated the vulnerability of Britain's sea communications. He realized that submarines operating independently dissipated much of their value. He realized, too, that the principle of concentration of force worked for both the defender and the attacker. Before the war Doenitz trained his submarines to operate in groups, initially in a long extended concave patrol line into which an enemy convoy would enter. The submarine making the first sighting would report the enemy and direct the other members of the group on to the convoy in order to attack it from the flanks and rear. The favoured position of the shadowing submarine was naturally behind the convoy. In carrying out attacks on convoys the submarines came to prefer approaches and attacks on the surface at night, even to the extent in some cases of entering the lines of merchantmen and attacking the convoy from the inside. In attempting this the submarine commanders were confident that once inside the convoy they would be immune from attack since the escorts would be too concerned with perimeter defence. In attempting to get inside the convoy the submarines had the advantage of first sighting since their low silhouettes against a dark sea made them hard to detect while the escorts and merchantmen could be seen far more easily. In this role the submarines were employed as torpedo boats that could dive to avoid an escort rather than as a submerged craft *per se*. Moreover, attacking on the surface made submarines invulnerable to detection by ASDIC. Doenitz wanted to stake all on a submarine campaign against British trade and he wanted priority given to the 300 submarines he deemed necessary to force Britain to her knees. He reckoned that of this total one-third would be on station at any given time, the remainder equally divided between vessels moving to and from operations and those undergoing refits, training and 'on leave'. In addition, he wanted small 500-ton submarines armed with about fourteen torpedoes. The smallness of these vessels made them very manoeuvrable and they were able to submerge in twenty seconds. Unfortunately for Doenitz the German Navy did not agree with his order of priorities and in any case were inclined to build larger submarines with strong gun armament and long endurance. Doenitz went to war with only fifty-six

The German battleship *Bismarck* at the beginning of her first and last cruise. German naval doctrine was to destroy British shipping with U-boats and powerful surface vessels like the *Bismarck*. If they sank enough they would starve Britain into surrender.

submarines, some of which were totally unsuited to long-range operations.

Doenitz's opponents, on the other hand, were fatally weak. The British had less than thirty escort ships in the Western Approaches when war broke out, and less than one hundred overall. They could not easily be reinforced by fleet destroyers since these ships were needed for other tasks and were in any case not easily adaptable to escort duties. Given their fleet role, destroyers tended to be high speed craft with heavy gun, anti-aircraft and torpedo armament: for defence of convoys endurance, small turning circles and good anti-

submarine weapons were needed. Moreover the performance of ASDIC tended to fall away at high speed. In addition to these handicaps the British operated under two severe difficulties. Firstly, the British government during the 1930s relinquished its treaty ports in Eire, with the result that escorts had to work out of home ports; secondly, the Royal Navy had neglected replenishment at sea (RAS) and a fleet train during the inter-war period (in marked contrast to the Americans and Japanese). This meant that British escorts could give support for convoys only within 600 miles of the UK coast; beyond this the merchantmen were more or less on their own until they approached the New World. Such were the major weaknesses of the two sides in September 1939.

World War II: General Comment

World War II was essentially two quite separate wars: one fought basically in Europe and the Atlantic, the other in the West and South Pacific (and certain parts of the Asian mainland). Only very occasionally did the two overlap and then in no meaningful strategic sense. The wars were largely fought in isolation of each other, the unifying factor being the involvement of the British and Americans (and to a lesser extent the French and Soviets) in both conflicts. In large measure, events shaped the strategies of Germany, Japan and Britain. Germany, given the British unwillingness to come to terms in 1940 and lacking a surface navy of real strength, was forced into unrestricted submarine warfare against British trade. For the most part the British strategy was defensive in that the Navy had to struggle to secure the homeland against direct invasion and to keep open the trade routes with the rest of the world. The maintenance of her sea communications was at the very heart of Britain's survival and capacity for any kind of offensive action: if they had been severed she would have had to surrender. Except in the secondary Mediterranean theatre, British naval policy was defensive and, given the absence of a balanced German fleet and a determined Italian naval effort, the European war at sea was fought along the trade routes between British (and Allied) escorts and German submarines (and aircraft). There were surface actions and the Germans used their surface ships to try to pin down British forces, particularly the escorts, in order to facilitate the tasks of the submarines, but for the most part this was a secondary effort. Japan, in 1941, was similarly committed by the march of events. Because of her over-commitment and the elusiveness of decisive strategic success in China, the thrashing administered her by the Soviet Union in Mongolia in 1939, her desperate reliance on the resources of South-East Asia, and American opposition to her that hardened implacably during the course of 1941, she was forced to attempt the neutralization of American naval power and the provision of a distant defensive perimeter, held by the carriers and battle fleet, behind which she could exploit the natural resources of her intended conquests. The Japanese Commander-in-Chief, Admiral Yamamoto,

was not sanguine about the prospects of such a plan, but he had no option. Japan could hardly attempt the conquest of South-East Asia with the American battle fleet intact on her left flank and the American possession of the Philippines astride the sea routes between South-East Asia and Japan. Yamamoto doubted whether Japan could hold the US Navy once the Americans fully mobilized their industrial resources, so infinitely superior to those of Japan and had cause to ponder the immense problems of forming a defensive perimeter consisting mostly of sea and sky without the necessary merchant and naval ships needed to give that perimeter teeth. In addition, the policy of securing a defensive line and then standing on the defence for the counter-attack against an enemy superior in strength and resources had little to recommend it. But the Japanese had no choice: their foreign policy in the thirties drove them into the cul-de-sac of the early forties.

The Americans, on the other hand, did have strategic choice, largely conferred by their geographical isolation and invulnerability. Before the war they had drawn up a series of war plans to cover every possible contingency (including war with Britain) and had decided that, in the event of war in both the Pacific and Europe, priority should be placed on the latter. The decision was made on the basis that any Japanese victories could be redeemed in time whereas a German victory in Europe could prove final and irreversible. When war came to the USA in 1941 these priorities were confirmed and maintained, though the revelation of Japanese weakness in 1942-3 enabled the Americans to undertake a more vigorous and aggressive policy on both fronts than they had considered possible before the war. Such a situation arose not simply because of Japan's inherent weaknesses but because of the seemingly inexhaustible capacity of American industry: in 1942 and 1943 it was completing a destroyer every three days; in the last quarter of 1943, merchant ship construction was running at an annual rate of 16.4 million tons. At the end of the war American shipyards were building aircraft carriers that, had they been completed, would have almost doubled the Navy's carrier strength of twenty-three fleet carriers.

Such strength was witness to the eclipse of British sea power, finally relegated to the second rank for the first time in 250 years. It also marked the end of the domination of the battleship. Admittedly for the operations against the Marianas in 1944, the Americans were

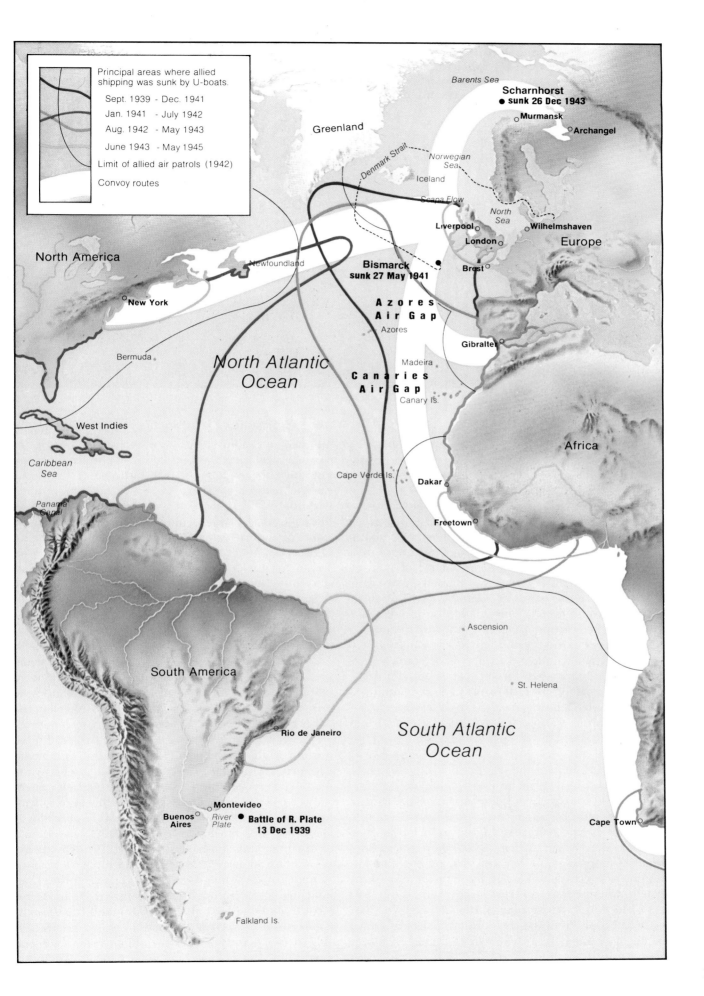

Principal areas where allied
shipping was sunk by U-boats.

Sept. 1939 - Dec. 1941

Jan. 1941 - July 1942

Aug. 1942 - May 1943

June 1943 - May 1945

Limit of allied air patrols (1942)

Convoy routes

Barents Sea

Scharnhorst
● **sunk 26 Dec 1943**

○ **Murmansk**

Archangel

Greenland

Denmark Strait

Norwegian Sea

Iceland

Scapa Flow

North Sea

Liverpool ○

London ○

Europe

Wilhelmshaven ○

North America

Newfoundland

Bismarck
sunk 27 May 1941

Brest ○

○ **New York**

A z o r e s
A i r G a p

Azores

Gibraltar ○

Bermuda

*North Atlantic
Ocean*

C a n a r i e s
A i r G a p

Madeira

Canary Is.

West Indies

Africa

*Caribbean
Sea*

Cape Verde Is.

Dakar ○

*Panama
Canal*

Freetown ○

South America

Ascension

St. Helena

*South Atlantic
Ocean*

● Rio de Janeiro

Montevideo ○

**Buenos
Aires** ○ *River
Plate*

● **Battle of R. Plate**
13 Dec 1939

Cape Town ○

Falkland Is.

117

The *Admiral Graf Spee*, the so-called 'pocket battleship'
because her weight was only 12,100 tons, but she had
six 11-in (280 mm) guns and could reach 27.7 knots.
A potent commerce raider, she was scuttled after the
Battle of the River Plate in 1939.

able to deploy fourteen battleships (more than the
Royal Navy had in commission at the time) and they
were able to play a vital role, but the real teeth of the
navies from this point was in the carriers and their
aircraft. (In the Marianas operation the Americans
employed fifteen fleet carriers and ten light carriers.)
Gradually the battleship was relegated to the second
rank – important primarily in pre-invasion bombardment and for close fire support for land forces once
ashore, and with a vital role in defence of convoys
(the unsung British R class saved many convoys from
annihilation at the hands of German surface raiders
simply by being there). They could also provide vital
cover for the carriers against both surface and air
attack: indeed carriers with their lack of guns and vulnerability often sought the comfort and reassurance of
massed anti-aircraft batteries of battleships. But these
were all secondary tasks: the role of finding and destroying the enemy fleet had passed to the carriers.

The European War

From the very start of the war the British and French
Navies were engaged in imposing blockade on Germany and in convoying military formations to areas of
operations both in Europe and throughout the world.
The latter particularly affected the French and their
possessions in North Africa, as did the need to keep
watch on unpredictable but unfriendly Italy. The imposition of blockade was naturally the main task of the
British, who used exactly the same methods as they had
in World War I – patrolling in the Channel, the fleet
based at Scapa Flow and the northern patrol of armed
merchant cruisers. In World War II, however, blockade never had anything like the devastating effect that

it had had in World War I. This was partly due to
German stockpiling before the war, partly because of
German development of effective substitutes for many
now missing goods, partly the outcome of the Nazi-
Soviet honeymoon of 1939-41 which meant that trade
with the USSR more than offset any losses caused by
blockade. And it also stemmed in part from the sheer
extent of German conquests and her rapacious stripping
of these conquered territories. It was not really until the
end of the war that she began to feel the full rigour of
economic shortages; by the time that economic collapse
did occur, she had been decisively defeated on land and,
in any case, the contribution of air power to her economic collapse was more spectacular, immediate and
profound than that of naval blockade.

At the start of the war Hitler did not launch complete all-out submarine warfare. Restrictions were
placed on the sinking of merchant ships though these
were progressively relaxed as it became obvious that the
Allies and later Britain alone would not come to terms.
In the early months of the war the Germans used mine
warfare off the east coast and surface ships, both naval
and auxiliary, in the prosecution of war against commerce. After 1941 the effectiveness of surface raiders
greatly diminished as British counter-measures, particularly in the fields of intelligence and the checking of
identity of individual ships encountered by naval units
on the high seas, gradually improved. In their heyday
the surface ships had some considerable success in
stopping or disrupting the flow of convoys rather than
inflicting losses through the auxiliaries *Atlantis* and
Pinguin, and the warships *Scharnhorst* and *Gneisenau* in
the January-March 1941 operations enjoyed considerable success (a total of sixty-two ships of about 400,000
tons sunk). But submarines, despite their role against

Below: A coastal U-boat. By 1940 Germany had bases for submarine war, but not enough vessels to wage it. Had Doenitz been allowed to build up the U-boat fleet before 1939 the outcome of World War II might have been very different. Bottom: On the lookout in the Atlantic. The advent of radar removed the cover of darkness and poor weather that had been used by the U-boats for stalking.

way. Strategically, the Germans concentrated on the UK-US and coastal UK trade routes, and their possession after mid-1940 of bases in Norway and western France enabled their submarines to reach out into the Atlantic far beyond the range of most British escorts. In effect, the Germans were blockading Britain as they had in World War I but from a position of much greater strength than had been possible between 1914 and 1918. Forty-nine per cent of all Allied losses between 1939 and mid-1942 were in the North Atlantic; between 1939 and mid-1941 32 per cent of all Allied losses were in and around UK coastal waters. Tactically, the only limitation on German submarines was the scarcity of the submarines themselves, the lack of co-operation from the Luftwaffe, and the small numbers of torpedoes they could carry. In carrying out this scale of destruction the U-boats enjoyed considerable immunity: only twenty-three submarines were lost in 1940 and only thirty-five in the whole of 1941. And in the last quarter of 1941, replacement exceeded the whole of the losses suffered during the war to date. In the first two years of the war the paucity of escorts, their limited range and, most importantly, the fact that they were seldom ever able to train together but were put in teams on the basis of what was available rather than what was needed, meant that the escorts laboured under immense difficulties. By the end of 1941 the situation at sea was becoming increasingly grave for the British. Merchantmen were being lost twice as quickly as they could be replaced; German U-boat strength was nearing 250 with about 97 at sea at any one time. Clearly things were moving towards a climax.

the British fleet, were the main means of striking at British trade, and as more submarines entered service, Allied losses mounted. Nearly 4 million tons were lost in 1940, half to submarines: roughly the same figures were reported for 1941. In the first thirty months of the war German submarines had things much their own

Two developments took place in the course of 1941 that showed that U-boats need not necessarily have things all their own way. Firstly, between July and

119

U-boat hunters in the Atlantic: Top left: HMS *Hydrangea* a Flower Class corvette. Top right: The destroyer HMS *Scimitar* and Bottom: HMS *Walker* a veteran of World War I. During escort duties with convoy HX112 in March 1941, she depth charged U-99 and captured her commander the 'ace' Otto Kretschmer.

December, losses on the North Atlantic route fell to about 100,000 tons a month – an indication of the growing presence of American strength in the western and central Atlantic where Germany feared to move because of the obvious danger of war with the US. But the decline of losses was also an indication that convoys were becoming more effective. Secondly, and related to the latter point, in December 1941 a convoy of thirty-two ships was fought through from Gibraltar to the UK with the loss of only two ships. Two escorts were also lost but five German submarines and two aircraft were destroyed. This convoy (HG 76) was exceptionally well defended, however, leaving Gibraltar with 10 escorts and a small escort carrier. It was commanded by the most famous of the British escort commanders, Captain F. J. Walker, and clearly showed what an aggressive, balanced and well-trained force trained together could achieve, particularly when supported by a carrier.

Despite HG 76 the convoy system came under great strain in 1942 and the first quarter of 1943, because of the extension of the war through the Atlantic and Pacific areas. This stretched Anglo-American resources far beyond their capacity and it took some time for the Americans to organize themselves and begin to draw on their potential strength. When the tide turned spectacularly in the spring of 1943 it was the result of a combination of factors, many of which had been clearly seen with the success of HG 76.

The nature of the victory of the convoy system was two-fold. Firstly, the Allies halted the massive scale of sinkings that took place in early 1943, which would have forced Britain out of the war had it persisted. Allied measures proved successful in preventing a rate of loss that could not be covered by fresh American construction. Secondly, German submarines in 1943 took losses that were totally unacceptable – 237 for the year, including 41 at the climax of the battle in May.

Of all the factors that contributed to the Allied victory on the sea routes probably the most important was the provision of more and better trained escorts.

A depth charge with quick-sinking attachment. Used in two world wars, it was very effective once a definite contact had been made with a submerged U-boat. Dropped or projected in a pattern and set for different depths, they would explode causing pressures that would crush the hull of a U-boat.

Early convoys proved fatally weak in escorts with all too predictable results. By 1943 more escorts were available with the result that the perimeter defence of convoys was far better. It was also realized that, tactically, an area of convoy (and hence the number of merchant ships in it) could be greatly increased relative to the perimeter by an increase in radius (the mathematical formula for area of circle as opposed to the circumference) and that there was an optimum size for a convoy and its escorts. The result of such deductions enabled strong defences to be prepared for convoys and even led to the formation of 'trouble-shooters' that could patrol routes to and from the U-boat bases or submarine-infested waters, giving aid to any convoy in the vicinity.

Technologically, too, the balance shifted away from the submarines in the course of the war. The development of radar and its use by escorts gave the defender the critical advantage of identifying the submarine before, and not after, its attack: the submarine thereby lost its immunity and the advantage of first sighting. Moreover, new weapons began to appear during the course of the war: mortars capable of firing twenty-four contact bombs, forward-throwing fast-sinking depth charges, depth charges with a 500-ft capability – all began to take an increasing toll. Part of the problem in destroying a submarine in the early years of the war had been that an escort in contact with it by ASDIC lost that contact as it moved into the attack, and also gave notice of intent by the sound of its engines; an alert submarine could therefore always try to turn away from the attack at the last moment. The new weapons allowed ASDIC to maintain contact as the contact was made. Walker developed one particular ploy to overcome the U-boats' evasive manoeuvres even before the new weapons came into service on a large scale: he used an escort to hold contact and to bring two or three other escorts at very slow speeds either across or over the U-boat, depth charging along both the U-boat line itself and either side of it. In this way any late evasive action brought the submarine into the line of depth charges to the side of its original course. No German submarine ever survived such an attack.

Walker was also notable for his aggressive defence, even when he had small forces at his disposal. The defence of HG 76 unveiled the hitherto unheard of tactic of weakening the defence screen in an effort to keep down or destroy the submarine with the first contact; he also encouraged aggressive lunges at U-boats moving into the attack, even if this meant further

weakening the defences. As more escorts became available more aggressive action around the perimeter was possible; Walker was exceptional in that he employed such tactics when such strength was not available. Such was the effectiveness of the escorts in this role that the Germans were forced to develop accoustic torpedoes designed to home on to the sound of ship propellers. They intended to use their limited supply of such torpedoes against the escorts with a view to clearing a route through to the merchantmen. Some initial success was achieved, mainly because of the element of surprise, but several tactical ploys were evolved to overcome their effectiveness. Noise-making equipment was developed that could be towed astern of the escorts to draw off the torpedoes (the weakness of this was that it interfered with ASDIC); (Walker's preference) high or low speed steaming when the effectiveness of the torpedoes fell away; or the dropping of depth charges to detonate the torpedoes themselves.

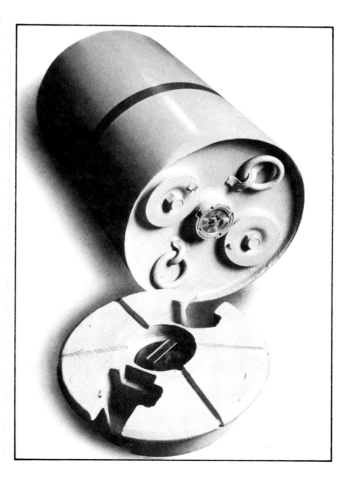

The death of a U-boat. Caught on the surface by an RAF aircraft it has been depth charged and machine-gunned. German submarines had been built with the assumption that they would operate under friendly or neutral skies and unlike their British counterparts were slower at crash dives. Depth charges with a shallow setting could rupture the pressure hull on or just below the surface.

A further factor in the decisive Allied success in the Battle of the Atlantic was the advent of air power on a major scale in the course of 1943. In the early years the British effort was severely handicapped by the lack of either shore- or ship-based aircraft on any scale. Aircraft for convoy work were vital in three respects: firstly, to try to prevent reconnaissance and bombing by the Luftwaffe, (which became increasingly less effective as the strength of the Luftwaffe was sapped in the course of the war); secondly, for aggressive patrolling of the perimeter; and thirdly, for general attacks on surfaced submarines. In the early part of the war aircraft were simply not available. One expediency was to arm merchant ships with a single catapulted fighter but this could not be recovered and there were considerable problems involved in deciding to produce a weapon that could never be used again. It was not until 1943 that the solutions began to appear in strength. A massive in-

crease in long-range aircraft operating from the UK, Iceland and the New World (and later the Azores) enabled the Allies to cover the whole of the Atlantic, thus denying German submarines a safe area in which to run on the surface in order to recharge their batteries, and enabling the convoys to have some protection for parts of their passage. After 1943 such aircraft were equipped with either 1.5m or 10cm radar sets and were able to locate a surface U-boat in the foulest weather or at night; and shallow-depth charges gave them a means of destruction totally lacking up until that time. By 1943 not only were shore-based aircraft increasing in numbers and effectiveness, but continuous air cover was being provided by growing numbers of rugged little escort carriers, mostly American built. Very small with about fifteen to twenty aircraft, these ships could sweep the areas around the convoys – particularly to the rear where submarines tended to concentrate and where the escorts were naturally weak. Although their anti-submarine armament was weak, their ability to search and direct escorts proved a major factor in increasing the effectiveness of convoy protection. Such was the decisive impact of Allied air power that, in 1943, aircraft accounted for 116 German submarines.

German tactics as a result of this changing balance of technology were hesitant. In the crisis of 1943, as German submarines came under increasingly frequent and heavy air attack, they were armed with more and heavier anti-aircraft guns and were ordered to move together to provide mutual protection. This proved ineffective: aircraft took heavy losses but still managed to sink them. The only answers available were the snorkel, which allowed a submarine to recharge its batteries and change its air while still submerged, or the development of new submarines. The snorkel was used extensively after 1943 but only at the price of low submerged speeds and decreased fighting effectiveness; the new submarines which emerged in 1945 came too late to reverse the tide.

The war in the Mediterranean was similarly a war largely fought along the sea lanes – the British sea lanes to Malta and the Italian-German convoy routes from Europe to North Africa. Few campaigns illustrate more graphically the critical importance of sea power and the inter-dependence between the land, sea and air theatres than this campaign. Put at its simplest, the armies in North Africa were utterly dependent on sea power for their supplies. Given the superior geographical position of Italy, and the shortness of the Axis sea routes to North Africa, the British had to sever this supply route for the army to have any chance of clearing the North African coast. This could only be achieved if naval forces operated out of Malta – and Malta could be supplied only with difficulty as long as the North African coast remained in hostile hands. Air cover for a convoy would be minimal as long as the British did not hold the Western Desert. In this case the chances of resupplying Valetta were very poor. Ultimately the war in the Mediterranean lasted some three years, in the course of which both Italian and British merchant seamen displayed persistence and bravery of the highest order, matched only by the sacrifice and gallantry of escorts on both sides.

In the first six months of the war, the British had things much their own way. The heavy ships of the Italian Navy were timidly handled and in the early exchanges the British achieved a striking moral ascendancy over the Italians that the latter never fully shook off, even in later months. In large part Italian difficulties stemmed from their lack of a naval aviation arm; relations between the Italian Navy and Air Force were, to put it mildly, erratic. The British, especially when they had carriers, were far better served, though on many occasions, particularly in 1941, the Royal Navy had to operate with no air cover at all – as in Greece and Crete where twenty-two warships and five transports were sunk or severely damaged, and a further fourteen ships were less extensively damaged.

In the opening exchanges, the British dominated the central Mediterranean by aggressive sweeps in order to lure out the superior Italian fleet to a battle the British were convinced they would win decisively. No engagement ever took place, however, the Italian battle fleet declining action wherever possible. They were badly shaken by the aggressiveness of the British and by such actions as the Toranto attack of November when the British used carrier aircraft against the Italian battle line in harbour: the Italians lost three battleships in this attack. Respect for British naval aviation was further enhanced in March 1941 off Cape Matapan when Royal Navy and Royal Air Force aircraft delivered up part of the enemy battle fleet in flight to the guns of the pursuing British battle line – just as the *Bismark* was to be cornered and destroyed by avenging Home Fleet units in May 1941 after having been crippled by torpedo-plane attack.

At Matapan the Italians lost three fine cruisers and two heavy destroyers and were perhaps lucky not to lose more. Fighting blindly and without air cover, they were extremely prudent in their subsequent actions – on no occasion more so than at the second battle of Sirte in March 1942. In order to fight in a convoy of four merchant ships to Malta from Alexandria, the British provided a cruiser and six destroyers as close escort and a covering force that at one time numbered four cruisers and ten destroyers. The Italians put in ineffective air and torpedo-boat attacks but placed their faith in a force of one battleship, two cruisers one light cruiser and four destroyers. The British were organized as close escort, a smokescreen laying force and five divisions intending to stand out from the convoy if it was threatened. When the Italian cruisers were sighted the convoy turned away under cover of smoke that was blown by a rising 25-knot wind. The British divisions repelled the first attack but when the battleship came up, the Italians attempted to

work their way around the smokescreen (which they naturally feared entering) towards the west: the rising wind and sea deterred their attempt to move to the east directly into the teeth of the storm. As the Italians moved to the west the British followed, always keeping the smokescreen between the Italians and the convoy and making repeated lunges from the smokescreen against the enemy battle line with gunfire and torpedoes. This forced the Italians to turn away repeatedly. Ultimately the Italians broke off action and retired for their bases, two of their destroyers floundering en route. The battle was an almost perfect example of the importance of 'the weather gauge' (almost unknown since the days of sail) in the course of the action, but also of the effectiveness of an inferior but aggressive force, skilfully handled as an entire formation, beating off a superior enemy. (The similar tactics of standing between convoy and enemy with inferior forces was also successfully employed by the British in the action with the *Scharnhorst* on December 26 1943. After having frustrated several attempts by the *Scharnhorst* to work her way around the flank of the British cruisers, the latter trailed the German battlecruiser to the south after she had broken off the action in order to bring her to a rendezvous with the battleship *Duke of York*. In a classic night-time action involving co-ordinated attack by gun and torpedoes from destroyers, the German ship was destroyed.) At Sirte, however, the Italians did have some compensation for the action delayed the arrival of the convoy at Malta with the result that two of the merchantmen were sunk by aircraft the following day: had there been no delay then almost certainly these ships would have survived.

In a sense this was exactly the same result as the Germans had achieved with the *Tirpitz*, by her very presence in Norwegian waters, against convoy PQ 17. In one of the most disastrous episodes in British naval history, this convoy was ordered to scatter by the Admiralty and the escorts withdrawn in the mistaken belief that they were shortly to be attacked by overwhelming force. The result was that the hapless merchantmen were picked off individually by submarines and aircraft, only thirteen surviving from an original convoy of thirty-six. This was another superb example of the tactical value of a fleet in being and the effect its presence could have on a superior enemy's dispositions.

Neervtheless with the Allied victories in the battles of the sea lanes in the Atlantic and Mediterranean by

mid-1943, the way was clear for Allied sea power to perform another of its vital tasks – putting an army ashore on an enemy coast and supporting its actions against an enemy field army. Five major seaborne landings were made after May 1943 by the Allies – Sicily (July 1943), the Italian mainland (September 1943), Anzio (January 1944), Normandy (June 1944) and the south of France (August 1944). With the exception of Anzio, which was a deliberate attempt to turn a fixed enemy position further to the south, these invasions were direct assaults on an enemy coast, the techniques being gradually and carefully evolved to ensure success. Though Sicily was the largest of the invasions (seven divisions being used), Normandy is generally considered to be the classic of its kind.

Few people realize the extent to which the Allied decision to land in Normandy, as opposed to the Pas de Calais, was determined by purely naval considerations. The strategic choice was limited by the need to provide searoom for the 1213 warships and the 2470 landing ships and landing craft allocated to the assault phase (plus 1656 other landing ships for support operations and the subsequent convoys needed to put more troops ashore and supply the armies once they were established on the continent). Only in the area to the south of the Isle of Wight in the English Channel was there sufficient room to form up such an armada and to allow the feeding in of forces from the small ports on either flank of the Southampton-Portsmouth area. The Straits of Dover were too narrow, the ports in Devon and Cornwall too far away for ships to make an

Below: HMS *Warspite* shells German positions in Normandy during the D-Day landings in June 1944. Naval firepower was an important part of the Allied success in Normandy. Right: Protected by barrage balloons and the guns of the fleet, Allied forces land from LCT's beached in Normandy. Far Right: Soldiers crammed in LCP's start the run in past a cruiser to land on their beaches.

undetected night passage to the other end of the Channel, and the ports of south-east England were too small to take an invasion force for the shorter, more direct sea route. The timing of the assault was also determined by naval considerations. Accurate pilotage and the needs of naval gunnery necessitated a daylight assault and hence moonlit passage; daylight was also needed to allow the engineers to clear the beach obstacles. The obstacles themselves demanded that the invasion take place on a rising tide on a day when two high tides in daylight occurred in order to allow the follow up forces to be moved ashore. These considerations meant that an invasion had to take place some forty minutes after dawn and four hours before high tide: such conditions, when combined with moon phase, only occurred on three or four days in a month – a good example of the manner in which natural factors affect naval and military strategy.

In Operation Neptune, the naval side of the Normandy invasion, the emphasis was placed on massive firepower to subdue the enemy (assisted of course by heavy bomber raids that could deliver far more weight of explosive but not so accurately as naval gunfire) during the actual invasion phase. This proved to be of vital importance, particularly on Omaha beach where the Americans lost much of their artillery to the sea and where uncleared obstacles prevented reinforcements getting into action. Direct naval gunfire was critical in suppressing enemy gunfire and in breaking up counter-attacks – just as the *Warspite* had broken up German counter-moves at Salerno and German counter-attacks at Anzio had not been facilitated by some 20,000 rounds fired at them by Allied cruisers and destroyers. This firepower was vital in allowing the armies to get ashore, reorganize and then fight their way inland beyond the range of the guns. Thereafter, the navies' task remained as it had always been, namely the continued supply of the armies in their operations against the enemy field forces. Indeed that the Allied armies liberated France and drove deep into Germany to contribute to the forcing of the Nazi surrender, liberating as a result the Benelux countries, Denmark and Norway, was a sign of the total victory obtained by Anglo-American sea and air forces in the struggle. Without victory on the convoy routes, the British would have been forced to surrender: the Americans might well then have been helpless to affect the European situation. Sea power was the basis of the Allied victories in the west.

The Pacific War

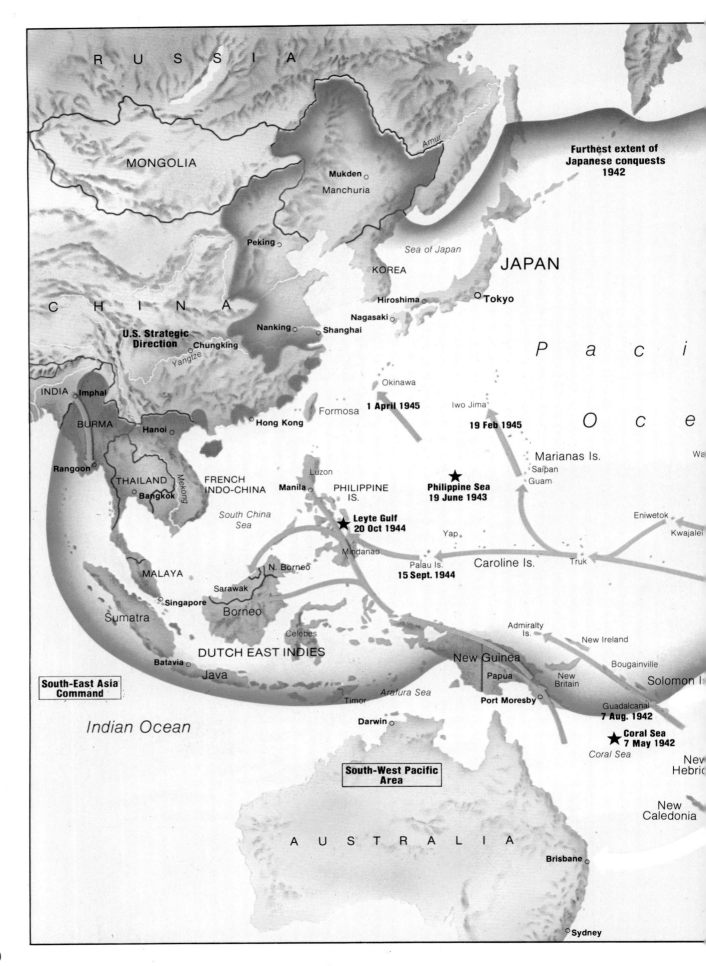

RUSSIA

MONGOLIA

Mukden ○
Manchuria

Peking ○

Sea of Japan

KOREA

JAPAN

Furthest extent of
Japanese conquests
1942

Amur

C H I N A

U.S. Strategic
Direction

Chungking ○

Yangtze

Nanking ○

Shanghai ○

Hiroshima ○

Nagasaki ○

○ Tokyo

INDIA ● Imphal

BURMA

Hanoi ●

Hong Kong ○

Rangoon ○

THAILAND

● Bangkok

Mekong

FRENCH
INDO-CHINA

South China
Sea

Formosa

Okinawa

1 April 1945

Iwo Jima

19 Feb 1945

P a c i

O c e

Marianas Is.
Saipan
Guam

Wa

Luzon

Manila ●

PHILIPPINE
IS.

★ Leyte Gulf
20 Oct 1944

★ Philippine Sea
19 June 1943

Yap ○

Eniwetok

Kwajalei

Mindanao

Palau Is.

15 Sept. 1944

Caroline Is.

Truk

MALAYA

Sarawak

N. Borneo ○

● Singapore

Sumatra

Borneo

Celebes

DUTCH EAST INDIES

Batavia ○

Java

South-East Asia
Command

Timor

Arafura Sea

Indian Ocean

Darwin ○

South-West Pacific
Area

New Guinea

Papua

New
Britain

Port Moresby ○

Admiralty
Is.

New Ireland

Bougainville

Solomon I

Guadalcanal
7 Aug. 1942

★ Coral Sea
7 May 1942

Coral Sea

Nev
Hebri

New
Caledonia

A U S T R A L I A

Brisbane ○

○ Sydney

130

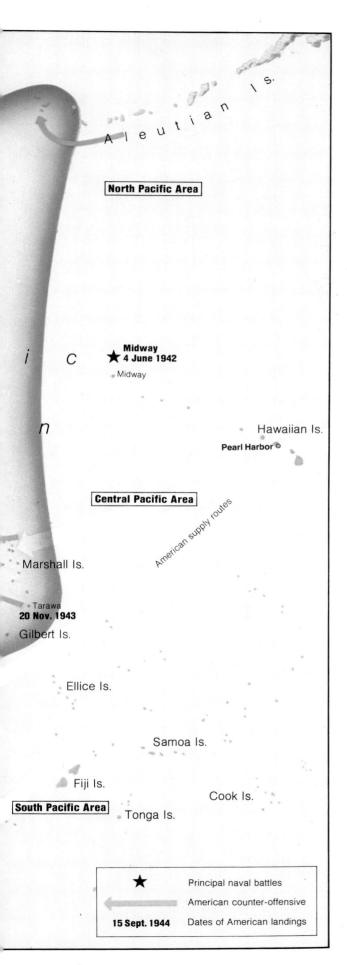

North Pacific Area

Midway
★ **4 June 1942**
Midway

Hawaiian Is.

Pearl Harbor ○

Central Pacific Area

American supply routes

Marshall Is.

Tarawa
20 Nov. 1943
Gilbert Is.

Ellice Is.

Samoa Is.

Fiji Is.

Cook Is.

South Pacific Area
Tonga Is.

★   Principal naval battles

    American counter-offensive

15 Sept. 1944   Dates of American landings

The Japanese spoke of a Victory Disease when they described the vast areas of the Pacific and Far East that they had captured during their first blitzkrieg. The strains on their manpower and resources retaining these areas was one of the factors that led to their defeat.

The war in the Pacific is often seen in terms of the great carrier engagements – the Coral Sea and Midway (1942), the Philippine Sea and Leyte Gulf (1944) – that marked the utter and total destruction of the finest fleet in the world in 1941, the Imperial Japanese Navy. In the course of this destruction, the US Navy increased in size and quality to become utterly unchallenged in power and effectiveness. Less well documented is the war that began immediately after Pearl Harbor whereby the Americans, temporarily paralyzed by the losses sustained in the attack, began unrestricted submarine warfare against Japanese commerce. Ultimately this campaign was to prove of immense strategic importance since in effect the Americans imposed an economic blockade on Japan that became a stranglehold. In the course of the war Japan lost 90 per cent of her merchant fleet and, by the time the atomic bombs brought her to surrender, she was economically, industrially and financially exhausted. Totally dependent on seaborne trade for the import of raw materials and the transport of men and materiel to the theatres of war, the Japanese were fatally vulnerable to commerce warfare in the same way as the British. And trade and the transport of resources were totally annihilated in the course of the war. Such was the power of the Japanese Navy, however, that it was not until after 1943 that losses exceeded replacements and that merchant ships were forced to go into areas controlled by American aircraft in order to supply their threatened or beleaguered garrisons. The most spectacular phase of the commerce war was at the end, when US naval air power roamed the skies around Japan and her approaches, destroying the few remaining merchantmen at will. But the real damage lay in the steady rate of attrition inflicted by American submariners throughout the war on the Japanese merchant fleet: 57 per cent of all losses were inflicted by US submarines. The American strategic blockade of Japan was one of the most decisive examples of economic warfare waged by aggressive sea power.

In the course of this war the Americans used their submarines in exactly the same way as the Germans – in hunting packs that closely co-ordinated their efforts to increase their effectiveness. The Americans had great technical superiority over the Japanese in terms of radar and communications: they were also presented with a supreme opportunity because of Japanese neglect of their trade. With the Japanese Navy committed to fleet action, and training geared to that eventuality, the unglamorous defensive nature of convoy protection was initially scorned. The Japanese patrolled the sea lanes in the same manner that the British had before 1917, achieving next to nothing, and shipping was not concentrated but left to sail independently. When, belatedly, the Japanese switched to convoy they afforded protection on a scale totally inadequate to deal with the aggressiveness of the attack; sometimes the escort was as weak as one escort for five to ten merchantmen. And this against American submariners who were prepared to stay at periscope depth and take on escorts with a spread of torpedoes in order to eliminate them and get at the helpless merchantmen.

The Japanese, on the other hand, did not use their submarines in the same manner against the massive American logistics train that stretched across the Pacific. Perhaps naturally, given the overall and growing American superiority of warship numbers, they used their submarines in an effort to write down US naval strength, as the Germans had in World War I. While this policy had some isolated successes – such as the sinking of the *Yorktown* at Midway – it never had any real chance of altering the balance of power. Moreover, such a policy forced the Japanese to attack the most heavily defended part of the American effort at sea and, as a result, their submarines took heavy losses. They would have been well advised to have concentrated on the merchantmen, effecting an even greater dispersal of American striking power than was in fact the case.

After Pearl Harbor the Americans were to a large

Below: Smoke streams from the USS *Yorktown* as she swings hard to port during Japanese air attacks in the Battle of Midway in June 1942. Inset: A Japanese submarine. Despite having the excellent 'long lance' torpedo, the Japanese failed to use their submarines as aggressively as the Americans.

Damage control teams at work on the flight deck of
the USS *Yorktown* after Japanese attacks on June 4,
1942 during the Battle of Midway. American carriers
did not have armoured flight decks which made them
vulnerable to air attack, though this did save weight
and therefore increase speed.

extent the prisoners of circumstances, both strategically and tactically. Strategically, they had to stand on the defence, for they lacked the strength to contest the Japanese conquest of South-East Asia. To the Americans, the defence of the island chain from Hawaii to Midway, and the sea routes to Australia and New Zealand, were paramount. Tactically, Pearl Harbor had shown that the torpedo and the bomb were the decisive weapons of naval warfare, that carriers could deliver massive and strategically decisive blows in their own right – even though the Japanese actually failed to achieve decisive success at Pearl Harbor since they missed the carriers, dockyard and oil storage depot. (Had they been destroyed, it is difficult to see how the Americans could have avoided withdrawing the remaining fleet to California, with incalculable results.)

Because of the absence of an effective battle line the only means of active defence for the Americans after Pearl Harbor was bound to be centred on the carrier. They basically evolved the notion of the fast carrier striking force, a carrier or carriers operating with a close cruiser and destroyer escort. Such forces operated in semi-independent groups whose movements were co-ordinated to give mutual support and concentrated offensive power where possible. In the early stages of the war a carrier group, if it contained more than one carrier, divided in order to launch or recover its aircraft: at Midway Task Force 16 divided into two groups, one centred on the *Hornet*, the other on the *Enterprise*. By 1943, however, task forces stopped dividing and stayed together under all circumstances in order to increase the effectiveness and strength of the continuous Combat Air Patrols (CAP) and the firepower that could be put up by the escorts against enemy aircraft. By 1944, the Japanese use of suicide aircraft against American naval ships – one in four caused some damage and one in thirty-three sank a ship – forced further changes in the tactical deployment of the carrier forces.

In December 1944 the new tactics were employed for the first time in support of operations against Mindoro in the Philippines. Task Force 38 was divided into three groups: TF 38.1, with two fleet carriers, two light carriers, two battleships, three heavy and one anti-aircraft cruisers, and eighteen destroyers, was the weakest of the three and only a little weaker than the whole of the force that the Americans had deployed at Midway. In order to give advanced warning of suicide attacks advanced destroyer pickets were

posted some sixty miles before the fleet, and equipped with modern radar and homing devices. American aircraft returning to the carriers were obliged to 'report' to the pickets and circle them, thereby allowing any Japanese aircraft that attempted to join the stream to be identified and eliminated. These pickets, which were under the CAP, were posted wide in order to leave a clear passage for Japanese aircraft, and an uncluttered radar picture for the fleet itself. In addition, the Americans altered the balance of aircraft on their carriers. Formerly an *Essex* class carrier on average carried thirty-eight fighters, thirty-six dive bombers and fifteen torpedo-carrying aircraft; after December 1944 such carriers had seventy-three fighters, fifteen bombers and fifteen torpedo planes – a far superior defensive capability than had previously existed, but also an increase in offensive power since the change in

balance was accompanied by modifications to the *Hellcat* and *Corsair* fighters that effectively made them general-purpose aircraft. With a 2000-lb bomb load and a capacity for unescorted bombing operations, such fighters in fact doubled the striking power of the carriers.

For the Mindoro operation the Americans employed a tactic known as the Big Blue Blanket, which was effectively a Day and Night CAP not over the fleet but over the enemy's airfields. When fighters were due for relief, bombers took over to keep the airfields neutralized. For Mindoro, the Americans flew 1671 sorties (1427 of them by fighters) over the Japanese airfields on Luzon, with the result that the invasion forces went untouched by Japanese aircraft based there: overall the balance of losses during these operations decisively favoured the Americans.

The USS *Enterprise* **about to launch Douglas Dauntless fighters on May 4, 1942 during the Battle of the Coral Sea.**

Such were the major tactics adopted by the Americans in the heady days of 1944-45 as their forces triumphantly swept across the western Pacific, taking losses of men, aircraft and ships but at a cost totally exorbitant to the Japanese. American strategy, so tentative and defensive in the dark days after Pearl Harbor, had been able to contest Japanese control of the central Pacific in June 1942, when the latter attempted to complete the task bungled the year before at Pearl Harbor. In attacking towards Midway, the Japanese had hoped to secure their defensive perimeter and possibly bring American carriers to battle, but it was the latter that secured victory. Fighting defensively and trying to keep at maximum distance from the Japanese, the Americans had the supreme advantage that they had broken the Japanese naval codes: they were able to catch the divided Japanese forces and,

concentrating against the carriers, were able to sink four of them for the loss of the *Yorktown*. Most of the Japanese carriers were lost when they were caught in the process of re-arming and refuelling their aircraft on the decks by a providential coincidence of a torpedo-plane and dive-bomber assault – just as the text book had always stressed, but in this case somewhat fortuitous in its timing. As a result of this battle a rough balance of forces in the central Pacific came into existence.

With the defeat of the Japanese in the central Pacific and the earlier checking of the Japanese southern thrust at the Battle of the Coral Sea, the Americans were actively able to contest the Japanese advance in the Solomons by landing on Guadalcanal on August 7 1942. Japanese resistance on the island ended in February 1943 when they evacuated their remaining forces and cut their losses. The landings on Guadalcanal were made to deny the Japanese a forward air base and the possession of this air base brought about a series of naval battles in the seas around the Solomons that were of immense strategic and tactical importance.

In the early exchanges, the sheer professionalism and expertise of the Japanese, particularly in night fighting and torpedo attacks from both cruisers and destroyers, provided them with a decisive superiority over the Americans, even though the latter had radar. The Japanese were also able to achieve a tactical success at the Battle of Santa Cruz where the Americans lost the *Hornet*. Over time however the Japanese, for all their fighting qualities, could not stand up to the sheer volume of the American resources being fed into the battle when this was combined with a more effective use of radar and growing battle experience. Though worsted in many of the engagements, the Americans achieved decisive strategic success at Guadalcanal and inflicted losses that the Japanese could ill-afford.

The slackening of the Japanese impetus and the steady accumulation of American strength, allowed the Americans to assume an offensive that became increasingly dynamic and imaginative with the passing of time. Their strategy essentially involved the by-passing of resistance where possible, leaving the strength of the Japanese to wither like a severed limb. The process, known as 'island-hopping', basically went for the gaps attempting to seize islands from which aircraft could operate. Nevertheless this policy involved the Americans in many severe actions, costly in blood and effort, against an enemy that until almost the end of the war fought to the last man. Yet few campaigns better illustrate the great flexibility of sea power than the American drive across the western Pacific in 1944. Starting from their secured positions in the Solomons and the Gilberts, they drove through the Marshalls to the Marianas (by-passing the scattered Carolines) – an 800-mile jump. At the same time, they conducted a series of landings along the Papuan coast and thrust towards the Philippines. The policy of switching the point of attack along two separate axes of advance, with the choice of timing and target, enabled them to put the Japanese on the horns of a dilemma: as the threat from the Solomons developed, the Japanese were immobilized in 'no-man's land' at Truk, unable to move against the American strength in the Gilberts because of the developments on their right flank. Only when the Americans assaulted Saipan did the Japanese come out to give battle in the Philippine Sea and here their painfully rebuilt carrier forces were annihilated in a cautious defensive action. Though severely criticized at the time, the defensive tactics of the Americans allowed them to concentrate their fighters for battle over the American fleet and by destroying Japanese carrier aircraft they destroyed the effectiveness of the carriers as effectively as if the carriers themselves had been sunk. In all, the Japanese lost three carriers (two to submarines) and had two more heavily damaged: over 400 irreplaceable aircraft and their crews were lost. The Japanese Navy was ruined in the Battle of the Philippine Sea for even though many battleships and lighter surface ships remained, they were of small account. Victory paved the way for the American invasion of the Philippines where, again, the Japanese were forced to give battle. In this battle, the Japanese deliberately divided their forces and used their empty carriers as bait to draw away American carrier forces in order that their surface ships could get among the invasion force. The plan almost worked but in the end the Battle of Leyte Gulf showed that the Japanese were virtually at the end of their tether. With the invasion in 1945 of Iwo Jima and then Okinawa, the way was clear for a concerted air attack on the Japanese home islands themselves: the air bombardment was joined in July by the first ship bombardments – an indication in itself of the totality of US naval and air power.

Total sea supremacy had been obtained by the Americans by the time the Japanese were brought to surrender. It was indeed appropriate that the signing of the instrument of surrender should take place in Tokyo Bay aboard a US Navy ship, for it had been sea power that had decided the issue in the Pacific. Yet by an irony the surrender was signed aboard the battleship *Missouri*, of all the types of ship involved in securing the American victory, perhaps the least important. In some ways, however, the choice of the *Missouri* was perhaps pertinent after all, for the surrender marked the end of an era, the end of the line for the battleship. No longer would such ships play a major part in war at sea: Tokyo Bay marked the passing of the ship that had been synonymous with sea power itself for over 300 years.

Sea Power in the Nuclear Age

The defeat of the Axis powers in 1945 in no way lessened the importance of sea power: it provided, in fact, the basis for many of the Western Allies' subsequent actions – the surrender of the former enemies (most notably Japan) and the reduction and repatriation of the American and British armies overseas to name only two. The disarming and repatriation of the defeated enemies, the despatch of armies of occupation (as in China and Japan), the shipment home of prisoners of war and demobilized soldiers, the imposition of order in certain areas (such as Greece) and the sending of urgently needed supplies and aid to liberated territories were also actions only made possible by the immense naval power of the Western democracies. For years after the war clearance of the debris of war – the removal of wrecks, and the clearing and destruction of mines and bombs – were also tasks that required considerable efforts on the part of naval forces.

The basis for such actions was American naval power. Following the sun's path from the Elbe to Vladivostock ran the writ of the American Navy; nothing on the surface of the seas could move except by her permission. Strong though her forces on land and in the air were, the backbone of American strength was her incomparable Navy beside which even the Royal Navy was dwarfed into insignificance. Local areas of control and influence remained to the British but British naval power was a complement and not a rival to or independent of US naval strength. For the reality of the situation was that an impoverished Britain, dependent on the Americans for almost all her escort carriers and many of her high performance aircraft, could not maintain her position. In the disastrous winter of 1947 the commissioned strength of the Royal Navy in home waters was reduced to one cruiser and three destroyers: the rest were being scrapped, held in reserve or were being used as training ships. The Pax Britannica had indeed passed, and control of the seas had been assumed by stronger friendly hands.

The advent of the nuclear age did not initially affect navies a great deal. The 1946 nuclear tests by the Americans at Bikini Atoll in the Pacific demonstrated the vulnerability of warships to direct or close nuclear attack, but the wisdom of the time decreed that for the most part nuclear attack would not wreak too much damage on a reasonably dispersed naval force and that, in any case, the paucity of nuclear weapons for the next few years would probably mean that any likely enemy (i.e. the Soviet Union) would be far more likely to use nuclear weapons against the homeland and against naval bases than against a fleet at sea. The development of nuclear weapons, therefore, had little effect on tactics. Moreover, strategically, navies were not immediately concerned with them because they were incapable of delivering them. The great size and weight of nuclear weapons, and the need to have heavy aircraft in order to lift them, meant that naval aircraft and, more importantly, aircraft carriers, were utterly unsuited to deliver them. This did not mean that the US Navy did not want to have a nuclear capability and did not fight hard to secure one, but it did lose the initial contest for the control of such weapons to the newly formed US Air Force, even though at the time, only the heavy strategic bombers of the latter were able to deliver nuclear weapons on their targets. So the strategic role of the navies – particularly the US Navy – remained conventional.

The fleets were a powerful weapon of diplomacy, capable of demonstrating a nation's interests, influence and determination. They could be used to exert pressure, without necessarily crossing a threshold of violence in some crisis situation. For the British and French, the need for, and importance of, sea power in colonial operations was quickly shown as their respective empires were quickly involved in countering insurgency in various areas. The French ability to reestablish their position in Indo-China by transportation of troops to that area, to give close fire support to coastal operations, to launch riverine operations and to patrol coastal waters to prevent infiltration or insurgent operations, all depended on sea power. In part the failure of insurgency movements in Malaya and the Philippines can be traced not only to their isolation from external sources of support and supply by the sea but also to the naval might of the British in the first instance and the reality, if distant, of American sea power in the second. Later the Korean and Vietnam Wars were to demonstrate the vital importance of sea power in conventional conflict fought under the nuclear umbrella. During the Korean War it was US sea power that saved South Korea from communist aggression. The desperate position of the United Nations forces in the Pusan perimeter was held only because of the massive contribution of US sea power – when the UN forces were virtually at the end of their tether and confronted by a strong and aggressive enemy, the defence and reinforcement of Pusan was achieved by the US Navy, particularly in the form of naval gun

support and close air support. In all naval ships fired some 4 million shells and naval aircraft flew over 250,000 sorties in the course of the Korean War. Important though these contributions were, they somewhat pale into insignificance when set against the sheer audacity and inspired brilliance of the Inchon landing of September 1950. While still in contact with a superior and attacking enemy, the Americans divided their forces to launch an amphibious attack against the communist flank where the combination of sea to the west and mountains to the east forced the enemy lines of communication through a narrow, restricted gap. Attacking defended position in waters where some of their craft drew less than one foot of water under their keels, the Americans fought their way ashore and then inland to stand across the communist line of retreat, thus bringing about a massive battle of encirclement and annihilation that was almost total in its extent. In subsequent operations the naval forces performed vital tasks in the recovery of ditched aircrews, the patrolling of the coasts and in evacuating United Nations forces from Korea. Later, in Vietnam, the great strength and invulnerability of sea power was most clearly shown as US naval forces pounded communist positions both north and south of the 17th Parallel. The losses that US aircraft took on the ground to night-time communist rocket and gun attack was in marked contrast to the invulnerability of aircraft far out to sea on the decks and in the hangars of the carriers. Flexibility, invulnerability and immense destructive power were clearly revealed by such operations.

Sea power, therefore, was of immense importance in such circumstances as 'limited wars'. It was also critical in demonstrating power, interest and intention in a crisis situation. The appeal for American intervention by the Lebanese authorities in 1958 was only met because the US Navy could send marines ashore and aircraft overhead almost immediately; the imposition of quarantine on Cuba in 1962 as the means of forcing the USSR to conform to US wishes was possible only because America at that time enjoyed almost total supremacy in the western Atlantic. The quarantine enabled the Americans to make an overt political and diplomatic move that provided time for the opposition to reflect on the options open without the immediate pressure of direct military confrontation that would have been present in a situation where land forces were mobilized. The invasion of the Dominican Republic in 1965 was a naval operation, an immediate and flexible response to a situation in which the Americans felt that vital US interests (and credibility throughout Latin America) was at stake.

Although the South Koreans' position was secure, mainly as a result of US sea power, it must also be noted that the Korean conflict went a long way to restoring American naval power, for by the time the Korean War broke out the US Navy had declined to a seven carrier fleet with hundreds of ships either stricken or in reserve, and with almost no new construction in hand. Virtually the only exception to this near halt in construction was the building of the massive *Midway* class carriers which had two novel features – they were the first American carriers to incorporate armoured flight decks, the value of which had been amply demonstrated by British carriers during the latter stages of the Pacific war and they were also the first American warships incapable of passing through the Panama Canal. In this they relinquished strategic flexibility for the tactical and technological requirements of broad beam and extra displacement.

The Korean War reconvinced the Americans of the need for strong carrier forces and indeed by the end of the war eighteen carriers had served off Korea, of which sixteen were kept in commission for many years after the war had ended. Technological developments

143

The cutting edge of a carrier: a US Navy Phantom laden with missiles, weapons pads and fuel tanks at the moment of take-off. Right: A British Hawker Siddeley Harrier VTOL fighter bomber during trials on HMS *Ark Royal* off Portland.

necessitated the construction of new classes of carriers after 1950: the *Forrestal*, laid down in 1952, needed longer flight decks than had previously been incorporated into carriers, in order to handle the new generation of jet aircraft. She was also given an enclosed prow to improve her seaworthiness, and during construction she was modified to incorporate three British inventions – the angled flight deck, steam catapults and the mirror landing aid. The angled flight deck was a major step forward since it allowed the simultaneous despatch and recovery of aircraft with comparative safety. The *Forrestal* and her three sister ships were followed by two ships of the *Kitty Hawk* class and then the *Enterprise*. With the building of the latter, the sheer cost of such ships began to make itself felt – the nuclear powered *Enterprise* cost $451 millions compared to the $265 millions of the *Kitty Hawk* class (the *Midway* class cost $81 millions) – and this caused a reversion to conventional power in the *John F. Kennedy* class ($280 millions), even though the nuclear propul-

sion of the *Enterprise* gave her immensely high speeds and long-range endurance. On her original cores the *Enterprise* steamed 200,000 miles in her first three years, though her great flexibility was somewhat limited by the fact that most of her escorts were conventional. The limitation imposed upon capability by rising costs can be gauged by the fact that the US Navy is now a thirteen carrier force since the cost of replacing the older carriers is now very nearly prohibitive. The *Nimitz*, commissioned in May 1975, initially cost $1881 millions and her two sister ships, the *Dwight D. Eisenhower* and the *Carl Vinson*, are confidently expected to break the $2 billion ceiling. The staggering cost – an eleven-fold increase in twenty-five years – has effectively put the acquisition of such ships beyond the reach of the Europeans, even without considering the difficulties they would have in finding the 6300 men needed to man a ship such as the *Nimitz*. Such costs may soon prove to be beyond the reach of Americans themselves. In order to seek a way around the problem

144

in 1975, the American Navy sought approval for a 14,300 ton ship of an escort type known as a Sea Control Ship (SCS) armed with three VSTOL aircraft and sixteen helicopters, many of the characteristics approximating those of the British *Invincible* (launched May 1977). The US Congress, however, threw out the request on the grounds that the ships were too small, too slow and lacked offensive capability, even though trials on the *USS Guam* in a SCS role between 1972 and 1974 had proved satisfactory. The result has been that the US Navy has made proposals for a new class of 'light' carrier, something between 40,000 and 50,000 tons or similar to the *Ark Royal*, that could operate fixed wing VSTOL aircraft. Such ships would be suited to sea control operations (that is, securing control of the seas surrounding the areas in which the ship operated), supporting amphibious operations and providing close air support, conducting mine warfare and for operations in which her aircraft would not be involved in a direct fight for air supremacy. Although her

aircraft could be used to deal with reconnaissance aircraft and bombers, they would not be equipped to fight high-performance fighters or attack aircraft – that task would remain the role of the fleet carriers with whom the light carriers could keep pace.

It is precisely in this increasingly costly field of carrier aviation that the Western navies still retain their most decisive advantage over the Soviet Navy at the present time. In the fifties, at the time of Korea and the building of the *Forrestal*, the US Navy emerged from the shadows of the US Air Force and secured for the carriers a major nuclear role. The miniaturization of nuclear weapons and the development of long-range jet aircraft capable of operating off a carrier deck allowed the Navy to emerge, not as a competitor, but as a complement to the Air Force as the means of delivering nuclear weapons. Moreover, they had one great advantage over the Strategic Air Command in this role in that the carriers, unlike airfields, were mobile and could pose immense problems of detection and destruction

HMS *Fearless* an assault landing ship with a self-flooding dock area aft. Not only can she launch and recover landing craft, her dock area has a deck which serves as a landing pad for Wessex helicopters. She is equipped to serve as an off-shore HQ for a joint naval and land task force.

for the defender. Nevertheless, the role of the US carriers as a major part of the strategic nuclear deterrent was relatively short-lived. The development of other means of delivery meant that the carriers, though important, became somewhat downgraded in the purely nuclear sense.

By the early sixties, particularly with Vietnam beginning to make itself felt, the role of the carriers in limited warfare operations began to become more important at the expense of the nuclear role. Today the carrier still has a nuclear role but the overwhelming part of its *raison d'etre* remains its conventional capability. Any amphibious landing or seaborne reinforcement of a threatened area – such as the northern flank in the event of a war with the Soviet Union – would have to be made under the protective umbrella of carrier aircraft: major reinforcements of the European theatre by the Americans could involve carriers, granted the strength and range of the latest Soviet naval aircraft. Support for land forces in contact with the enemy would also have to be made under air cover. In this role the carrier is absolutely vital and the task forces formed to discharge such tasks would have to be formed around the carrier. Such task forces besides the carrier(s) would have to include solid- and liquid-replenishment ships, and naval vessels armed with weapons capable of protecting not only the individual ship but the force as a whole. A task force would have to be screened, particularly to the fore, by anti-submarine warfare ships, whose sonar searches overlapped: these would probably be preceded by their helicopters working in front searching for submarines or surface ships of the enemy. In immediate support of the carriers would have to be the heavier of the escorts that were capable of dealing with submerged or missile attack and, most importantly, some anti-aircraft capability to supplement the carriers own Combat Air Patrols. The CAPs would probably be well forward of the task force, perhaps some sixty to eighty miles in advance, in order to give as much warning as possible of the approach of hostile aircraft. Given the existence of stand-off weapons, carrier aircraft would have to think in terms of intercepting and destroying enemy bomber forces several hundred miles before the task force, rather than relying on the missiles of the task force to deal with the enemy weapons. (The task force could also be scouted by patrol lines of conventional submarines and hunter-killer submarines).

The carriers were the first means by which the US

Navy secured a nuclear role. In 1954, however, the US Navy launched the first nuclear propelled submarine, the *USS Nautilus*, a patrol submarine armed with conventional torpedoes. Nuclear propulsion enabled the submarine to become a proper submarine craft rather than a ship that could submerge; it also gave great underwater speed and endurance and hence invulnerability from surface ships. (In one of her earliest voyages the *Nautilus* sailed nearly 1400 miles at 20 knots submerged.) The logic of nuclear deterrence pointed the way to a further dispersal of the means of delivery by evolving a nuclear-powered submarine armed with strategic nuclear missiles. The first US submarine to carry nuclear missiles was the *Halibut*, initially designed with conventional power. At first the *Halibut* and her sisters were armed with the 575-mile range *Regulus I* missile that could only be fired from a surfaced submarine; this, combined with the limited range

of the missile, meant that the submarines were vulnerable to detection and destruction since they had to come quite close to their targets and show themselves. The only solution to the tactical problems thus caused was the evolution of longer-range missiles that could be fired underwater; indeed, the *Halibut* and her sisters were intended only as an interim measure until such weapons were available. The first occasion on which a submarine (the *George Washington*) fired a strategic

HMS *Ark Royal* and the USS *Forrestal* during joint naval exercises in July 1976. Conventional carriers like these will in time be replaced by 'through deck' versions.

missile while submerged was on July 20, 1960, the missile being the 1200-mile range *Polaris A-1*. The role of the submarine as the most effective means of delivering strategic nuclear weapons on account of

149

her endurance, mobility and comparative invulnerability has grown from this time, though only at the expense of developing longer-ranged missiles and larger submarines capable of carrying them. The initial *Polaris* submarines, costing about $100 millions, were subsequently replaced by longer-ranged Marks of the *Polaris* and then by submarines armed with the 2800-mile *Poseidon* missile. The *Poseidon* in its turn will be replaced by the 4000-mile range *Titan*, with a 6000 Mark II projected. The cost of new submarines capable of delivering such weapons is enormous: in 1977 the US Navy programmed $1969 millions for just two.

Such escalating costs – roughly parallel to the rising cost of the carriers – have to be borne by the Americans in order to hold diplomatic cards in the Strategic Arms Limitation Talks (SALT) and to maintain the whole credibility of the American nuclear deterrent upon which the security of both the United States and NATO depends. The *Titan* missiles are almost literally intercontinental in their range: without moving from their West Coast base they can hit virtually any major city in China or the Soviet Union. No time need therefore be lost in moving to and from patrol areas, and even greater areas of ocean will be made available for nuclear submarines to try to hide in – multiplying the difficulties of the defence and making it harder to take effective counter-measures. Heavy though the cost may be, there would seem to be no alternative to such expenditure, granted that the Americans must begin to replace many of their older nuclear submarines and that the Soviets already have equivalent submarines and missiles.

Since the end of World War II one of the more remarkable developments at sea has been the growth of the Soviet Navy. For a country that is largely land-locked, which has very little need for seaborne trade and which in 1945 had a navy that was virtually irrelevant in equipment and wartime performance, the change from impotence to a position whereby she can challenge the naval power of the US on an almost equal footing is most profound. While they still have many difficulties to face – most notably the physical separation of forces by the sheer size of the Soviet homeland – and while there remain certain areas of Western superiority at sea, the continued growth of the Soviet Navy, both quantitative and qualitative, is bound to be of great concern to the West. For while it was possible to see its development in the forties and early fifties as a reflex action to Western maritime

supremacy, that supremacy has already passed and some degree of nuclear parity has now been obtained, so the continued relentless production of Soviet warships can hardly be seen in purely defensive terms or as a defence of marginal maritime interests.

The Soviet Navy, taking its place alongside the Army, strategic rocket and air defence forces in attempting to fulfill distinct political and strategic objectives, exists for three basic purposes. Initially it secures the defence of the Soviet Union and the Soviet-bloc countries. To this end it plays a part in the deployment of the Soviet nuclear deterrent and possesses forces for operations against American nuclear submarines. It also possesses a capability in conventional

surface and air units that could prevent an orthodox attack from the sea by the West and is also capable of conducting offensive conventional operations on the high seas. As such, it exists in order to 'write down' the conventional power of the Americans, Western Europeans and the Chinese. The third role is the promotion of Soviet interests and the cause of communism (mutually identifiable in Soviet eyes) through such matters as intervention in 'wars of national liberation' – such as Angola. They are also aware, from the way in which naval power has been used by the British and Americans, that a fleet is a powerful instrument of diplomacy, not simply to show the flag and demonstrate power and determination, but also in a subtle use of force or pressure below a threshold of violence that could lead to wider conflict. Conversely the Soviet presence at sea at the present time means that certain responses that have been available to the West in the past may not now be possible, for arguably the recent build-up of the Soviet fleet must be seen in conjunction with the Soviet build-up in land and air forces and not simply in terms of defence or keeping Eastern Europe in check. One does not need long-range bombers and nuclear submarines to hold Warsaw in line.

The Soviet naval performance in World War II was very poor. This was the result partly of poor training and equipment (particularly with regard to radar and

A Soviet Whiskey Class submarine showing signs of a long stay at sea. Russia has the world's largest submarine fleet, which would give her the ability to wage a crippling campaign against islands such as Britain and Japan in a conventional war.

sonar) and partly because the Soviets, particularly in the early years, were forced to use their sailors in many of the great land battles where their losses were immense. Soviet historians have denigrated the importance of the Anglo-American naval contribution to Allied victories and have claimed considerable successes for their own forces, but the truth of the matter is that the Soviet naval effort in World War II, particularly when it is remembered that in 1941 the Soviets had more submarines than the Germans, was derisory. In only one area did the Soviet Navy perform at all well: their river flotillas, especially when they took part in operations in support of the land forces, as at Stalingrad, were very effective. It is worth noting that Sergei S. Gorshkov, now Commander-in-Chief of the Soviet Navy first came into prominence as commander of the Sea of Azov flotilla during the war.

In the years immediately after World War II the Soviets naturally placed their priorities on national

recovery, the needs of the Army and the development of atomic weapons. (Nuclear weapons were secured in 1949; thermo-nuclear weapons after 1953.) Nevertheless, impressive progress was made during this time in expanding the Navy – in itself a major task given the massive destruction of naval bases, construction facilities and ports during the war. Equally importantly, a massive missile research and development programme must have been undertaken during the ten years after the war, given the Soviet Navy's deployment of missiles in the later fifties and early sixties.

Just what they were aiming to achieve during this period is hard to discern. It may be that they were aiming to build a substantial balanced oceanic fleet with carriers, battleships and cruisers with attendant ships, but that this dream never materialized. And it may have been abandoned as a result of the patent inability of Soviet industry to meet all its objectives, or when the realization of the scale of American rearmament after

Korea meant that any such idea of a balanced surface fleet was tantamount to giving the US Navy live target practice in the event of war: there really was little point in building a carrier or two when the Americans had sixteen or more ready for operations. But Stalin was known to favour a big navy and was attracted by the notion of ocean-going ships that could push the defences, interests and capabilities of the USSR even further from the Soviet heartland. On the other hand, however, it would seem that the Soviet Navy was built along more limited, defensive and prudent lines and that their forces were finally built up in order to fulfill three distinct objectives: firstly, to provide sufficient forces to deny the Western navies control of certain waters washing Soviet and Soviet-controlled territories; secondly, the provision of a coastal capability for operations in conjunction with the Army; and, thirdly, an ability to carry out operations on the high seas against Western commerce and American military

movements across the Atlantic to Europe. In the immediate post-war period the Soviets concentrated upon completing various ships on which work had stopped because of the war; once these were completed new programmes involving modern vessels were put in hand. Of these new vessels probably the most important were the submarines of the *Whisky* class, seemingly based on the German Type XXI submarine and superior to any submarine then in service with Western navies. Perhaps as many as 230 were built by 1957, and there were some fifty of the less successful *Quebec* and (larger) *Zulu* classes completed by that time. The overall strength of the submarine arm by late 1958 was about 470 – more than the Germans had possessed at any single time between 1939 and 1945. At the same time the Soviets pressed ahead with cruisers and destroyers. Fourteen of the graceful if obsolete *Sverdlov* 6-in cruisers were completed while the powerful *Skoryi* class destroyers were followed by the

larger *Kotlin* class.

The death of Stalin seems to have caused some wavering in naval construction, just as it did in the whole Soviet political sphere. The direction of naval policy had certainly entered a new phase by 1956 with the supremacy of Khrushchev within the Soviet political hierarchy and that of Gorshkov as Commander-in-Chief of the Navy. This new regime did inherit certain considerable assets. Firstly, Krushchev's great concern to build up strategic nuclear forces – later to lead to conflict with the military because of the cuts on conventional forces as a result – coincided with the technological developments that made possible submarine-launched strategic missiles. The first tests on ballistic missiles for submarines were carried out in 1955 by the Soviet Union, the same year that the first six *Zulu-V* class submarines began conversion in order to carry 300-mile SS-N-4 *Sark* missiles. It seems that these submarines pre-date the *Halibut* and, in a sense, this was understandable. Given the fact that the Soviets lacked forward bases and long-range bombers, it was natural that missiles and submarine launchers should be of immediate interest to them: the fact that the missiles were of such short range was to the Soviets the spur that the *Regulus* proved to be for the Americans – to implement further development in order to secure invulnerability.

By the time that the *Zulu* conversions were complete, work had already started on new submarines capable of carrying strategic nuclear weapons. Some of these were nuclear-powered, others conventionally fuelled. These were the nuclear *Hotel* and the conventional *Golf* submarines: both classes were initially armed with the *Sark* but then re-equipped with the 700-mile *Serb* missile. By the early sixties the Soviets were building roughly along the same lines as the Americans though slightly behind them: moreover their submarines were neither as good nor as quiet as the American ones. The Soviet equivalent of *Polaris* was the *Yankee* class with sixteen SS-N-6 missiles. These 1300-mile range missiles meant that Soviet submarines could not strike central USA; although this target was subsequently made possible with the development of the *Delta* class with twelve 4200-mile SS-N-8 missiles, which were superior in range and warhead size to any contemporary American naval missile. The acquisition of such missiles enabled the *Delta* class to be effective against the USA even in Arctic waters, without having to enter the Atlantic and

A Russian Krupney Class guided missile destroyer. This type of vessel has gun and missile firepower vastly superior to destroyers of World War II. She is armed with a range of surface-to-surface and surface-to-air missiles as well as anti-submarine rocket launchers, torpedo tubes and radar controlled light anti-aircraft guns.

Pacific Oceans. (Western sources estimate that the Soviets have some fifty to sixty SSBN submarines, most of which are with the northern fleet based on Sveromorsk.)

The development of SSBN submarines was obviously a major part of Soviet submarine development and was vital to the deployment of their nuclear deterrent, but it was not the only area of development. In addition to the SSBN and the continued construction of conventional patrol submarines (such as the plentiful *Foxtrot* class built after 1958), they developed submarines that were equipped for a hunter-killer role (against Western SSBN submarines) and for operations against Western surface ships by virtue of cruise missiles. The latter type of missile seems to have been built specifically with Western carriers and task forces in mind, possibly intending short- or medium-range missiles (with either conventional or nuclear warheads) to be used in conjunction with an aircraft relay system against surface targets. Such submarines included the *Juliet* class (conventionally-powered) and the nuclear *Echo* class, both of which were commissioned in quite large numbers in the mid-sixties, and which are now mostly deployed with the northern fleet.

Overall at the present time the Soviet Navy deploys about 400 submarines of all types, just over half of which are conventional patrol submarines (of which half of them are of the *Whisky* class). The total capability of this force is impressive not only in its deterrence role but also in the conventional role against trade and military convoys on the oceans. Its importance in the latter role is likely to increase in a situation of Mutually Assured Destruction, particularly if a war did not result in a short nuclear exchange but in a long, drawn-out war of attrition where numbers and not quality were of the essence. The quality of Soviet submarines has definitely improved and the number of nuclear-powered submarines is constantly increasing – although this must be balanced against the decline in the number of older submarines, particularly of the *Whisky*, *Quebec* and *Zulu* classes that must now be approaching the end of their active service lives.

Throughout the Krushchev era, there were important developments in the field of strategic missiles, and his successors have continued the pattern he helped create in his ten years of leadership, by enhancing even further the conventional surface strength of the Navy. The most marked feature of these developments has been the arming of most new ships with missiles.

Kiev, the first Soviet aircraft carrier during a cruise in the Mediterranean in July 1976. Right: An Osa Class fast patrol boat launches STYX missiles. Small vessels equipped with surface-to-surface missiles have a punch which makes them a major threat to larger vessels which can be hit at long range.

After the *Sverdlov* class was cut back from twenty-four to fourteen ships, there was an inter-regnum of some six years before the first of *Kynda* class appeared in 1962. The *Kynda* class was seemingly the first purpose-built guided-missile warship: earlier the Soviets had modified certain of their destroyers to take either SS-N or SA-N missiles (in the case of the *Kildins* between 1957 and 1962; with the *Krupnys* after 1960). Much of the missile development was directed to fill the one glaring weakness in the Soviet position at sea – the lack of an organic air defence. The first air defence missile to be fitted in Soviet ships was the SA-N-1 or *Goa* missile, believed to have a 15-mile slant range and a ceiling of 12,000m: subsequently the SA-N-2 (*Guideline*), SA-N-3 (*Goblet*) and SA-N-4 have been introduced, and the latter two are now used very extensively. (The SA-N-4 is believed to be the naval equivalent of the Soviet Army's *Gecko* missile.)

Attention has also been paid to the provision of a considerable punch against surface and submerged enemy ships, the Soviets arming their ships with increasingly formidable SS-N missiles and later anti-submarine weapons. The first SS-N missiles to enter service were the *Scrubber* missiles, followed by various others, most notably the *Shaddock* (SS-N-3) and the *Styx* (SS-N-2). The latter is probably the most famous of all Soviet missiles since it has found service in seventeen different foreign navies and was responsible for the sinking of the Israeli destroyer *Eilat* in 1967. The *Styx* is employed extensively in light fast patrol boats of the *Osa* and *Komar* classes and has a 40km range at subsonic speeds. Its proven effectiveness – four missiles fired at the *Eilat*, four hits – indicate that, despite the smallness of the patrol craft, it carries a very heavy punch and can deny coastal waters to a powerful enemy. The *Shaddock*, on the other hand, is believed to have a 500km range and to be capable of carrying either a nuclear or conventional warhead. These missiles are also carried on certain Soviet submarines though in this case the range is almost certain to be very much smaller. The whole of this first generation of SS-N missiles is now in the process of being replaced by more modern weapons.

Soviet warships, generally speaking, have been built along general-purpose lines, designed to be able to do a variety of tasks. They seem to be universally the same in that they bristle with armament, radar and electronics, and have not specialized in a given role as the Americans did in the case of the *Spruance* class of destroyer. Com-

missioned in 1970, these are the largest ships, other than carriers, to carry virtually no anti-aircraft protection. Besides two 5-in guns they are designed around helicopters, and ASROC missiles and torpedo tubes – a sure indication that they are designed specifically for work with task forces and will rely on carrier aircraft for air defence. Whether the Soviets will follow this lead when they acquire a number of carriers remains to

be seen, though one rather suspects this will not prove to be the case.

The first Soviet step towards an integrated air capability at sea came in the shape of the *Moskva* in 1967. This was initially thought to be a commando carrying ship but the presence of the small *Hormone* class of helicopter identified her as being an anti-submarine cruiser. Her heavy array of AS weapons and sensors confirmed this, but in addition *Moskva* and her sister ship, *Leningrad*, are equipped with considerable facilities for A-A warning and defence, EW and for carrying out a command role. Their rear flight deck would enable them to operate a very limited number of VTOL aircraft. The lack of organic air defence has in part been filled by VSTOL aircraft operating from one of the latest additions to the Soviet Navy, the *Kiev*.

The first Soviet aircraft carrier the *Kiev* photographed in the Mediterranean by an RAF Nimrod of No 203 Squadron.

Although designated as an anti-submarine cruiser the *Kiev* displaces about 40,000 tons and has a 600 ft angled flight deck; her carrying capacity has been estimated at being about fifty aircraft, equally divided between *Hormones* and VSTOL aircraft. She is exceptional in that, in addition to her aircraft, she carries SS-N missiles and four Gatling guns for air defence as well as SA-N-3 and SA-N-4 missiles. (The latest American carriers do not carry guns and have no SS capability other than their aircraft.) It is believed that the *Kiev* carries an anti-submarine missile system and may be followed by as many as five sister ships. Overall, though she might not be able to compete with the latest American fleet carrier (though possibly with a light carrier), the *Kiev* marks a considerable advance for the Soviet Navy, both in terms of her political and strategic importance. Her considerable troop lifting capabilities and the strength of her surface-to-surface armament, make her a powerful instrument in the event of a Soviet desire to intervene in some area in the future. Her aircraft enable her to provide some form of defensive umbrella for the fleet at sea and are a possible sign that the Americans will not have matters all their own way in the air over the oceans. As such, this must be a point that marks some shift, however small,

in the balance of forces at sea.

Until the time that the Soviets have more *Kievs* at sea, however, the Soviet Navy must still rely on land-based aviation with all the difficulties that such an arrangement implies. They have considerable numbers of long-range aircraft and, in the event of war, could use them *en masse*, possibly in regimental strength of forty bombers, against a Western task force. Any lesser strength might in fact prove inadequate in the event of an invasion force or vanguard task force, the invasion element and rear task force being spread over thousands of square miles of ocean during the approach and possessing considerable anti-aircraft and missile defence capabilities. When all these elements are set alongside her capabilities in mine warfare, and the great problems that they pose for the defence, one can see why the Soviet Navy is causing great concern to the Western Allies. While some take a more sanguine view of Soviet naval developments, it is perhaps timely to make the observation that naval exercises such as *Okean* 75 showed that the Soviets have a world-wide capability that has been considerably enhanced by ever improving RAS facilities: overall, it may be safely noted that the Soviet Navy is an ever growing force that has to be reckoned with.

The first experiments

The Wright *Flyer* on its historic flight at Kill Devil Hills, Kitty Hawk. Its brief journey was the beginning of a new era in peace time travel and the prosecution of war.

On 17 December 1903, at Kill Devil Hills, four miles south of Kitty Hawk, North Carolina, the brothers Wilbur and Orville Wright, bicycle manufacturers from Dayton, Ohio, made what is generally regarded to have been the first manned flight in a heavier-than-air machine. Their aircraft, appropriately known as the *Flyer*, stayed in the air for about a minute on its longest flight before being overturned and destroyed by a strong gust of wind. With the possible exception of Otto Hahn's splitting of the atom in 1938, that flight in 1903 was the most important and far-reaching event of the twentieth century so far. It represented the realization of one of man's most persistent dreams, for he could now, like a bird, travel through air, free from the strictures of topography and, to a certain extent, from dependence upon the wind.

The Wright brothers were by no means the first to devote their lives to the dream, but were unusual in their belief that the answer lay in heavier-than-air contraptions. For centuries the ingenuity of man had been devoted to lighter-than-air machines, ranging from the Chinese man-lifting kites of 2300 years ago, to the successful experiments with hot-air balloons by Joseph and Etienne Montgolfier in the 1780s. But there were serious limits to such machines: all were dependent upon the wind – indeed, the majority were totally unusable in anything but the calmest conditions – and all lacked manoeuvrability, even in the hands of the most skilful pilot. As a result, although there were occasional bursts of military enthusiasm, with balloons being used for battlefield reconnaissance and observation, the art of flying was restricted to those who could afford it as a sport. Experimentation went on, initially along the lines of attaching oars or manually-operated airscrews to the balloons, and then, in the mid-nineteenth century by slinging a steam-driven engine beneath the gas-bag, but the problems remained. Man did not have the energy or muscle-power to direct a free-floating machine, and the existence of red-hot steam pipes next to a bag full of hydrogen or coal-gas was hardly the height of safety. Slight improvements were made at the beginning of the twentieth century, when the internal combustion engine seemed to offer possibilities. Indeed for a time the development of dirigible airships, notably by the German Count von Zeppelin, suggested a breakthrough, but overall the lighter-than-air machines were something of a dead-end. If speed and manoeuvrability were desired, very large engines had to be used and, as these were necessarily heavy, bigger

and bigger airships had to be built to get them off the ground. Eventually, they became so big that their aluminium or wooden "skeletons" could not bear the weight, leading to a number of spectacular accidents. All of which makes the Wright Brothers' achievement seem even more revolutionary.

It would be wrong to assume, however, that the 1903 flight was immediately recognized as an event of historic importance, or that a track to Dayton Ohio was beaten to congratulate the Wrights on their achievement. In fact, the international press barely covered the flight, and many of the reports that did appear were so inaccurate that foreign observers discounted their veracity. One of the few men who showed more than a passing interest was Lieutenant-Colonel J. E. Capper, Commandant of the Royal Engineer's Balloon School at Aldershot, but although he personally visited the Wrights and urged their invention upon the War Office in London for military purposes, neither the British nor any other government showed any real interest. Too little information was available and too many unrelated, yet potentially-fruitful experiments were going on elsewhere for the Wrights to receive the credit that was their due. Nevertheless, their achievement probably provided the impetus that was needed, for as early as 1909 viable aircraft, of widely-differing designs, had appeared in a number of countries, clearly based upon the experimental work of the two brothers. The dream of manned flight, in relatively fast and manoeuvrable machines, had finally become reality.

It is still less than seventy-five years – or slightly more than an average life-time – since that initial flight, and one only has to compare an aircraft such as Concorde with the original *Flyer* to realize how far and with what phenomenal speed the art of manned flight has developed.

However, man rarely uses his skills for purely peaceful means and, in common with so many other inventions, the aircraft was soon adapted to the purposes of war. Theoretically, the possibilities were limitless: by flying over the battle area, whether at sea or on land, the whole panorama of opposing forces could be seen at a glance, enabling more accurate intelligence to be gathered, more quickly; and the enemy could be attacked directly from the air (a possibility foreseen as early as 1670 by an Italian Jesuit priest, Francesco Lana). Nor did it take men long to appreciate the usefulness of carrying troops or supplies by air or, eventually, of destroying the enemy homeland

Above: Wilbur Wright at the controls of a later Model A in 1911. The pilot is now seated and the wing warping and rudder controls are separate.
Left: Orville Wright.

itself through aerial bombardment. The evolution of these practices and their effects upon both the strategy and tactics of modern warfare constitute the primary themes of this book.

Since both the strategic and tactical roles of air power as they have developed, basically from the First World War to the present day are discussed at length, an early definition of the terms "strategic" and "tactical" is necessary. In a war, if aircraft are used in direct support of armies or navies – hitting the *manifestations* of enemy armed power in the immediate vicinity of the battle area or contributing directly to the movement, supply or defence of land or sea forces – this is usually regarded as tactical, whatever the size or depth of the battle area.

If, on the other hand, they hit the *sources* of armed power in the enemy homeland, away from the battle area, with the aim of destroying or impairing the enemy's capability to produce such power, then it is regarded as strategic. Or to put it simply: the destruction of a tank or ship in the battle area is tactical, the destruction of the factory or shipyard which produced them, is strategic. The difference between the two is worth bearing in mind as a number of specific air-power roles are examined in turn – strategic bombing, reconnaissance and observation, tactical strike support and interdiction, airborne troop landings and air transport, naval support, and the maintenance of air space.

165

The death of a Zeppelin. These lighter than air craft were the first strategic bombers to attack the enemy homeland and attempt to undermine civilian morale by indiscriminate bombing. The early fighter aircraft were not powerful enough to gain height in time to put in an attack, but as soon as more modern aircraft became available, daylight operations became suicidal for Zeppelins.

The possibilities of aircraft as potential weapons of war were first recognized in 1911. In the summer of that year the Italians, intent upon achieving a position of dominance in North Africa declared war on the Turks and occupied the town of Tripoli, then a Turkish possession. The Italian expeditionary force included a small air detachment under a Captain Piazza, which proceeded to demonstrate its usefulness not only in reconnaissance but also in elementary bombing, when modified hand-grenades were dropped on to a Turkish camp. Relatively little damage was done, but the feasibility of aerial bombardment, admittedly on a tactical level only, had been firmly established. The extension of this to a strategic level, with the bombs being dropped onto the enemy homeland and areas of war-production, followed almost as soon as the European powers entered their next major conflict.

In the First World War strategic bombing was begun by the Germans. The 1914 version of the Schlieffen Plan, designed to outflank and destroy the Western Allies before Russia could effectively enter the war in the East, included a project for the capture of Calais and its use as a base for aerial attacks upon southern England. The aims were unclear, although it may have been hoped that elements of the British expeditionary force, particularly its aircraft, would have to have been withdrawn from France to counter the threat, so making the German advance on Paris that much easier. In the event, however, the Germans did not get as far as Calais during the 1914 offensive, and the plan was dropped. Nevertheless, they did not give up the idea of aerial bombardment entirely, for in 1915 and 1916 Zeppelin airships – the massive end-products of the lighter-than-air experiments – regularly set out at night from their bases in northern Germany to harrass and attack the industrial towns of the north of England and Midlands. A few even managed to make the long and dangerous journey to London, which was always regarded as the prime objective, but little damage was done.

Even at this early date, however, a number of lessons about strategic bombing and its effects emerged. Despite the large size and slow speed of the airships, the first point to be noted was that defence against their incursions was apparently ineffective. The progress of the Zeppelins could often be tracked from the North Sea to their targets, but regardless of the number of interceptor fighters sent up against them, very few were shot down or even damaged during the early raids. This was partly due to the high altitude at which the airships, flew, for by the time the heavier-than-air machine had struggled up that far, the intruders had gone, and partly the result of poor defence co-ordination around the major English towns, which had not been expecting such attack. Even so, the advantage seemed to be firmly on the side of the offensive power. In addition, there were significant signs of panic among the civilian population whenever the Zeppelins were reported, regardless of the lack of damage incurred through their operation. Sir Basil Liddell Hart, the British armoured warfare theorist of the inter-war years, for example, witnessed a raid in late 1915, the effect of which, he stated, was such that "in the weeks that followed, thousands of the population streamed out into the surrounding countryside" whenever the sirens sounded, whether it was a false alarm or not. Gradually, the home-based fighter pilots learned to go up at night without causing more damage to themselves than the enemy, the numbers of anti-aircraft guns were increased around the major towns, and a number of Zeppelins were destroyed. But although the enemy virtually admitted defeat by late 1916, the lessons remained. They were to be re-inforced within the year.

In the spring of 1917 the Germans began a more serious strategic offensive, this time during the hours of daylight. They established air-bases in occupied Belgium and from these Gotha bombers began to attack England with immediate success. In one of the first raids on the south coast, ninety-five people were killed, and although a total of seventy-four interceptor fighters went up to attack the Germans, only one bomber was destroyed. This set the pattern for the future and, as the Gotha crews gained experience, London itself came under sustained attack. On 13 June 1917 twenty-one Gothas dropped bombs in the area of Liverpool Street Station in London, killing 162 people and injuring a further 432. A month later another raid killed sixty-five and injured 245. In both cases large numbers of fighters took to the skies, but with negligible results.

These raids were important as they determined the future of strategic air thinking, not only in Britain but also elsewhere. The casualty figures may seem small compared to those of the Second World War, when it was not unknown for over 100,000 people to be killed in one raid alone, but in the London of 1917 they caused public outcry, signs of panic and a significant diminution of war production as workers stayed at home

to avoid being caught by the bombers in crowded factories which were likely to be the primary targets. The Lloyd George Government reacted by setting up a special committee, chaired by the South African Jan Christian Smuts, to investigate the lamentable state of British air defence and recommend improvements. The Smuts Committee made two reports, the first of which dealt exclusively with the defence system over London and suggested an immediate increase in the numbers of anti-aircraft guns and fighter aircraft, even at the expense of the Western Front. This was privately regarded by the Committee members as little more than a sop to public opinion, and it was the second report, submitted in September 1917 (less than three months after the Gotha raids) that contained their true feelings and affected the development of strategic thinking.

Its central assumption was sweeping: "The day may not be far off when aerial operations, with their devastation of enemy lands and destruction of industrial and populace centres on a vast scale, may become the principal operations of war, to which the other forms of military and naval operations may become secondary and subordinate. . . ."

In other words, Smuts and his colleagues were of the opinion that in the bomber was to be found a potential war-winner, capable of destroying the industrial base upon which any technological nation's armed forces had to depend. Furthermore, they were obviously thinking that the German Gotha raids were merely the beginning of such an offensive against Britain, for they went on to recommend an immediate counter-offensive as the best, if not the only form of defence. For this reason it was proposed not only that the strength of British air services should be doubled, but that a large strategic bombing force should also be created. Since the formation and direction of such a force would lie entirely outside the experience of existing military or naval staffs, who controlled the Royal Flying Corps and Royal Naval Air Service respectively, it necessitated the institution of an independent Air Service, provided with a separate administration and general staff of its own. Opposition to this idea was strong, particularly among those who saw it as merely contributing to a weakening of the Royal Flying Corps on the Western Front, but a series of night-time Gotha and Zeppelin raids during the winter of 1917-18, which proved almost impossible to counter successfully, ensured the implementation of the Committee's reforms. On April 1 1918 the Royal

Air Force came into existence, owing its separate identity almost entirely to the concept of a strategic counter-offensive against German cities. Unfortunately, although an independent bombing force was set up in France, operating the new Handley-Page 1500 aircraft, the war was over before it could be really tested in action. A few raids were carried out, but for most of the time up to the Armistice on November 11 1918 the force operated in long-range tactical support of the Allied armies, hitting German fuel dumps, communications and reserves behind their front line.

There can be little doubt that this had a detrimental effect upon strategic air theory. The Smuts Committee had met and reported in considerable haste, confronted with a series of extremely successful air raids, and there is much to warrant a view that the evidence used by the Committee was unrepresentative of the true facts. If the German raids of 1917 are taken in isolation – something which Smuts was obviously obliged to do as they were the first of their kind – a number of conclusions appear to be valid. Firstly, that the bomber, with the element of surprise on its side, always holds the initiative and will more than likely be able to drop its load before interceptors can struggle up to its operating height. Secondly, that air defence is not a great deal of use, for exactly the same reason. Thirdly, that such attacks were to be the operations of the future, causing panic in the streets, widespread destruction of property and instant diminution of essential war production as workers are dehoused, demoralized and killed. Fourthly, that the only hope is for a counter offensive designed to do more damage to the enemy than he can ever inflict on you, resulting either in your victory or a nullification of the weapon through deterrence.

These were basically the conclusions of the Smuts

Committee and the reasons behind the founding of an independent Royal Air Force and it was indeed unfortunate that the First World War ended before they could be tested in a more general way. As it was, the strategic conclusions drawn from that conflict formed the basis upon which a number of air-power theorists built up the framework of an air strategy which, in general terms, continued to be believed and practised by many at least until the 1960s if not to the present day.

The most important and influential of these theorists was probably Guilio Douhet, an Italian who gained his air experience operating with the Allies against Austria during the First World War, although it is interesting to note that he was never involved in a strategic bombing campaign. As a theorist, he was certainly the most revolutionary of his time, for in his book *Command of the Air*, published in the 1920s, he took the lessons of the late conflict to their extreme. Two basic assumptions formed the framework of his theory: firstly, that aircraft were instruments of offense of incomparable potential, against which no effective defence could be foreseen; and secondly, that civilian morale would be shattered by bombardment of centres of population. Taking these ideas, he followed them through until convinced that, in the event of war, the side with the larger strategic bombing fleet would automatically gain complete command of the air, since no effective defence existed, and would end the war swiftly by bombing the civilian population into a state of panic which would force the enemy to sue for peace. As a natural extension, neither armies nor navies would really enter into consideration and would play merely subsidiary roles, mopping-up and occupying territory. It mattered little to Douhet whether the bombers flew by day or night, but it was to his mind essential that the air force enjoyed

complete independence of administration and command, for the simple reason that tactical roles in support of armies or navies were totally unnecessary.

Douhet was so sure of the correctness of his arguments that he even entered into rather spurious mathematical calculations and worked out exactly how many bombs would be needed to destroy a given area of a city. Basing his hypothesis upon the fact that one bomb from a Gotha in 1917 killed, say, five people and devastated twenty-five square yards of buildings, he simply multiplied these figures so that ten bombs would kill fifty people, one hundred bombs devastate 25,000 square yards of buildings. In retrospect, one can perhaps appreciate the false logic which this entailed – after all, bombs do not fall in an exact pattern twenty-five square yards apart – but Douhet seemed, at the time and in the absence of further evidence, to be so convincing that as late as 1939 the authorities were sure that in the first week of hostilities alone a city such as London would suffer up to 66,000 fatal casualties.

Hence the mass evacuation of children from urban areas and the provision of over 100,000 hospital beds in Greater London alone for potential air-raid victims in September 1939.

Douhet was not the only air theorist to think along these lines in the 1920s and 1930s. In America Brigadier William ("Billy") Mitchell, a serving airman, was so vociferous about the war-winning potential of aircraft and the lack of official interest in his ideas that he was eventually court-martialled and forced to resign his commission. He too was convinced that, in an age of aerial warfare, military and naval campaigns, particularly so far as America was concerned, were subsidiary to the main air effort, if not totally unnecessary. He pressed for the defence of the American mainland to be put into the hands of an independent air force, demonstrating his belief that the navy was obsolete in this sphere by destroying the ex-German battleship hulk *Ostfriesland* from the air in July 1921: a lesson for the future that was completely ignored. In addition Mitchell saw no reason why, in the event of war, America should not depend upon strategic bombing for, according to his theory, waves of self-defending bombers, gaining command of the air as they flew through it, would operate during the hours of daylight and hit vital parts of the enemy war machine, undermining his capacity to continue the conflict. Unlike Douhet, however, he saw no reason to terrorize the

Handley Page HP 0/400

Engines *Two 350hp Rolls Royce Eagle VIII-cyl vee, water-cooled; four bladed wooden propellers.*
Crew *3, 4 or 5*
Span *upper wing, 100ft; lower wing, 70ft*
Length *62ft 10¼in*
Height *22ft*
Max speed *97.5mph at sea level*
Armament *nose, double .303in Lewis MGs on Scarff ring; dorsal, single .303in Lewis MG; ventral, single .303in Lewis MG, fired through fuselage chute*

Bomb load *16x112lb; 8x250lb; 3x520lb or 550lb; 1x1,650lb; a 'supply' of 25lb Cooper bombs*

1 *The Office: control-wheel and main dashboard of the HP 0/400 pilot's cockpit. Lower left shows door to the forward cockpit.*
2 *and* **3** *The 1,650lb SN bomb, with the 25lb Cooper bomb displayed by personnel of 207 Squadron, 29 August 1918.*

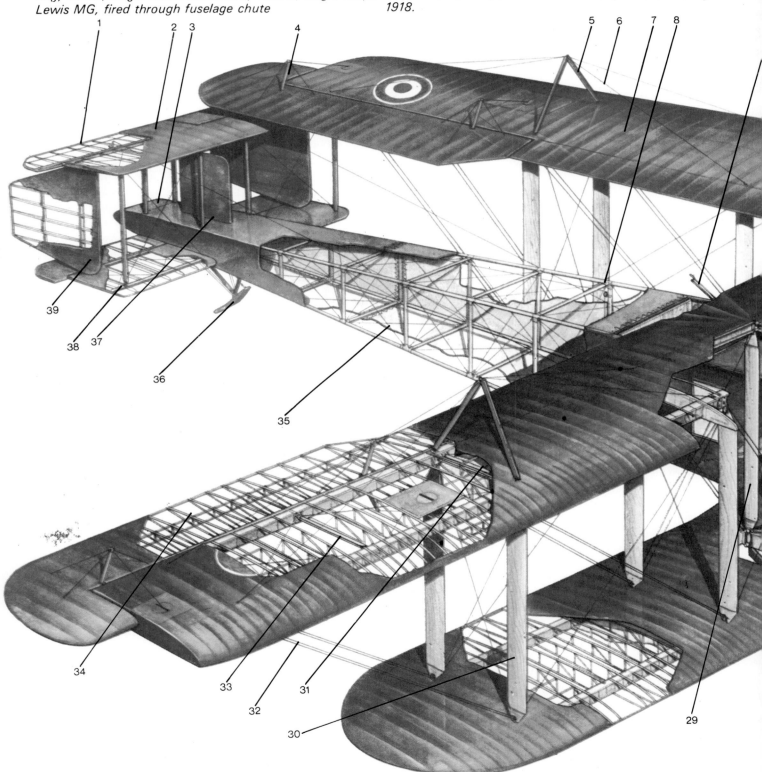

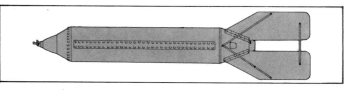

C. Bowyer

C. Bowyer

1 Elevator
2 Upper tail-plane
3 Plywood tail cover
4 Aileron control horn
5 Steel cabane
6 Cabane braces
7 Port wings, shown in folded position
8 Fuselage frame
9 Dorsal .303in Lewis MG
10 Air-driven fuel pumps
11 Leading-edge gravity-feed fuel tanks
12 Forward entry hatch
13 360hp Rolls Royce Eagle VIII engines (2)
14 Radiator
15 Observer's seat
16 Pilot's seat
17 Twin .303in Lewis MGs
18 Access to gunner's position
19 Pitot tube
20 Pilot's foot controls
21 Slat flooring
22 Batteries
23 Fire extinguisher
24 Bomb bay below fuel tanks
25 Transparent panel
26 Faired rubber cord shock strut
27 Twin main-wheels
28 Fuel tanks (2) each holding 130 Imp. gall
29 Hinge strut
30 Plywood-covered spruce interplane struts

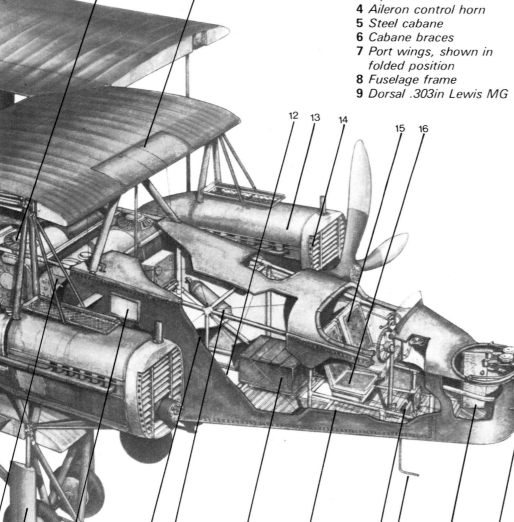

31 Plywood covering
32 Double flying braces
33 Drag strut
34 Aileron
35 Multi-strand cable bracing
36 Tailskid
37 Vertical stabiliser
38 Lower tailplane
39 Rudder

171

civilian population, probably because he recognized that America could, with its huge industrial potential and lack of vulnerable land frontiers, maintain a bombing campaign for long periods, and did not, like Italy or other European powers, need civilian panic to end a war quickly. Despite his court-martial and failure to achieve an independent air force – the Americans continued to operate separate Naval, Marine and Army Air Forces until 1946 – some of Mitchell's ideas gradually took hold in America in the 1930s. The results will be examined later.

Meanwhile, what was happening in Britain, the source of so much evidence about strategic bombing and its effects? First of all, it needs to be made clear that neither Douhet nor Mitchell had a noticeable effect upon the Royal Air Force strategists. Despite a fairly widespread belief that Douhet's theories in particular affected the development of air power in all countries except Russia and Japan, it is highly improbable that many people in Britain between the wars had even heard of Douhet, let alone studied *Command of the Air*. It is probably safer to say that British air power, building on the considerable experience of the First World War, tended to develop on its own, expecially in the 1920s. There were two main reasons for this. Firstly, there was no need, immediately after the First World War, to pursue theories like those of Douhet or Mitchell, which had as their central theme the necessity for the creation of independent air forces, for the Royal Air Force had achieved its independence in 1918; secondly, as it had been formed specifically to carry out long-range strategic bombing, all the air administrators in London had to do to ensure a future strategic role was to maintain the *status quo*.

But this was not as easy as it sounds. Once the First World War was over, many politicians and military leaders pressed for the abolition of the Royal Air Force as an unnecessary peace-time luxury and the British air chiefs had to fight very hard indeed to maintain their independence. The fact that they succeeded was due almost entirely to one man – Hugh, Lord Trenchard. Born in 1873, he saw active service in South Africa, India and Nigeria as an officer in the Royal Scots Fusiliers before deciding, at the relatively late age of 39, that he wanted to fly. His regimental experience made him a welcome addition to the Royal Flying Corps – formed in 1912 as a unit of the Royal Engineers – when he transferred to it in the summer of that year. Between then and 1919 he progressed from Major to full General, holding nearly every important air post, including that of Commander of the Independent Bombing Force of the Royal Air Force in 1918, before becoming Chief of the Air Staff. He held the latter post from 1919 until December 1929 and was therefore in the forefront of the battle to maintain its independence. He succeeded in winning that battle by stressing three main points, and although it seems pertinent to describe him as an organizer and administrator rather than a theorist of air power, it is surprising how similar his final conclusions were to those of both Douhet and Mitchell.

Firstly, Trenchard was an ardent believer in air offensive, arguing that regardless of the numerical strength of the enemy, it was impossible to defend every cubic foot of air space above one's country. Just as it is extremely difficult to put up an effective barrier to a swarm of bees, some of which will simply fly round, above or below that barrier, so it was almost

Britain's answer to the Gotha was the Handley Page HP o/400. Though this aircraft could have been employed as a strategic bomber she arrived late in the war and was used principally against tactical targets behind the front lines.

impossible to prevent the passage of aircraft through all air space, at least in the context of the 1920s. For this reason, according to Trenchard, air defence was a waste of time and a negation of air power, since to devote aircraft and men to such operations would not prevent the enemy getting through in some form or other: you might inflict casualties but you would never stop him completely. Therefore, if the Royal Air Force was to be used, it had to be constantly on the offensive and, as his second point, because all Britain's potential enemies were situated a long way off, this had to be carried out by the long-range bomber. There was little room for co-operation in the tactical sphere with the Army or Navy, as this would merely dissipate valuable resources, and this in turn, as the final point, necessitated the continued independence of the Royal Air Force. It is interesting to note that Trenchard never said that his bombers would end the war without the need for military or naval campaigns, but he did feel that the strategic air offensive would be so vital to the overall war effort that no one could doubt its necessity.

As has been already intimated, Trenchard managed to persuade enough influential people round to his way of thinking to ensure that the Royal Air Force did not disappear, and when he resigned as Chief of the Air Staff in 1929 to make way for a younger man, it looked

as if the strategic bomber had been accepted in Britain as a potentially useful weapon for the future. Unfortunately, further efforts to undermine the autonomy of the R.A.F. were made in the 1930s – and it is in the light of the battles between military and naval administrators on the one hand and the air chiefs on the other, basically over who was to get what share of an increasingly stringent peace-time defence budget, that led Trenchard's successors to take his ideas one stage further, into the realms of the extreme. From his argument that air defence was not a great deal of use came the expression, first used by Prime Minister Stanley Baldwin in the House of Commons in 1932, that "the bomber will always get through" – something which Trenchard had never categorically stated. Similarly, in an effort to show that strategic bombing was not only viable but also essential, an argument which was designed to obtain an expansion of the Royal Air Force, the air chiefs began to expand their claims. Basing their opinions more and more upon the Smuts Committee and the effects of unopposed bombing by the Royal Air Force in places like Iraq and North-West India, it was argued that strategic bombers, operating by day, would be able to attack enemy cities with impunity, hitting selected targets of vital economic importance and rapidly undermining the morale of the civilian population. In the end, as it may be appreciated, the British ideas began to look very like those of Douhet and Mitchell, even though they were arrived at by different routes and for slightly different reasons.

At the beginning of the Second World War the various ideas, theories and specifically the aims of strategic bombing could be summarized as follows: the undermining of civilian morale, which would, it was hoped, force the enemy government to sue for peace; and the destruction of key targets which would destroy the capability of the enemy to wage technological war. The method of achieving one or both of these aims was to bomb by daylight and with accuracy, a method based firmly on the belief that the bomber would always get through.

What needs to be remembered before the validity of these ideas is examined in detail, is that in 1939 the theory of strategic bombing was just that, only a theory. It was based upon incomplete evidence from the First World War which had been taken to extremes by people intent upon achieving or maintaining air force independence, and had never been put into practice, so the problems and shortcomings were simply not known.

Strategic Bombing

The instrument of night strategic bombing — an RAF Lancaster taxis prior to take-off for a raid on Germany.

The three strategic bombing campaigns to be examined in this chapter are those against Germany and Japan during the Second World War and that against North Vietnam between 1965 and 1973. These are not the only campaigns which have taken place since 1939 – the German attacks on Britain in 1940 and 1941 are not included, for example, because they fit so conveniently into the Battle of Britain as a whole, which will be examined in a later chapter – but for the purposes of testing the validity of strategic theory they are by far the most important. In the course of this examination, the Allied attacks upon Germany between 1939 and 1945 will be emphasized, partly because they involved the air forces most affected by the pre-war theories and partly because they have been the subject of more research and comment than any other strategic attacks. This does not mean that less can be achieved by looking at Japan or North Vietnam as individual campaigns but it seems logical to use them to illustrate how poorly the lessons of the offensive against Germany were assimilated by those in high command. What those lessons were constitutes the central theme of this chapter.

When war broke out in September 1939 the bomber arm of the Royal Air Force was not prepared. It had a theory of strategic bombing worked out, based upon the two-fold assumption that the bomber would always get through and be able to destroy vital parts of the enemy's war-machine, but it had neither adequate equipment with which to carry this out nor experience upon which to base its course of action. In addition, the Chamberlain Government did not wish to initiate strategic bombing, not only because it might cause a reaction from the enemy that would be more devastating and decisive, but also because neutral countries whose aid might be essential in the future – notably America – would regard it as an unnecessary escalation of the conflict. After all, the Washington Conference on the Limitation of Armaments, held in 1922, had expressly condemned "aerial bombardment", and the American President in 1939, F. D. Roosevelt, was known to be opposed to unrestricted air warfare, even in a conflict which did not yet involve his country. Even before it had started, therefore, the theory of strategic bombing had come up against the problem of world opinion, which negated one of Douhet's basic ideas – that future wars would begin, and probably end, with waves of bombers devastating centres of civilian population. This problem was to appear again later.

Nevertheless, during the early "Phoney War" period of the Second World War, Royal Air Force Bomber Command did carry out two forms of limited attack upon the enemy homeland. Neither of these can be strictly termed as strategic in aim, but their existence was to have radical results upon future air policy. On the one hand bombers carried out daylight raids against enemy shipping, chiefly in the North Sea and the Baltic, and on the other they dropped leaflets over Germany itself by night. The anti-shipping raids, carried out by Vickers Wellingtons of No. 3 Group, failed to make much headway against German fighters and anti-aircraft defences and twice, in September and December 1939, the dispatched force lost 50 per cent of its aircraft; a loss-rate which if it had continued would have wiped out Bomber Command in less than a week. The British Air Staff began to realize that the heavy bomber could not survive in daylight, and this feeling was reinforced by the apparent success of the leaflet raids, for the Armstrong Whitworth Whitleys of No. 4 Group, operating at night, suffered few casualties. An idea arose – understandably enough – that a switch from day to night bombing might well be prudent. The basic aims of strategic bombing – the undermining of civilian morale and the precise destruction of key targets – were not to be abandoned, but the method of achieving them was to be revised. By May 1940 night bombing raids were becoming more frequent, and by the autumn of that year daylight attacks had virtually ceased.

Night bombing, however, created its own problems. During these early months of the offensive the standards of navigation and bomb-aiming were poor, and on most night-time raids it was lucky if the aircraft – designed for daylight operations and crewed by men who had been trained accordingly – actually reached the target, let alone hit exactly what they were aiming at. This was discussed as early as March 19 1940, before the switch to night bombing had even been ordered, when a group of fifty bombers attacked the German seaplane base at Hornum on the island of Sylt.

Most of the crews believed that they had located the target and placed their bombs accurately, but reconnaissance photographs the next day showed no sign of damage whatsoever. In fact at the end of the war it was discovered from captured German records that the enemy was completely unaware that any raid had taken place at all! This lack of effectiveness continued until August 1941 when Churchill's Scientific Adviser,

Lord Cherwell, was directed to organize an official investigation into the accuracy of the bomber offensive. His chosen investigator, a civil servant by the name of Butt, looked at some 600 aerial photographs taken by bombers after they had released their bombs on raids in June and July 1941.

Taking into account the necessarily selective nature of his statistics – after all, not every bomber had returned – Butt's overall conclusion was that of the bomber crews who thought they had located and hit a specific target, only about one third had managed to drop their loads within five miles of it. Thus the target area, far from being a circle of 300, 600 or even 1000 yards around an aiming point, as some optimists imagined and precision bombing required, was in fact a territory up to five miles in radius. Two bombs landing within this target area might be up to ten miles apart. Moreover, it was apparent that only a small proportion of the more successful raids were achieving even this degree of success.

The Butt Report showed the inevitable result of the switch from day to night bombing, and suggested that before the prospect of precision bombing by night could become a reality the efficiency and equipment of Bomber Command had to be much improved or an alternative mode of operations found. The obvious alternative was a return to day bombing, but since the "Circus" operations of summer 1941, this was

regarded as still potentially dangerous. (When Germany invaded Russia in June 1941 the Russians insisted upon a bomber offensive in the West to draw German air power away from the Eastern Front, and the Royal Air Force obliged by mounting a series of daylight sorties, using both bombers and fighters over occupied France. At first with the protecting escort-fighters much in evidence, the Germans had refused to rise to the bait, but when the bombers came alone, the enemy fighters had a field day, which suggested that any return to daylight bombing as a central policy was sure to end in disaster.) In such circumstances, night-time raids had to stay but in the light of the problems of navigation and accuracy the method of carrying them out had to be revised.

The Chief of the Air Staff, Air Marshal Sir Charles Portal, produced such a revision in early 1942 when he suggested the substitution of area for precision bombing, so that in the case of a city or large town, the entire urban complex not merely the industrial targets within it, would be attacked. This had two distinct advantages, for on the one hand it would normalize the results already being achieved – if, as Butt said, the target area was being missed by five miles, then make the target area five miles square – and on the other it might achieve the aim of disrupting war-production not by hitting the factories but by de-housing, terrorizing and killing the working population. The new Bombing

Directive consequently appeared on February 14 1942 laying down specifically that the raids on places like Duisberg, Essen, Dusseldorf, Cologne and Berlin were now to be focussed upon the morale of the civil population and, in particular, its industrial workers. Precision attacks upon key targets were no longer to be the norm – although this did not preclude them entirely if the circumstances were right – and a note attached to the Directive by the Chief of the Air Staff emphasized the true nature of the new offensive, pointing out that in the urban attacks of the future "the aiming points are to be the built-up areas, *not*, for instance, the dockyards or aircraft factories." In other words, in a relatively short time, the original theory of strategic bombing as it had emerged by 1939, had been altered out of all recognition. Far from being an offensive of precision bombing by day, practical problems, unforeseen by the theorists, had turned it into one of area bombing by night.

Area bombing presented yet another disadvantage, however, for if it was intended to hit huge urban complexes night after night, as it had to be if industrial workers were to be demoralized to the extent that important factories no longer operated, a very large bomber fleet was needed – something which did not exist in early 1942. Furthermore, even if the aircraft were available, little was likely to be achieved unless it could be guaranteed that the majority would find the target in the dark and, once over it, drop their bombs in concentrations which would swamp the civil defence services and destroy large areas of urban housing and industrial facilities. In the light of these considerations, Bomber Command was in no position to carry out the Area Bombing Directive effectively in early 1942, and it is small wonder that it was around this time that pressure for an end to strategic bombing reached its height in Britain with influential politicians and military men pressing for a full-scale transfer of heavy bombers and their crews to tactical support or naval co-operation. If Bomber Command was to survive and strategic bombing to be tested to the full, a great deal of development had to take place quickly and a number of improvements made both to efficiency and equipment.

The first sign of improvement came on February 22 1942, only eight days after the Area Bombing Directive had been issued, when Air Marshal Sir Arthur Harris was appointed Commander-in-Chief of Bomber Command. He was wholeheartedly in favour of area bombing, later in the war he maintained what were known as "Blue Books" showing, by means of perspex overlays on aerial photographs, the amount of damage done to German cities. He fully realized the need for a large bombing fleet, something which was unlikely to materialize in the prevailing climate of influential opposition. His first task, therefore, was to mobilize public opinion in his favour and gain official recognition for the bombing offensive, basically by making it appear more effective than it was. The method he and his Deputy, Air Marshal Sir Robert Saundby, chose was to attempt the seemingly impossible by organizing a raid to be carried out by 1000 aircraft. Nothing like this had ever been tried – indeed, in order to gather together 1000 planes capable of carrying bombs to Germany, Harris had to commit his entire front line force, its reserve and even elements of its training cadres – and the risks were frightening. Even at the accepted level of casualties (then about 5 per cent of any committed force), Bomber Command could expect to lose over fifty aircraft, and this took no account of midair collisions, aircraft being hit by falling bombs, or the dubious flying ability of some of the participating crews, particularly those who had not even finished their training. But the gamble paid off. When the British public was informed that on the night of May 30-31 1942 1046 bombers had attacked the city of Cologne, their approbation successfully vaporized official opposition. In the event, little irreparable damage was done to Cologne, but the relatively small losses sustained by the attacking force – forty-four aircraft, or 3.9 per cent – and the apparent strength of Bomber Command put the strategic offensive firmly back on the map. Any talk of transferring bombers to Coastal Command or tactical support in other theatres would now produce an immediate public outcry.

Having obtained this vital breathing-space, Harris set about improving the equipment and techniques of his command, bearing in mind throughout that he was involved in a night-time area campaign. On the equipment side he was fortunate improvements to air-

Left: Window tumbles through the sky. This was an early form of E.C.M. By dropping foil strips in the sky Allied aircraft could reproduce reflections on German radar that looked like incoming bombers. Below: A USAAF B-17 plunges down, disintegrating as it burns. American losses in daylight raids were heavy until they coordinated their fighter protection and flight patterns.

craft design had been taking place before he was appointed, for by early 1942 the twin-engined, short-range Wellingtons and Whitleys had been replaced by long-range bombers like the Short Stirling and Handley-Page Halifax. This development trend culminated in the introduction of the Avro Lancaster, the first few of which were ready for use in the Thousand Raid on Cologne. Developed from an abortive twin-engined machine known as the Manchester, the Lancaster was undoubtedly the best British bomber of the war. By 1942 the Stirling and to a lesser extent the

Halifax, had shown performance shortcomings, but the Lancaster seemed to offer a great deal of potential. Its four Rolls Royce engines were powerful, capable of carrying it to high altitude if necessary and fully able to lift large bomb loads. It was relatively fast, reasonably well armed for night flying and, most important of all, popular with the air crews.

But the development of such a good aircraft, although giving Bomber Command the means to do the job as early as 1942, was not a great deal of use as long as the problems of navigation and bomb-aiming remained.

Principal Bombing Targets

- ⓐ Aircraft
- ⓑ Ball-bearings
- ⓓ Dams
- ⓤ U-boats
- ⓥ V-bombs
- General industrial and urban targets
- Limits of allied fighter cover

0 — 150m
0 — 200km

North Sea

GREAT BRITAIN

DENMARK

Thunderbolt with belly tank
Aug. 1943

Thunderbolt
June 1943

Spitfire
May 1943

ⓤ Kiel

Lübeck

Wilhelmshaven ⓤ   ⓞ Bremerhaven   ⓞ Hamburg

ⓤ Bremen

NETHERLANDS

Amsterdam ⓐ

Hanover

The Hague ⓞ
Rotterdam ⓞ   *Rhine*

ⓞ London

Dortmund
Essen   *The Rhur* ⓓ   **G E R**   **R**

Düsseldorf ⓞ

Antwerp ⓞ   Cologne ⓞ   ⓓ

ⓥ   Brussels ⓐ

ⓥ   Lille ⓞ   **BELGIUM**

Coblenz ⓞ

ⓥ   *English Channel*

Frankfurt   Schwei...

ⓑ

Le Havre   **LUX.**
Rouen ⓞ

Mannheim   Nuremb...

Seine

Paris ⓞ

Strasbourg ⓞ   Stuttgart ⓞ

F R A N C E

ⓐ   *Loire*

Rhine

Basle ⓞ   ⓞ Zurich

SWITZERLAND   A

180

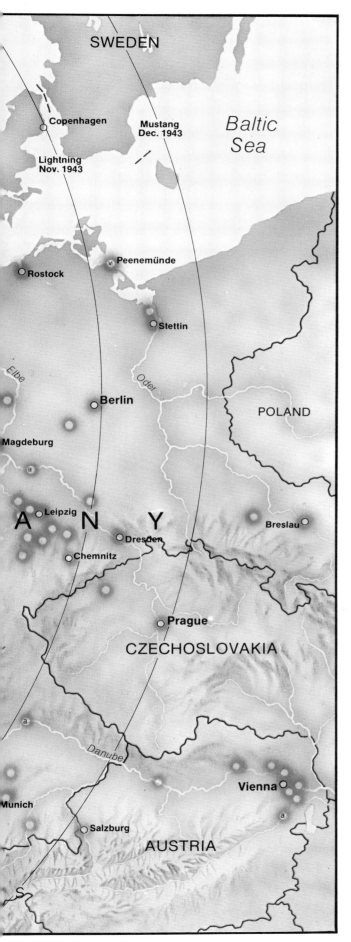

Fortunately, research had been carried out by air scientists and, even before the Area Bombing Directive had appeared, the first steps had been taken to improve these crucial aspects of the campaign. So far as navigation was concerned, a range of radar inventions helped the bombers to find the targets in the dark. The first of these, known as *Gee*, was available from early 1942, enabling a bomber's navigator to fix his position by consulting an instrument which received special signals from three widely separated stations in England. The instrument worked out the difference between receipt of these signals and gave an instant "fix", but did suffer from defects of range, being unable to operate more than 400 miles from the English coast because of the curvature of the Earth. In December 1942 a new device – *Oboe* – appeared, which enabled aircarft to follow radar beams to pre-selected targets, but once again effective range was restricted. It was not until January 1943, when a third invention – *H2S* – was introduced, that the navigator could be provided with a radar map of the ground over which he was flying and although this too had deficiencies, being most effective only when a contrast between land and water could be made, it did ensure a chance of arriving on target.

At about the same time it became common policy for the bombers to attack in a stream rather than individually or by squadrons. This was introduced initially to defeat the German defensive system known as the Kammhuber Line – a series of radar posts, anti-aircraft sites and night fighter stations stretching from Denmark to Northern France – which, by dividing the defended area into a series of "boxes" and stationing night-fighters in each, had managed to destroy many individual bombers. In 1942 the British realized that one way to defeat this system was to concentrate the bombers and swamp selected boxes, at the same time confusing German radar by dropping massive amounts of *Window* – small metal strips, cut to the correct wave length, which showed up on the radar screens as bomber formations and caused the enemy to commit his defending fighters away from the main attack. The scheme was an instant success. It even produced an unforeseen navigational bonus, for so long as the leaders of a stream found the target, all the other bombers had to do was follow the aircraft in front. As the leaders then tended to be chosen from among the more experienced crews (they being the most likely to locate the target correctly), it did not take long for their duties to be extended to include marking the target area, so that the

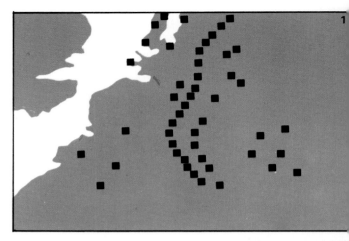

following waves had something definite to aim at and concentration of destructive power could be achieved. The effectiveness of this "Pathfinder" technique was shown as early as March 28 1942 when a selected group of bombers, operating the new *Gee* radar, was directed to mark the Baltic city of Lubeck with red flares and incendiaries. The results were impressive, with reconnaissance photographs later showing nearly half the city in ruins. Thereafter the idea was used on a regular basis. Indeed, by 1944, the stream leaders were not only marking the aiming-point but remaining over the target area to guide the other bombers in, which was usually the responsibility of a Master Bomber. When techniques like this had been fully developed, Bomber Command was potentially at its most effective.

Meanwhile, America had come into the war, and its vast human and industrial might promised a reinforcement to Bomber Command which should have made the campaign decisive. But this did not happen immediately, for two main reasons. Firstly, the Americans refused to act as a mere reinforcement, wishing instead to make their own individual contribution to the air offensive. Secondly, they too had ideas about strategic bombing inherited from Mitchell and, secure in their development of the "self defending" bomber in the B-17 Flying Fortress and B-24 Liberator, refused to be dissuaded from delivering their attack upon Germany by daylight. Experiments had been carried out in California before the war which apparently proved that high-flying aircraft could hit extremely small targets with an impressive degree of success, and the Americans saw no reason to doubt that such results could also be achieved over Europe. Unfortunately, certain important problems had been overlooked, as the U.S. 8th Army Air Force found to its cost in 1942 and 1943.

The first of these was the weather. For high altitude precision attacks clear skies and good visibility were essential and, although such conditions may have been usual in California, they were conspicuously absent from the skies of North-West Europe for much of the year. The result was long periods during which no operations were possible or raids were aborted because of cloud cover over the target area, and this led to a dangerous undermining of crew morale, to say nothing of a lack of damage inflicted upon the enemy.

Secondly, and perhaps more importantly, the California experiments had taken no account of enemy opposition. If the skies were clear and visibility good for the Americans, it was an ideal situation for the Germans too, for interceptors could attack the bombers with ease while the anti-aircraft guns needed only visual sightings. Needless to say, the initial American casualties were heavy, culminating in two raids on ball-bearings factories at Schweinfurt in 1943. In the first of these, on August 17, thirty-six bombers out of a force of 229 were lost, and when this was repeated on 14 October, with sixty out of 291 aircraft destroyed, the Americans were obliged to revise their ideas. As the majority of losses had been caused by the activity of interceptor fighters, despite the introduction of

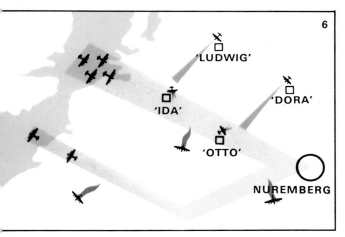

The pattern of radar interception. The chain of stations covered occupied Europe and Germany. They would first locate a bomber and vector in a circling night fighter. Once the fighter was within its own radar range it would attack. A typical raid on Nuremberg could catch the bomber stream on its approach to the target and as they returned home.

destroy the enemy aircraft one by one in the skies above Europe by mounting raids against almost anything that the Germans would be forced to defend. But the bombers could not do this alone, as the recent loss rates showed, and special long range escort fighters had to be developed. The use of escorts had never been expressly precluded from the American offensive, but in the early months the only available machines P-38 Lightnings, P-47 Thunderbolts, P-51 Allison-engined Mustangs and R.A.F. loaned Spitfires, lacked the range to escort bombers much beyond the borders of occupied France. It was not until late 1943 when Rolls-Royce engines were fitted into the Mustangs, that fighter aircraft appeared which could escort the bombers almost anywhere in Europe, engage the enemy and shoot him out of the sky. Then, and only then, did the Americans begin to gain the air superiority they so desperately needed.

With this American breakthrough on the one hand and the new British techniques of night bombing on the other, early 1944 should have seen the beginning of a true and decisive Combined Bomber Offensive, the orders for which had existed on paper since the Casablanca Conference and *Pointblank* Directive of January 1943. The Allied invasion of Europe took precedence, however, and between April and September 1944 the bulk of both bomber fleets was switched to tactical attacks upon the French Coast. Thus, when the strategic offensive began again in earnest in autumn 1944, the war was drawing to a close, and although the British and American bombers, flying by night and day respectively, were able to range far and wide over a rapidly-diminishing Germany for about eight months, it is arguable whether their offensive succeeded in the war-winning sense in which it had been undertaken.

The practical problems of mounting the type of air offensive envisaged in 1939 were immense for a start. On the British side it soon became apparent that Trenchard's belief in the impossibility of air defence was just not viable, and with loss rates of 50 per cent per operation experienced almost straight away, that the Royal Air Force's theory of daylight bombing needed revision. The subsequent switch from day to night bombing showed the problems of finding and destroying targets; the later switch from precision to area bombing necessitated the construction of an entirely new weapon. This took time and money – by the summer of 1943 some 40 per cent of British industrial effort was being devoted purely to the bomber offensive – and by the

"combat boxes" whereby the bombers grouped together for mutual protection, the only answer seemed to lie in the total destruction of the Luftwaffe. Until it had been lured out and destroyed, the daylight offensive could not even begin for, regardless of Mitchell's belief and the California experiments, the self-defending bomber needed complete air superiority to be effective.

The obvious method of achieving this superiority was to destroy the Luftwaffe and its support services on the ground by attacking airfields, oil installations and aircraft factories, but the casualty figures in the process were sure to be high. The Americans chose instead to time that Bomber Command was ready to wage an effective air offensive, the tactical demands of D-Day had taken precedence. The same thing happened with the Americans, for the practical problems of gaining complete air supremacy delayed the development of their offensive to its full potential. The overall result of these problems and delays was that in a war lasting nearly six years, full scale strategic bombing could only be carried out for about eight months. So strategic bombing, far from being the straightforward operation that the inter-war theorists imagined, was in fact a highly complicated affair, necessitating the devotion of huge amounts of money and scientific knowledge even to begin. When it is remembered that by May 1945 nearly 100,000 Allied airmen had lost their lives one begins to ask whether it was all worth the effort.

These doubts are reinforced when, as a second factor, the physical results of the offensive upon Germany are examined. Going back to the original theory, the offensive had two aims – the undermining of civilian morale and the destruction of German war industry – and, although the methods employed by the Allies were altered, these remained the aims throughout. Were they achieved?

So far as civilian morale was concerned, the answer must be no. Isolated examples of panic may be found – for example, the Hamburg fire-storm of July 1943 caused 900,000 people to flee the area and spread alarm but, overall, bombing had the same effect upon Germany as it had upon Britain in 1940/41: that is it caused a determination to carry on and work together in the face of common adversity. In Germany, of course, the process was aided by a repressive Nazi regime, imposing an iron rule which, if broken, resulted in punishment worse than aerial bombardment.

It is far more difficult to draw any conclusion concerning the effects of bombing upon German war industry. There is no doubt that the Allies grossly underestimated German industrial potential throughout the war. Thus, although attacks might destroy an industrial plant, it tended to be out of action for a comparatively short time as the machinery and workers could either be quickly replaced or moved elsewhere. In addition, German industry was mobilized only gradually, in step with military efforts, and it is a fact that by 1944 German war production was running at a higher level than in 1940, before the bomber offensive began; a fact which may be appreciated from the following table:

German War-Material Output 1940-1944

	1940	1941	1942	1943	1944
Aircraft	10,200	11,000	14,200	25,000	39,600
Tanks	1,600	3,800	6,300	12,100	19,000
Artillery	6,300	7,800	13,600	38,000	62,300
Ammunition (Million rounds)	2,950	1,340	1,340	3,170	5,370
U-Boats	76	218	238	279	229
Oil (1,000 met. tons)	4,652	5,542	6,368	7,508	5,412

On this evidence it would appear that the bombing failed to contribute a great deal to the winning of the war.

This is perhaps an extreme view, for a number of other factors do need to be considered. Firstly, there is of course no saying what tremendous heights of war-production would have been achieved by Germany if bombing had not taken place. Secondly, as a result of the bombing, by 1943 German industrial output had been forced on to the defensive, to manufacture defensive weapons and aircraft instead of tanks and artillery. Similarly, by early 1944, 1,000,000 trained soldiers and airmen were tied down in Germany itself manning anti-aircraft defences, and many Luftwaffe squadrons were committed to air defence instead of tactical attacks upon enemy armies. Their effect alone upon either the Western or Eastern Fronts could have been decisive.

These points undoubtedly balance the picture, but the question must still remain: Was it all worthwhile? Obviously, if the war had been won by the bombing offensive alone, one would have no hesitation in applauding the perspicacity of men like Douhet, Mitchell and Trenchard, but it must be remembered and emphasized that it was the physical defeat of German armies and occupation of German territory by Allied land forces which brought the war to an end. Strategic bombing undoubtedly weakened German strength and contributed to the final victory, but taking all the evidence together, the theory of strategic bombing as a war-winner, put forward in 1939, did not fulfil its promise. Not only did the methods by which it was to be executed need radical alteration in the face of practical problems, but the aims themselves were grossly overestimated. On the evidence of the offensive against Germany, air power did not have a strategic viability in the war winning sense.

But this view is based upon the results of one cam-

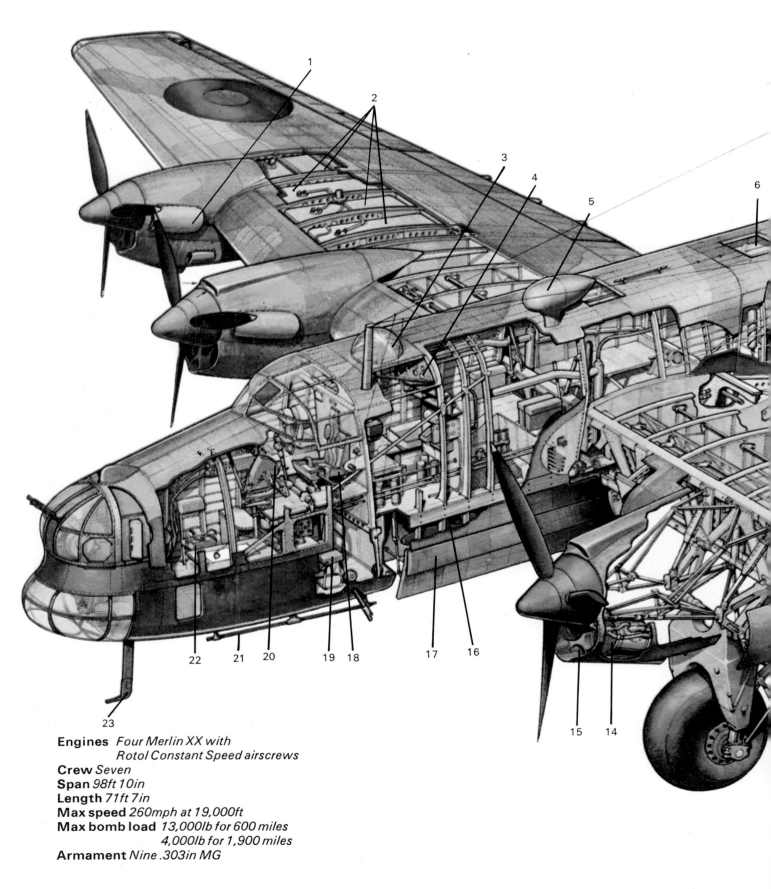

Engines *Four Merlin XX with*
Rotol Constant Speed airscrews
Crew *Seven*
Span *98ft 10in*
Length *71ft 7in*
Max speed *260mph at 19,000ft*
Max bomb load *13,000lb for 600 miles*
4,000lb for 1,900 miles
Armament *Nine .303in MG*

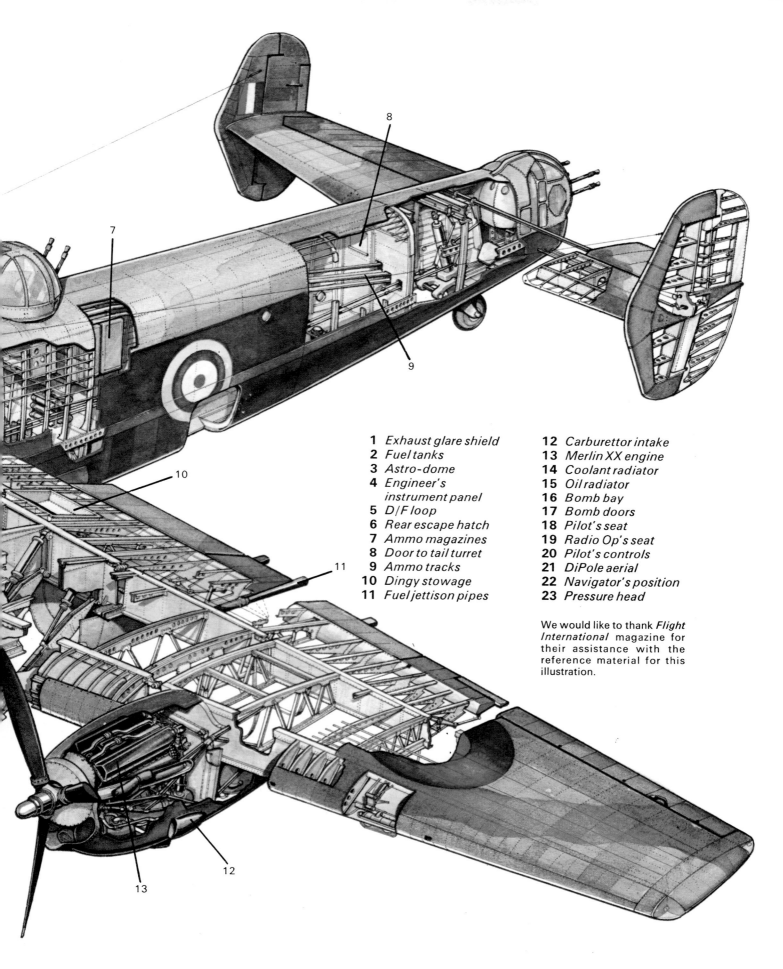

1 Exhaust glare shield	**12** Carburettor intake
2 Fuel tanks	**13** Merlin XX engine
3 Astro-dome	**14** Coolant radiator
4 Engineer's instrument panel	**15** Oil radiator
5 D/F loop	**16** Bomb bay
6 Rear escape hatch	**17** Bomb doors
7 Ammo magazines	**18** Pilot's seat
8 Door to tail turret	**19** Radio Op's seat
9 Ammo tracks	**20** Pilot's controls
10 Dingy stowage	**21** DiPole aerial
11 Fuel jettison pipes	**22** Navigator's position
	23 Pressure head

We would like to thank *Flight International* magazine for their assistance with the reference material for this illustration.

paign only, and in order to reach as balanced a conclusion as possible, it is necessary to examine, in general terms at least, the lessons of the offensives against Japan and North Vietnam.

Taking them in order, the Japanese declaration of war on America by attacking Pearl Harbour on 7 December 1941, found the American air forces, despite the influence of Mitchell's ideas, unprepared for an immediate strategic offensive. Plans for attacking the Japanese homeland existed on paper but, when it came to putting these into practice, a multiplicity of problems arose.

The most important of these was a complete lack of suitable bases from which to send the bombers for, with Japanese advances through the Pacific in early 1942, all the islands capable of maintaining airstrips within range of Japan had been lost. The only alternative was mainland China, where Chiang Kai-shek's armies had been fighting the Japanese since 1937, but once again the practical difficulties were awesome. So long as Japanese forces remained in the area, any airfields in China were in constant danger of being over-run, while the long and tenuous supply line over the Himalayas from India made the maintenance of a bomber fleet virtually impossible. Admittedly, as early as April 18 1942 Colonel James Doolittle did lead a raid on Tokyo with B-25 Mitchell bombers flown from the aircraft-carrier, *Hornet*, but this was never regarded as a long-term answer to the problem and may be seen purely as an exercise in American morale-boosting. An immense amount of organization was clearly needed before a true strategic offensive could be launched.

In the event, despite the disadvantages, the Americans chose to base their bombers initially in China, and it was from there that the specially designed B-29 Superfortress long-range aircraft began the assault upon Japan. But the first raids did not take place until June 1944, two and a half years after the outbreak of war, and even then were not particularly effective. Carrying out daylight precision attacks according to the Mitchell theory, the B-29s suffered heavy losses, chiefly because they had to cross so much Japanese-occupied territory before approaching their targets, and on a number of occasions the raids ceased altogether because of Japanese attacks upon forward air bases, a lack of supplies coming through from India, or most common of all, the atrocious weather conditions. It was not until the Americans had retaken the Marianas Islands in the Central Pacific that a relatively secure base became

available. And as that campaign did not end until August 1944, the islands could not be prepared to receive the B-29s until the following November.

As a result, however, the China-based operations were gradually phased out, and from December 1944 the offensive began in earnest from the Marianas. By that time tactics had changed dramatically, in much the same way as those of the Royal Air Force had changed during the early months of the offensive against Germany. By the end of 1944 it was more common for the B-29s to indulge in area bombing – with incendiaries and the newly-invented napalm being dropped on to Japanese houses rather than factories – and not unknown for the raids to take place at night. The use of these techniques culminated in the

A USAAF B-29 over its target. Though the bomb-load was not as great as the RAF Lancaster, the B-29 was pressurized which enabled the crew to take it out of range of anti-aircraft fire from the ground. Below: USAAF B-17s escorted by Mustangs form up over England prior to a daylight raid on Germany.

devastating fire-raid on Tokyo during the night of March 9/10 1945 in which, it is estimated, nearly a quarter of a million people died. So far as destructive capability was concerned, the tactics of the offensive could not be faulted but, once again, the strategy of ending the war through such raids did not work. The Japanese people did not panic and their industries, although badly affected, did not cease production. In other words, the lessons of this offensive would appear to be the same as those of the offensive against Germany: the mounting of a strategic bombing campaign is time-consuming, costly and fraught with problems; that the bomber does not always get through to hit precision targets by daylight, necessitating a switch to night-time area bombing to counteract losses

and a lack of results, and that, even then, civilian panic and the destruction of the enemy's war-industry does not necessarily follow.

But this was not the end of the story so far as the offensive against Japan was concerned, for on 6 and 9 August 1945 the Americans dropped atomic bombs on Hiroshima and Nagasaki respectively. The results of these attacks were immediately applauded as complete vindications of the theories of Douhet and Mitchell, for by dropping the atomic bombs a Japanese surrender was achieved and an extremely costly seaborne invasion of Japan averted. Arguments for the continued existence of air forces on a strategic level received a much-needed boost and, in the American case, led to the formation of an independent Strategic Air Command, charged solely with the delivery of atomic weapons. Indeed, some theorists in America even went so far as to suggest that, with such weapons available, there was little need for large conventional ground and sea forces: an interesting reversion to one of the more controversial arguments of Douhet and Mitchell.

Unfortunately, for the Americans, the Russians developed their own atomic bombs in 1949 and, with the realization that a strategic offensive involving such weapons would result in retaliation and an unacceptable amount of damage to both sides, atomic warfare entered the realms of deterrence, with neither superpower prepared to attack the other except under the type of provocation which has yet to appear. Nevertheless, as a direct result of the attacks upon Hiroshima and Nagasaki, it became widely accepted that strategic bombing could be a war-winner, without any differentiation being made between conventional and atomic weaponry. Despite the glaring lessons of the Second World War, it was argued once again that the decisive element was the air and widely believed that a strategic bombing offensive, regardless of the weapons used, could decide a future war without a great deal of dependence upon military or naval campaigns. The results of this interesting exercise in ignoring the lessons of the past is illustrated in Vietnam, particularly in the American attacks upon North Vietnam between February 1965 and February 1973.

Dispassionate and accurate information about these engagements is hard to find since we are fairly close to the event, but it is apparent that when they began in 1965 there were three basic aims. Firstly, to impede North Vietnamese infiltration into the south by hitting supply lines, bridges and rear areas north of the Demilitarized Zone around the 17th Parallel: a campaign more of tactical interdiction than strategic consequence. Secondly, it was foreseen that any raids upon the enemy would help raise the flagging morale of the South Vietnamese and it was later also seen as a boost to the morale of the American ground forces, but this too could hardly be described as strategic. Thirdly, and more importantly, it was argued that through a strategy of precision attacks upon key industries – petroleum, lubricants, hydro-electric power plants, coal, iron and steel – the Hanoi Government would be forced to sue for peace or at least to stop supporting the Viet Cong in the South. Moreover, this strategy was to include an element of "punitive bargaining", whereby the Americans in their aptly

named *Rolling Thunder* operations, would begin by attacking rural-based industries to show the capability of their air-power. This, it was hoped, would cause the North Vietnamese to stop and reflect upon their position. If that did not work, the next series of attacks would approach nearer to the cities of Hanoi and Haiphong before another pause gave the enemy one more chance to see the error of his ways. At all times, the emphasis was to be firmly upon the precise destruction of key industries, but in effect the Americans were holding the cities of North Vietnam hostage, subject to Hanoi's decision about the continuation of the conflict.

This was perhaps a rather vain hope, as one imagines any World War II bombing veteran could have pointed out, and was not really argued through to its logical conclusion. The American policy-makers in Washington do not appear to have contemplated what would happen once the strategic bombers and their escorts had reached Hanoi and Haiphong, and in the event the results were predictable. By 1973 the Americans had dropped ten times the weight of bombs on North Vietnam than had been dropped throughout the Second World War on Germany and Japan together, and were actually attacking targets within the urban centres, all to little avail. America came under intense pressure both from other World powers and from domestic opinion to stop the offensive entirely; fighter bombers were shot down by surface-to-air missiles and ground fire, and the crews who survived became useful hostages to the enemy in the eventual peace negotiations; the North Vietnamese did not panic and, as they possessed no real war industries, being supplied in large measure from other Communist states, felt few effects in front-line units. Moreover, on occasions the accuracy of the offensive left much to be desired (as the inhabitants of the Algerian Embassy in Hanoi – situated over a mile away from the nearest industrial target – found to their cost in 1970) and the North Vietnamese were bombed neither to the conference table nor "back into the Stone Age". Once again the lesson, which should by now have been apparent, had to be learned the hard way: strategic bombing, using conventional weapons, does not win wars.

This basically, stands as the main conclusion, although it does not mean that the theory of strategic bombing is entirely dead: far from it. Both America and the Soviet Union – who are about the only countries still able to afford strategic equipment on a large-scale

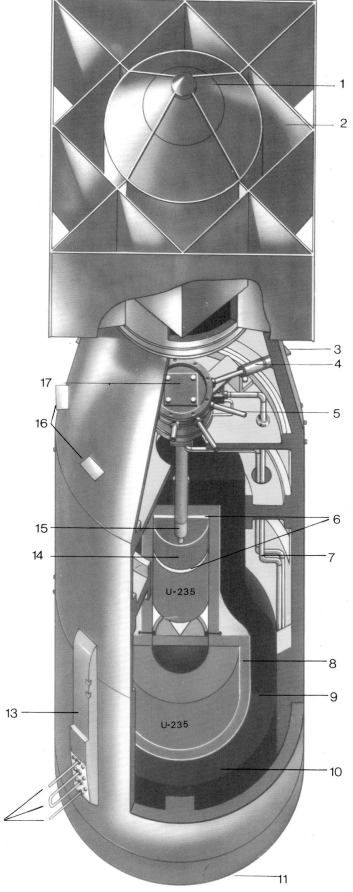

– are currently involved in the development and manufacture of weapons aimed specifically at undermining, through the element of the air, the enemy's moral and physical capability to wage effective war. Admittedly the majority of these weapons are nuclear and as such, because of their devastating power, may indeed be vindications of the theories of Douhet and Mitchell, but it is interesting to note that the use of conventional ordnance, delivered by the manned bomber, is not ignored. On the Soviet side, the Backfire bomber has been produced in fairly large numbers for both nuclear and conventional delivery, and although its makers state that it has the range for only tactical strikes within the European theatre, it could be equipped with refuelling facilities which would enable it to reach the eastern seaboard of America. Meanwhile the Americans, despite their recent cancellation of the B-1 bomber, are maintaining a substantial fleet of up-dated B-52s, primarily as delivery platforms for the revolutionary Air-Launched Cruise Missile (ALCM).

These ALCMs with their sophisticated contour-matching guidance systems, enabling them to "read" the ground over which they are flying, are able to approach their chosen targets at altitudes of less than 100 feet, below the radar and anti-aircraft defensive cover, and are accurate to within thirty feet over 2000 miles. They are undoubtedly the weapons of the future, and it can be argued that they alter the entire complexion of strategic bombing. They represent the latest outcome of a technological revolution which began during the Vietnam War, when the Americans developed "smart" bombs, guided by television cameras or laser beams on to specific targets: a development which seemed at last to solve the constant problem of bombing accuracy, so making the bombing of selected industrial targets more effective. Certainly, when such weapons were field-tested against oil-installations near Hanoi in 1972 the results were impressive, but they are expensive and may be susceptible to Electronic Counter-Measures (ECM). In addition, in any future war, particularly between the superpowers, they will probably be used against tactical targets only. If war reaches strategic level, nuclear warheads can do the job of destruction so much better, and if they are used, strategic bombing may well be so devastating that arguments about its effectiveness would be meaningless. In short, strategic bombing can only work if the devastation is so enormous that results are virtually instantaneous.

Reconnaissance and observation

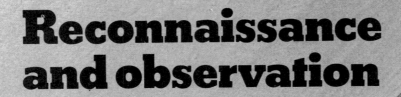

16 FISHBEDS

2 FAGOTS

An airfield in Cuba with Soviet-built fighters on dispersal points along the main strip.

Despite the rather negative conclusions reached so far, there can be little doubt that air power has revolutionized warfare during the present century, chiefly by adding a third dimension which offers entirely new concepts and capabilities to those involved in the management of organized conflict. The fact that the strategic potential of these capabilities was exaggerated in the past does not lessen the impact of air power, and it is the aim of this part of the book to analyze that impact in the tactical, or battlefield, areas of war.

The most obvious military use of aircraft when they first appeared was in the role of reconnaissance /observation. One of the basic principles of successful warfare is the element of surprise and to achieve it at times and places of your own choosing, it is necessary to know as much about the enemy as possible. Before the advent of aircraft, such reconnaissance and observation had to be carried out by spies or by elements of the army or navy acting well in advance of the main force. During the Peninsula War (1808-14) for example, the Duke of Wellington used both methods, sending out spies behind the French lines to sketch out enemy dispositions and to assess possible routes of march for the main army, and using his cavalry units to report on the situation "on the other side of the hill." In a naval context, and taking the same period of history, Lord Nelson substituted merchant sailors for spies and fast frigates or gun-boats for cavalry. But, in all cases, the results were poor. Information was restricted to the immediate area observed by a few men only; what they saw was subject to geography and terrain on a two-dimensional setting; and by the time their intelligence had been relayed to the commander, it was invariably out of date. The introduction of aircraft which could fly relatively quickly over long distances over the top of natural obstacles changed all this and the reconnaissance/observation potential was soon appreciated. It was given credibility on its way to becoming an integral part of military organization by a tradition of experimentation with balloons which had been going on since at least 1794 when, at the Battle of Fleurus, the French observed enemy positions and altered their scheme of attack accordingly. Indeed, by the time of the Wrights' experiments in 1903 most European armies (and some navies) had balloon sections, but use of the balloon was restricted by its dependence upon calm conditions and attachment, by static lines, to one point on the ground. Balloon observers were useless in a fluid battle situation.

It was Captain Piazza of the Italian air service who gave the first intimation of the new potential over Tripoli in 1911, although many refused at first to accept his claims of success. Some of the more reactionary generals, not only in Italy but elsewhere, even went so far as to doubt whether anything distinct could be seen by someone flying above the ground at fifty miles an hour. Nowhere was this more apparent than in the British Army, where the tradition-conscious cavalry regarded the aircraft as a rival for one of their most coveted roles. But as early as 1912 even they were forced to accept the new weapon, for in the army manoeuvres of that year elements of the fledgling Royal Flying Corps changed the course of the mock battle. Trenchard, the new recruit to the Corps, flew as an observer for the northern force under General Grierson, with orders to locate General Haig's advancing southern force. This he did, reporting back to Grierson within an hour of take-off and reinforcing the lesson by then acting as an aerial messenger to Grierson's cavalry force, recalling it from a false advance, to counter Haig's attack. Afterwards it was admitted officially that the success enjoyed by Grierson had been largely influenced by the "intervention of aircraft" and, as the air historian Sir Walter Raleigh later wrote, "the aeroplanes rose to such esteem that they were asked to verify information which had been brought in by the cavalry."

With evidence like this available, it was hardly surprising that, in 1914, reconnaissance and observation was an accepted role for aircraft. In fact, however, the First World War saw little dramatic development in this area. While the land campaigns, especially on the Western Front, remained fluid, the great potential was recognized, and there is evidence to suggest that during the Allied retreat from Mons in September 1914 French and British air observers contributed to a relative lack of confusion by keeping commanders informed about the situation on the ground. Once the trench deadlock set in after December 1914, however, air reconnaissance/observation was affected by two important factors. Firstly, since the armies were static, it was not so necessary to assess enemy dispositions over a wide area, and this enabled the balloon to re-appear in an observation role at the front line. Aircraft still contributed, chiefly in the areas of deep reconnaissance and artillery spotting, but as an enemy build-up could usually be both seen and heard by ground forces in the trenches, much of the preparatory

work laid down by people such as Piazza and Trenchard was invalidated under the prevailing circumstances.

This was emphasized still further by the second, related development, for it did not take long for both sides to realize that it was possible and, of course, desirable, to blind the enemy by depriving him of his observation aircraft and balloons. There quickly developed the concept of the interceptor, or fighter aircraft, armed with machine-guns, which could shoot enemy reconnaissance/observation machines out of the sky before they could report what they had seen. Rather than risk losing such a valuable source of information in this way, it became usual for reconnaissance aircraft and observation balloons to be protected from the fighters – and what better weapon than another fighter? By 1916 it had become normal for all reconnaissance/observation missions to be protected and for air-to-air combat between protecting and attacking fighters to take place. The famous "dog-fights" of the First World War were the result, and this constant battle for air supremacy – defined at the time as the ability to observe the enemy from the air without fear of attack or destruction – continued right up to 1918. It constituted one of the most important tactical lessons of World War I – if air reconnaissance/observation is to be successful, you must have the ability to use the skies as and when you deem necessary, not merely when the enemy permits. The difficulties encountered as enemy counter-measures became more effective tended to relegate this role to one of only secondary importance, the prime necessity being the achievement and maintenance of air superiority.

Such a decline in importance was reflected in the relative lack of emphasis placed upon reconnaissance/observation between the two World Wars. The previously mentioned air power theorists virtually dismissed the idea as irrelevant to the more essential needs of strategic bombing, and few air forces devoted much time or effort to the development of skills beyond the level which had prevailed before 1914. But as the Second World War approached, air technology began to provide at least the basics for improvements in the reconnaissance and observation areas. The first and most important of these lay in the evolution of aircraft, principally for racing and the achievement of endurance and air-speed records. No longer would air observers be expected to hover around at fifty or seventy-five miles an hour, as in World War I, they could now streak over the area to be reconnoitred at three or four hundred miles an hour, surprising ground defences and standing a fair chance of outstripping opposing interceptors. In addition, they were no longer restricted to the lower

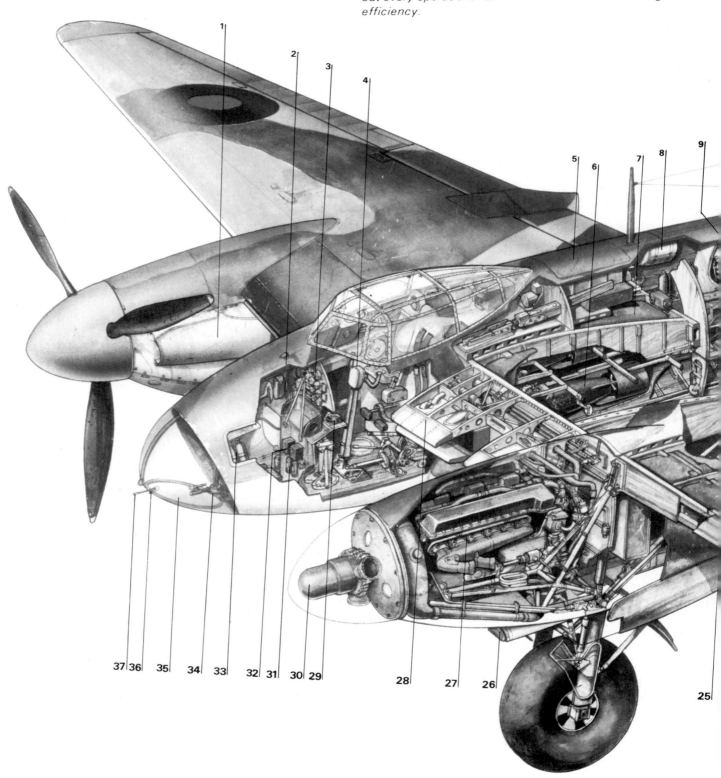

196

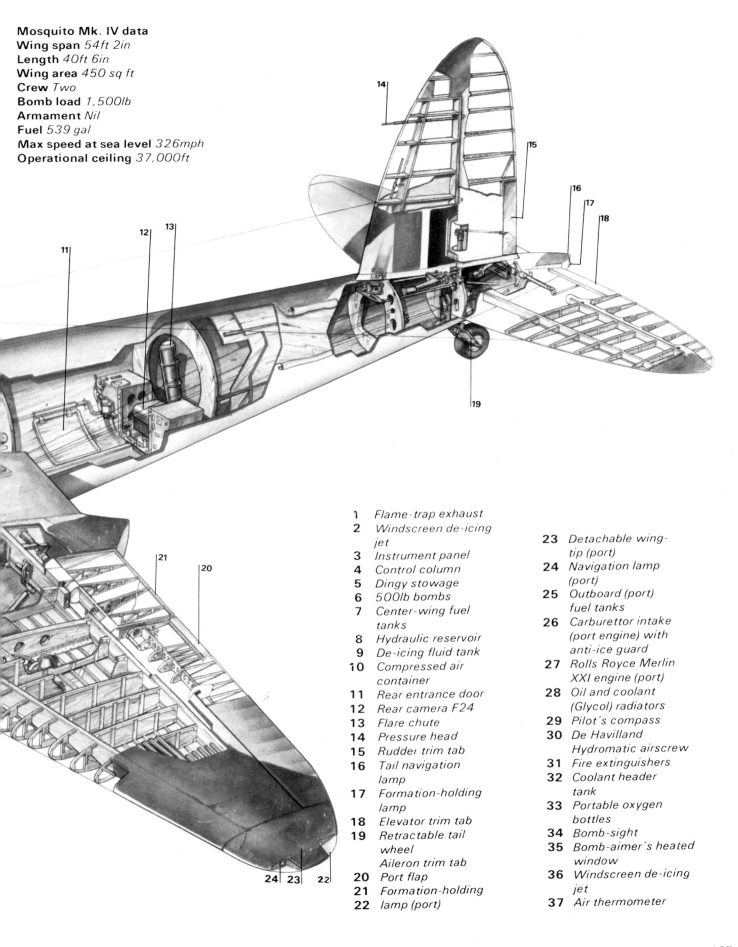

Mosquito Mk. IV data
Wing span *54ft 2in*
Length *40ft 6in*
Wing area *450 sq ft*
Crew *Two*
Bomb load *1,500lb*
Armament *Nil*
Fuel *539 gal*
Max speed at sea level *326mph*
Operational ceiling *37,000ft*

1 Flame-trap exhaust
2 Windscreen de-icing
   jet
3 Instrument panel
4 Control column
5 Dingy stowage
6 500lb bombs
7 Center-wing fuel
   tanks
8 Hydraulic reservoir
9 De-icing fluid tank
10 Compressed air
    container
11 Rear entrance door
12 Rear camera F24
13 Flare chute
14 Pressure head
15 Rudder trim tab
16 Tail navigation
    lamp
17 Formation-holding
    lamp
18 Elevator trim tab
19 Retractable tail
    wheel
    Aileron trim tab
20 Port flap
21 Formation-holding
22 lamp (port)

23 Detachable wing-
    tip (port)
24 Navigation lamp
    (port)
25 Outboard (port)
    fuel tanks
26 Carburettor intake
    (port engine) with
    anti-ice guard
27 Rolls Royce Merlin
    XXI engine (port)
28 Oil and coolant
    (Glycol) radiators
29 Pilot's compass
30 De Havilland
    Hydromatic airscrew
31 Fire extinguishers
32 Coolant header
    tank
33 Portable oxygen
    bottles
34 Bomb-sight
35 Bomb-aimer's heated
    window
36 Windscreen de-icing
    jet
37 Air thermometer

reaches of the sky, but could now soar upwards to altitudes outside the effective range of anti-aircraft guns and could, conceivably, come and go before the enemy realized what was happening. This clearly made air reconnaissance and observation a more viable operation, but the argument that little of value could be seen from the air naturally re-appeared; after all, the higher you fly and the faster you move, the less intelligence you are going to gain.

This is where the second technological development came in – the reliable air-photo camera. Pictures had been taken from aircraft since the earliest days – indeed many of the impressions we now have of First World War trench-systems snaking across a devastated landscape come from air-photos. But obviously the faster and higher you flew, the less clear these became. Moreover, in the early days, when speed and height were not essential, each aircraft could carry an observer in addition to the pilot, who leant over the side to take the relevant photographs. However as aircraft became faster they needed to lose weight, or at least concentrate it in a more powerful engine, and this meant losing the observer. No pilot could be expected to fly and photograph at the same time so the development of remotely-controlled cameras, attached to a firm base within the aircraft, was clearly a breakthrough of some importance. Allied to this was a growth in the ability to decipher and interpret exactly what the photograph contained, so that by 1939 aerial reconnaissance/observation was a well equipped, established part of air warfare.

Examples of the successful appplication of this role during the Second World War are many and varied. On the Allied side the Royal Air Force kept a careful watch upon German barge concentrations in the coastal ports of France and the Low Countries during the *Sea Lion* invasion scare of late 1940. They also contributed to a significant extent in the strategic bombing campaign of 1939-45 by observing weather patterns over Germany and assessing the damage done once the raids had been delivered. During the build-up to, and the actual execution of the D-Day invasion of Europe in June 1944, air reconnaissance provided vital information about enemy defences, troop dispositions and movements, and this was continued as the Allied armies pushed on towards Germany. In other spheres, it was air reconnaissance that first pin-pointed the German development of V-weapons at Peenemunde on the Baltic coast in 1943, and later helped to identify

the sites in Northern France from which the revolutionary VI ("Doodlebug") pilotless bombs were launched: a factor which contributed in no small way to the Allied decision to advance northwards to take out these sites rather than directly eastwards towards the centre of Germany. Indeed on all fronts, both Allied and Axis, many military decisions were taken purely on the basis of information from air photographs.

But perhaps the most dramatic examples of success in this role came at sea. Certainly so far as Britain was concerned, during the period up to 1943 the life-line with America was all-important and the battle against the U-boats and German surface raiders became an essential one to win as quickly as possible. Unfortunately submarines and single surface vessels are extremely difficult to find once they are at sea, so air observation of their ports, supply points and routes is obviously vital. During the battle of the Atlantic (1939-43), aircraft contributed in no small measure to the final Allied victory, and although their more aggressive roles will be dealt with later, their ability to keep track of enemy vessels does need to be mentioned now. When the German surface fleet began to show signs of activity, for example – a development apparent from as early as 1939 when the battleship *Graf Spee* appeared in the South Atlantic – aircraft were dispatched to maintain round-the-clock watches on known or possible anchorages. The results were impressive. When the battleship *Bismarck* escaped into the North Atlantic in 1941, it was reconnaissance aircraft from Britain which traced her to an obscure Norwegian fjord and provided the first steps in her eventual pursuit and destruction. Similarly when *Tirpitz* tried to follow her sister-ship a year later, air reconnaissance was so effective that she was kept under observation so closely that she found it impossible to move out of Norway without elements of the Royal Navy showing an immediate and unhealthy knowledge of her exact whereabouts. The same degree of success was achieved when it came to finding U-boat bases and directing bombing raids against them, so that overall the contribution of air reconnaissance/observation to this battle alone suggests a substantial restoration to its former primacy. Specially adapted Spitfires, devoid of all unnecessary weight, and the extra-light Mosquitoes, constructed almost entirely of plywood, showed that by flying fast and high the First World War problems of ground fire and interception in the air could be successfully overcome.

199

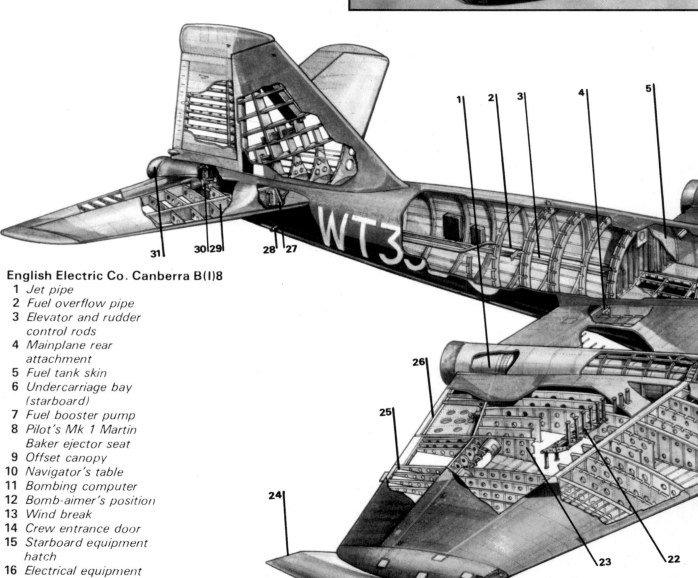

English Electric Co. Canberra B(I)8

1 *Jet pipe*
2 *Fuel overflow pipe*
3 *Elevator and rudder control rods*
4 *Mainplane rear attachment*
5 *Fuel tank skin*
6 *Undercarriage bay (starboard)*
7 *Fuel booster pump*
8 *Pilot's Mk 1 Martin Baker ejector seat*
9 *Offset canopy*
10 *Navigator's table*
11 *Bombing computer*
12 *Bomb-aimer's position*
13 *Wind break*
14 *Crew entrance door*
15 *Starboard equipment hatch*
16 *Electrical equipment hatch*
17 *Bomb bay doors*
18 *Bomb bay*
19 *Triple breech starter*

The English Electric Canberra B(I)8 was the night-intruder interdictor version of an aircraft which underwent a series of modifications and variant-types for 26 years, culminating in a number of one-offs for investigation into electronic counter-measures. Introduced in July 1954, the B(I)8, with a wing-span of 63ft 11½in, was 65ft 6in long and was powered by two Avon 109 turbojets each producing 7,500lb of thrust. The pilot sat in a cockpit off-set to port under a canopy which gave increased visibility. Access was through a hatch on the starboard side of the nose. Navigator/bomb-aimer/radio operator sat in the nose section. There was provision for 6,000lb of bombs in the bomb-bay and wing-racks. Top speed was in the region of 580mph. It was produced for the 2nd Tactical Airforce to deliver nuclear weapons and had a low-altitude bomb-sight.

20 Rolls Royce Avon
    109 turbojet
21 Integral fuel tanks
22 Air-brake drag
    channels
23 Mainplane structure
24 Jettisonable fuel tank
25 Aileron, starboard
26 Flap, starboard
27 Tailplane hinges
28 Fuel overflow pipe
29 Tailplane structure
30 Tailplane actuator
31 Tail-cone

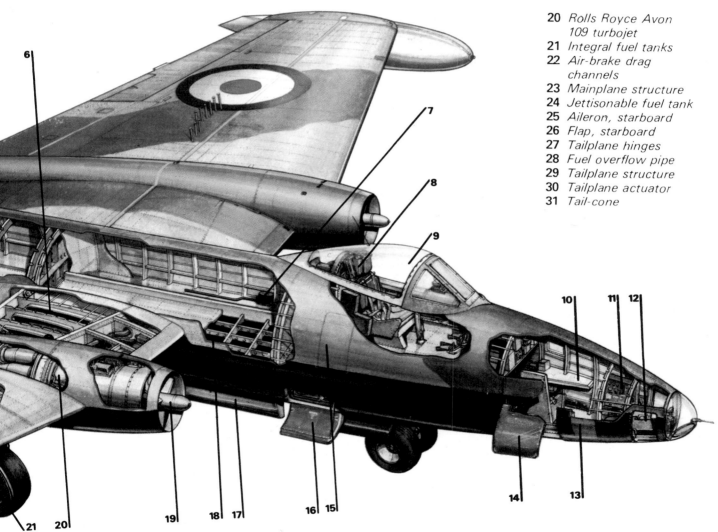

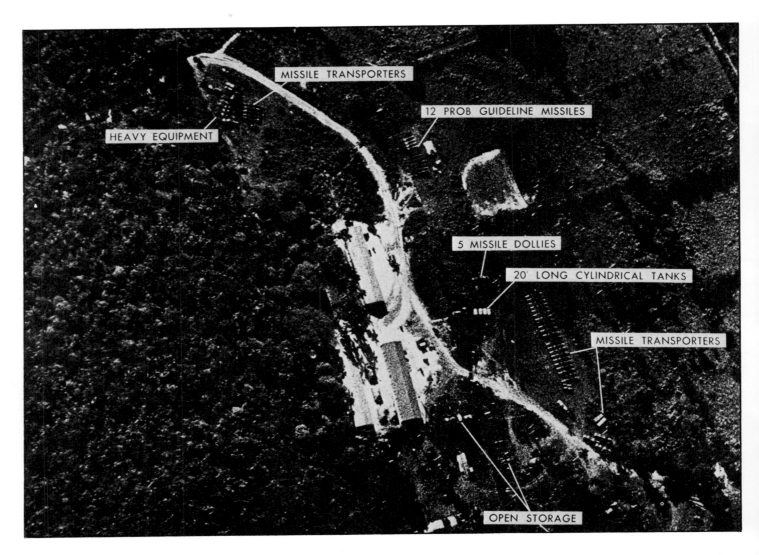

Left: One of the reconnaissance photographs of Cuba that triggered the Cuban Missile Crisis of October 1962. The missiles and equipment have been indicated for distribution to the Press.
Below left: An industrial target before and after an attack by the USAAF in World War II.
Right: An RPV, Remotely Piloted Vehicle, a pilotless reconnaissance drone which is difficult to locate on radar and relatively expendable.

Viewing the situation since 1945, it is impossible to conclude anything but a mammoth expansion in this area. This is partly a result of the Cold War and super-power confrontation which has characterized the nuclear age, for in such circumstances of wary, but non-violent, hostility, information about the potential enemy, his dispositions and possible intentions, is clearly essential. But this does not alter the fact that the massive technological leaps which have occurred since the Second World War have made the whole area of reconnaissance/observation much more effective. To take an extreme example, the existence of special spy-satellites capable, through infra-red photography, of taking detailed pictures of the earth from beyond the atmosphere, obviously take the lid off not only the battlefield but also the most inaccessible areas of the enemy homeland. This is particularly useful in the context of superpower dentente and arms limitation, for in the absence of information freely provided by either side such things as missile sites, ABM (anti-ballistic missile) complexes and submarine pens can be checked by air reconnaissance. The satellites are also less dangerous than aircraft for, as the U-2 crisis in 1960 illustrated (when the American pilot Gary Powers was shot down over Russia), it can be very embarrassing to be caught in the act of aerial recon-naissance during peacetime. In addition, satellites enable the two super powers to maintain a careful watch upon potential or actual trouble-spots around the world and advise any of their allies who may be involved of the true situation. This was shown to good effect during the Arab-Israeli War of 1973, for it was spy-satellite pictures, provided by the Russians, which showed President Sadat of Egypt the true extent of Israeli gains on the west bank of the Suez Canal just before the cease-fire agreement of October 22. Sadat could never have gathered such information from the confused situation on the ground, yet he needed it desperately in order to decide upon the advisability of the cease-fire.

But spy-satellites are an extreme example and in the event of a major war between the super powers they are likely to be blotted out almost straight away: both sides are reported to have contingency plans which even include sending astronauts into space to steal the enemy's equipment! If this is the case, aircraft are sure to return to the reconnaissance/observation role, and neither super power has neglected the development of reconnaissance machines, concentrating as before upon speed and altitude. The latest American contribution – the aptly named Blackbird – now holds the trans-Atlantic speed record, while the Soviet Tu-20 Bear is a constant visitor to the shores of Britain and Western Europe, probing air defence systems and monitoring radar wave-lengths for future jamming or ECM, should a war occur. In addition, both sides have developed multi-role aircraft which will be expected, as a part of their job, to do reconnaissance sweeps over the battle area itself.

Before leaving this role, however, it is worth con-sidering the latest developments in the reconnaissance sphere. During the Vietnam War the Americans were presented with the problem of keeping a constant watch upon possible infiltration and supply routes into the south, particularly around the Demilitarized Zone and on the Laotian and Cambodian borders. At first they used the traditional means of reconnaissance aircraft, equipped with such technological innovations as infra-red cameras, electronic surveillance devices and even "people-sniffers" (small dart-like objects dropped into the jungle and capable of warning the pilot of human movement through a sensitivity to body heat and odour), later the idea of Remotely Piloted Vehicles (RPVs) was put forward. These aircraft contained all the equipment used by conventional reconnaissance aircraft, but relayed their findings by television and radar to a secure ground controller, were expendable, relatively cheap and, of course, pilotless; considerations which soon led to their extension into the tactical strike and even bombing roles. So far as reconnaissance/ observation is concerned, however, they are now in front-line use – according to newspaper reports of July 1977, a number were shot down by the Libyans during their border war with Egypt – and are quite clearly the equipment of the future. The amount of money and research still being devoted to such developments shows how important the basic role of reconnaissance/observation is, and implies its con-tinuation for as long as the air is used for military purposes.

Tactical support and Interdiction

Bombing up a Hawker Hurricane IIc in North Africa. When the Hurricane became too slow to be an interceptor it proved an excellent ground attack fighter.

The RAF Mosquito. One of the most versatile and successful aircraft of the war, it saw action in many roles including tactical interdiction.
Right: A rocket-firing Mosquito in flight.
Centre: A coastal tanker explodes after being hit by rocket firing Mosquitos.
Bottom: A Mosquito roars over a factory at almost zero feet.

Early experiments in what later came be to known as tactical strike support coincided with those on reconnaissance/observation, when the Italians under Piazza, dropped small bombs on the Turkish camps around Tripoli in 1911 at the same time as they were observing dispositions and force levels. This was only logical, obeying the military maxim of attacking the enemy wherever he may be found, and immediately offered a new and important role to the aircraft. So far as military forces are concerned, any preliminary attacks upon an enemy, demoralizing his troops, cutting his immediate lines of communication or supply (a process now known as interdiction), disrupting his movement of reinforcements and destroying his more static elements such as airfields, railheads, artillery positions and troop concentrations, are extremely beneficial. They will weaken an attacking force by blunting his assault, or they will prepare the way for an advance by undermining enemy strength and efficiency. If, in addition, the strikes are maintained as the battle develops, then the side with the strongest air element will clearly enjoy a substantial advantage.

There was obviously nothing new about the principles behind this role – it had long been a basic task of the army artillery – but the extension of it to aircraft was soon accepted. As with so many air power roles, that of tactical strike support/interdiction evolved from the carnage of the First World War. At the beginning of that conflict, when aircraft were generally unarmed, it was not unknown for pilots on both sides to follow Piazza's lead and drop darts, grenades or small bombs on to the ground forces they were observing. This could be especially effective against massed troop formations (particularly if they included horsed transport or cavalry which was susceptible to animal panic) but was usually regarded as little more than an irritant through its lack of repetition. But things changed once the trench system became established. Not only were the armies situated in one place, which tended to increase their dependence upon static supply dumps and communications networks behind the front line, but their artillery came up against problems.

Gunners could not see their targets – vulnerable though such targets were – and could not observe the fall of shot. Observation aircraft and balloons could help to a certain extent, but to be effective the artillery bombardments needed to be both powerful and sustained. Preliminary barrages lasting days rather than hours became the norm by 1916, and although these could be effective, they were extremely expensive and eroded the element of surprise. In such circumstances the aircraft was an obvious alternative. Armed with bombs and machine-guns, it could appear over the enemy lines, attack the relevant targets and be gone before the ground forces had fully realized what was going on. If enough aircraft were used, the task of the artillery could be done literally in minutes, enabling the ground forces to advance against a surprised and confused enemy.

The Germans seem to have understood this first: in late summer 1917, General von Hutier was given the task of attacking and taking the town of Riga on the Eastern Front, so that the German armies could advance along the Baltic coast and turn the right flank of the Russian line. According to normal practice, Hutier should have planned a sustained artillery bombardment before sending his troops forward in a frontal assault, but rather than risk a repetition of the many defeats which had followed such tactics in the past, he chose instead to use aircraft to attack the Russian lines just ahead of his main force. He did not dispense with artillery altogether – in fact, his plan involved a five-hour bombardment, using a mixture of gas and high explosive – but as the enemy clearly expected a barrage which would go on for anything up to four days they would still have their heads down as the advance got under way. The tactic was a success, and was repeated on a number of occasions by both sides as the war progressed. Two months after the Riga offensive, the British used aircraft to support the newly invented tanks in their first major battle at Cambrai, hitting troop concentrations and other targets just in front of the advancing ground forces, and during the major German offensive on the Western Front in March and April 1918, Field Marshal von Hindenburg used Hutier's tactics to good effect. The groundwork had been well and truly laid.

If the First World War had continued for a few more months, into the spring of 1919, there is much to suggest that the principle of tactical strike support/interdiction would have been extended still further. When Colonel J. F. C. Fuller, a staff officer with the British Tank Corps, observed the confusion which accompanied the Allied retreat in spring 1918, he was struck by the ease with which such an organizational break-down could be achieved and by the advantages which were likely to accrue to the attacking side. Concentrating for obvious reasons upon the use of the tank,

he compiled a document known originally as "The Tactics of the Attack as affected by the Speed and Circuit of the Medium D Tank" but later shortened to "Plan 1919". As Fuller's tanks advanced in pincer movements on the selected ninety miles of front, air support was to be provided. According to the plan, elements of the newly-constituted Royal Air Force were to indulge in ground strafing just in advance of the armour to help punch the initial holes in the enemy line, while other aircraft bombed important targets in the rear. Chief among these was to be the sector GHQ, the aim being to destroy the "brain" of the enemy rather than his expendable "muscles" or front-line units.

The war ended before Fuller had a chance to test his ideas in action and, as with strategic bombing, a seemingly viable air power theory was left in limbo, unsupported by essential evidence. But in this case the future was not left solely to the theorists, for although cooperation between the army and a proudly-independent Royal Air Force in Britain was poor, other European states were quick to realize the potential. In Russia, for example, once the chaos of the Revolution and Civil War had died down, tactical strike support of ground forces was regarded as essential, and for much of the inter-war period research and development on the air side concentrated upon this role. Consequently, by the late 1930s and early 1940s, the Soviet Air Force consisted almost entirely of tactical strike aircraft, tied closely to the needs of ground forces, and throughout the Russo-German War (1941–1945) such machines as the Petlyakov PE2 and Ilyushin IL2 provided constant support to land units, acting as protection against enemy attack and as forward strike elements.

It was in Germany that the process was carried to its logical conclusion, however, when generals such as

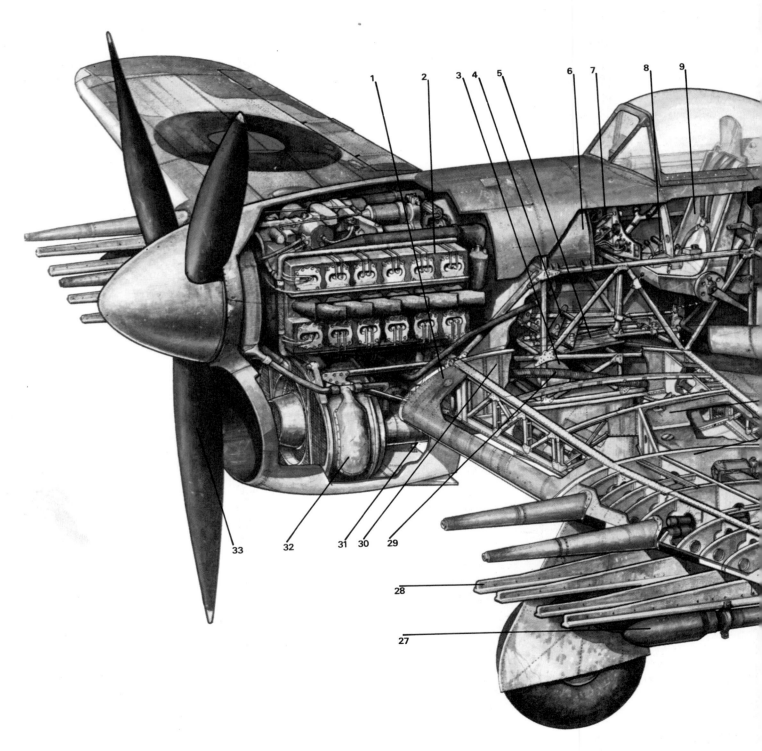

While the battle of Britain was in progress, with the superlative Supermarine Spitfire and Hawker Hurricane carving their names on the scroll of aviation history, another RAF fighter was being test-flown in great secrecy. This was a basic, no-frills single-seat fighter. But it had one distinction, in the shape of a huge power-plant that, while giving an incredible extra 100mph over the Hurricane, created real and unpleasant problems for the test-pilots who had to fly the prototypes.

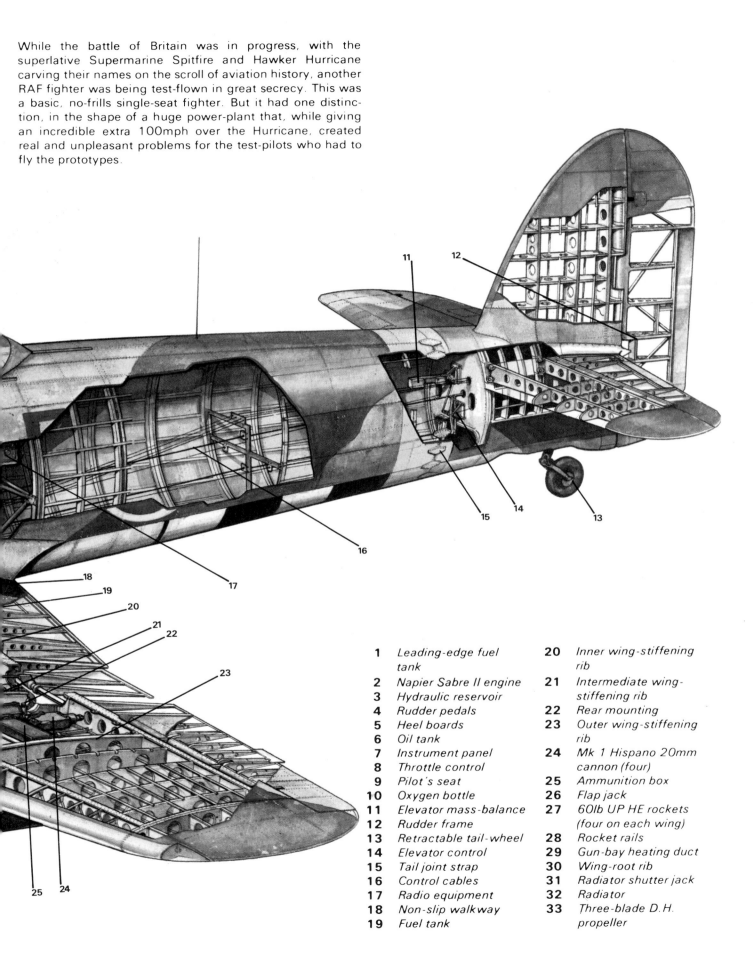

1	Leading-edge fuel tank	20	Inner wing-stiffening rib
2	Napier Sabre II engine	21	Intermediate wing-stiffening rib
3	Hydraulic reservoir	22	Rear mounting
4	Rudder pedals	23	Outer wing-stiffening rib
5	Heel boards	24	Mk 1 Hispano 20mm cannon (four)
6	Oil tank	25	Ammunition box
7	Instrument panel	26	Flap jack
8	Throttle control	27	60lb UP HE rockets (four on each wing)
9	Pilot's seat	28	Rocket rails
10	Oxygen bottle	29	Gun-bay heating duct
11	Elevator mass-balance	30	Wing-root rib
12	Rudder frame	31	Radiator shutter jack
13	Retractable tail-wheel	32	Radiator
14	Elevator control	33	Three-blade D.H. propeller
15	Tail joint strap		
16	Control cables		
17	Radio equipment		
18	Non-slip walkway		
19	Fuel tank		

Manstein and Guderian built up an entire structure of war based closely upon Fuller's ideas. Known as *Blitzkrieg*, it was first tested in Spain during the Civil War (1936–39) and brought to perfection during the campaigns in Poland (1939), France (1940) and Russia (1941). The system of *Blitzkrieg* did not merely consist of sustained tank assaults, gaining momentum as the factor of surprise confused a demoralized enemy but provided for the strike support aircraft – notably the Ju87 dive bomber – which contributed enormously to the remarkable string of German successes. Acting as mobile air artillery, such aircraft hit troop concentrations, communications centres, fuel dumps and even civilian refugees, clearing a way for the tanks to come forward. Their screeching sirens and apparent ruthlessness undermined the morale of opposing troops, especially in the French campaign. When the German land forces approached the city of Rotterdam in May 1940, for example, it took only one air raid by medium bombers for the garrison to surrender, and although there is evidence that the strike was unnecessary, its existence discouraged many other cities from even trying to hold out in the future. The lesson which emerged, still bearing considerable relevance today, was that very close cooperation between air and ground elements was an essential pre-requisite to success in modern war.

The importance of this lesson is re-inforced when Allied attempts at tactical strike support during the Second World War are examined. In the French campaign of 1940, for example, aircraft capable of carrying out the role were available, but they were largely of obsolete design while their pilots lacked training in low-level precision attacks or close cooperation with ground forces. This was partly a result of economic stringency during the inter-war years, especially in Britain, but more importantly was a by-product of the emphasis upon strategic bombing and Royal Air Force independence. Resources, both financial and human, had been devoted to the offensive capabilities of the manned bomber fleet, and although something of a *volte-face* had taken place when air defence was suddenly seen as important during the late 1930s, fighters had been preferred to strike aircraft. The abortive attempts to destroy bridges over the Meuse river and Albert Canal in order to stem the German advance in May 1940 show the inevitable outcome: unescorted Fairey Battle light bombers – slow, under-gunned and vulnerable – made little impact for very high losses. Some attempts were made to switch medium bombers such as Bristol Blenheims or Wellingtons to the tactical role, but with little success as their crews had even less experience or expertise. In addition, lacking air supremacy in the face of a large and well-organized Luftwaffe, the Allied aircraft came up against the problem of integrated air defence systems and interceptor fighters. It soon became apparent that the First World War experiments with tactical strike support – restricted as they were to a fairly static battlefield which could be covered quickly by attacking aircraft – had failed to emphasize the crucial point that the enemy may well be capable of preventing you from reaching the target, let alone destroying it.

Regardless of these basic lessons, however tactical strike support interdiction does not seem to have been afforded the priority it deserved by the Allied powers, until about 1944. During the British campaigns in North Africa (1940–43) for example, there was still a lack of specially developed machines, and for much of the time both bombers and fighters were switched to the tactical strike role as and when they were needed. Aircraft such as the Blenheim (designed for strategic bombing and incapable of attaining the speed necessary for successful tactical strike) and the Spitfire and Hurricane (interceptor fighters which, although enjoying the speed, lacked the payload capability were ill-suited. Attempts were made to rectify the situation in preparation for the D-Day invasion but were left too late. An entire air force, the 2nd Tactical, was formed, with bombers like the American Marauder being used for tactical bombing and interdiction, and the British

A Junkers Ju-87, known to Allies and Axis forces as the Stuka an acronym for Dive Bomber, starts the roll that precedes its dive on to the target. Dive bombing allowed bombers to hit small targets very accurately, and enabled the Germans to destroy transport, command centres and even gun positions prior to a land assault — it was a vital part of their Blitzkrieg tactics.

Typhoon for close support of ground forces. When the Allied High Command at last realized the desperate need for tactical strike support interdiction over the coastal areas of North-West Europe in 1944, they had to order a large-scale switch of strategic bombers away from the attacks upon Germany.

The results were impressive, but ill-considered. The invasion began with wide-ranging attacks along the length of the coast of northern France to confuse the enemy, with an ultimate aim of cutting off the entire area behind the proposed landing sites in Normandy, between the rivers Orne and Vire. The strategic bombers did their job well, destroying bridges, railroads, roads, communications centres and possible defensive systems but, if anything, went too far. Not only were the Germans paralyzed, and unable to move reinforcements into the battle area but, when the Allies emerged from the beach-heads in August 1944, they, too, found it difficult to advance. The bombers were too powerful, for instead of blasting a route for the ground forces, as the Stukas had done in the *blitzkrieg* operations, they had presented the advancing armies with a sea of rubble, much of which was impassable.

Take, for example, the case of Caen, a city which should have been taken on D-Day itself. When it proved a centre of resistance, the bombers attacked it with such force that no wheeled or tracked vehicle could pass through it, thus necessitating by-pass operations (*Epsom* and *Goodwood*) which were both lengthy and costly. In addition, instead of destroying defending forces, the bombing had presented the Germans with almost impregnable positions, which required bitter

house-to-house fighting before the Allies were successful. A similar situation had arisen during the battle for Monte Cassino in Italy during March 1944, when over 1000 tons of bombs had not only destroyed an historic monastery but also provided the Germans with good defensive positions.

In fairness, however, it should be added that improvements were made as the war drew to an end, with the specially designed light or medium bombers and fighter bombers, especially of the 2nd Tactical Air Force, learning to cooperate with the ground forces. Indeed, by late 1944, during the abortive German offensive in the Ardennes, the appearance of tactical strike aircraft over the American lines, after a period of bad weather had prevented them taking off, effectively turned the tide of the battle. Similarly, in the American "island-hopping" campaigns in the Pacific (1943–45), U.S. Marine Corps fighter-bombers perfected ground attack techniques with bombs, rockets, and napalm. By 1945, after a long and often difficult process of error and experimentation, the Allies seem to have appreciated the role of tactical strike support interdiction, but it is probably more than mere coincidence that much of their success occurred only after air supremacy had been gained by other means, notably the American strategic attacks against the Luftwaffe and its supporting services. In the absence of opposing fighters, experiments could be made in ground attack techniques.

Once the Second World War was over, the importance of tactical strike support/interdiction was overshadowed by the apparent success of strategic bombing using atomic weapons. The future seemed to be sure to involve atomic exchanges, leaving little room for conventional warfare. But this did not last. Once the Soviets had exploded their first atomic device in 1949, and the principle of mutual deterrence between the super powers began to emerge, the possibility of fighting non-nuclear limited wars for limited political aims soon became apparent, re-introducing all the old techniques of conventional conflict. This can be seen clearly in the Korean War (1950–53) when the Americans, in company with the United Nations, limited the size of committed forces, the scope of the geographical area of conflict and the political aims and types of weapons used in what was, to all intents and purposes, a peripheral theatre of East-West hostility. The limitation of weapons inevitably restricted the air element considerably, for although the American air force had the capability to launch strategic bombing raids on

Ground attack in theory and practice. A Hurricane IID starts its run firing armour piercing ammunition against an enemy tank. Below: A Typhoon equipped to carry bombs. Far right: How a rocket firing fighter would attack a target like a railway train. The pilot had to align his aircraft with the target and then fire the rocket when he was within range before peeling off.

North Korea and the Chinese bases across the Yalu river with either conventional or nuclear weapons, a political desire to keep both the Chinese and the Russians out of the war, necessitated a return to tactical air attacks. So far as ground forces were concerned, this resulted in little more than an extension of World War II techniques to a new theatre of operation, with fighter bombers giving close support and taking out enemy strong-points immediately in advance of the front line. But the process of interdiction reached new levels of application. Confronted by an enemy who received supplies and, after late 1950, reinforcements, over a lengthy border with Communist China, the Americans attempted to cut off North Korea by destroying the bridges, roads, tracks and supply-routes which connected the two countries. On the whole, the campaign was fairly successful, even when it was insisted that not one bomb should fall on Chinese territory for fear of political repercussions.

The situation in Vietnam in the mid 1960s was very similar and, as we have seen, the Americans tried to repeat the Korean offensive by instigating a campaign of tactical interdiction designed to cut off the North from all contact with the South. The North Vietnamese government was openly supporting the Viet Cong guerrillas south of the 17th Parallel, pushing both supplies and reinforcements across the Demilitarized Zone and down what was known as the Ho Chi Minh Trail, a long and tortuous route which wound its way through the neighbouring countries of Laos and Cambodia before emerging in the Mekong Delta around Saigon. Air strikes against these areas began in 1965, but the success enjoyed in Korea was not repeated. There were a number of reasons for this which, when combined together, showed how difficult the role of tactical strike support/interdiction had become.

The common denominator undoubtedly lay in the technological revolution which took place during the 1960s. On the air side, the trend was toward the multi-role aircraft, capable of carrying out a number of tasks where speed was essential – for example, reconnaissance or interception – and this tended to act against the tactical strike potential. As early as the Second World War, the accuracy of strikes had been dubious and it had become apparent that the faster an aircraft travelled, the less likely it was to hit a precise target which remained in the pilot's sight for a very short time. As aircraft became virtually supersonic, therefore, the chances of hitting a camouflaged supply dump or a

narrow trail in the jungle declined, leaving only two options open to the attacking side. The Americans tried both in Vietnam between 1965 and 1973. To begin with they attempted to substitute firepower for accuracy, dropping increasingly larger loads of high explosive and napalm on to the smaller targets in the hopes of hitting them with something. But this was expensive and, in the event, less than successful as the Viet Cong showed themselves to be remarkably adept at improvisation and recovery. The alternative was improved technology, particularly in the areas of directing bombs and radio controlled guidance; a process which began with the introduction of laser and TV-guided "smart" bombs and culminated in the development of tactical strike RPVs, armed with missiles, bombs and computer control systems. The results were promising, for in 1972 and early 1973 a number of strikes upon the infiltration areas appear to have succeeded, and many would argue that their introduction contributed to the North Vietnamese decision for a truce with the Americans.

Nevertheless, this is only half the picture, for although the Americans may have solved the problems of accurate delivery, they were also presented with enormous difficulties by anti-aircraft defences which destroyed a significant number of tactical aircraft. The development of air defence systems will be examined in more depth in a later chapter, but it is necessary to stress that as the role of tactical strike

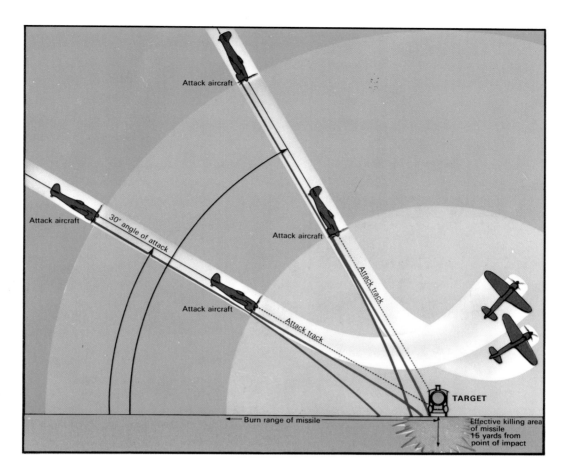

Attack aircraft

Attack aircraft

30° angle of attack

Attack aircraft

Attack aircraft

Attack track

Attack track

TARGET

Burn range of missile

Effective killing area
of missile
15 yards from
point of impact

support/interdiction evolved, so did the enemy's capability to destroy attacking aircraft. During the Second World War – and in Korea as well – interceptor fighters had been the main problem, but by the time of Vietnam ground-based units had increased in effectiveness and importance. Chief among these were the SAMs (Surface-to-Air Missiles), capable of homing-in on the exhaust heat of a jet-engined aircraft, and although the North Vietnamese and Viet Cong forces had access to only the first generation of these weapons – the Soviet-built SAMs 2, 3 and manportable 7 – they proved effective in destroying the American Phantoms and Skyhawks. By the early 1970s they also had Soviet self-propelled anti-aircraft cannon such as the radar-controlled ZSU-23/4 as well as conventional A.A. guns, so it may be appreciated that the Americans were encountering stiff opposition. They tried to counter the SAMs by re-introducing piston-driven aircraft and depending upon helicopter gun ships (a process which incidentally aided accuracy by reducing the speed of attack), and attempted to jam the ZSUs radar through ECM, but overall the problem remained. It is still applicable today, as the NATO air forces are well aware, for in the event of war with the Warsaw Pact Countries in Central Europe any attempts at tactical strike support/interdiction – against bridges, airfields and advancing enemy forces – are sure to be vigorously opposed. Technology appears to have caused a continuous battle between offensive and defensive capa-

bilities, and it is nowhere more apparent than in this particular role.

It would be wrong, however, to suppose that tactical strike support/interdiction is a declining air power task: far from it. The basic principles behind its original development still remain: for if an army is to operate successfully in any situation, it needs to attack the enemy in every possible way and, regardless of the problems, the aircraft still offers an unprecedented degree of mobility, speed and hitting power which military weapons short of tactical nuclear strength cannot hope to emulate. In addition, the technological developments continue apace and may in fact outweigh the defensive capabilities of the enemy ground or air forces. For tactical strike the Americans now have fleets of helicopters, designed to hug the ground before appearing suddenly to attack advancing enemy forces: the British have the Hawker Harrier "jump jet" which can land and take off vertically from extremely small areas, thus enabling it to survive counter-strikes and return to the attack with surprise on its side. At the same time, for the interdiction role, the ALCM, with conventional warhead, now has the ability to attack the most inaccessible and well-defended target through its contour-matching guidance system with an impressive degree of accuracy. Such developments suggest a technological swing in favour of the offensive, at least for the moment, and explain the importance placed upon the continued use of tactical strike/interdiction.

Transport and Airborne Landings

Dakotas stream across the sky as 9000 paratroops jump over Le Muy in southern France. The airborne attack supporting the Anvil sea landings in 1944 was one of the most successful attacks of its kind in history.

The third air-power role to be examined in a tactical context is that of transport/airborne landings. It inevitably covers a large amount of ground, but the two concepts involved are inextricably linked not only by the idea of movement through the air, but also by the very similar types of aircraft which tend to be used for both sorts of operation. Having said that, however, it is perhaps easier to take the two topics separately to a certain extent, if only because before 1940 airborne landings as such had never been practised under war conditions.

Air transport can be taken to cover the movement of conventional ground forces (as opposed to specially trained paratroop units), equipment and supplies from one place to another through the air. This has obvious advantages in both the planning and execution of military campaigns. If ground troops find themselves cut off from the main army by an advancing enemy, or are operating behind enemy lines as part of a definite strategy, or if the ground being fought over is unsuitable, aircraft can help solve the problems. They can be used to keep troops supplied, either by para-dropping material to them or, if an airfield is available, by landing to evacuate civilians, casualties or unnecessary administrative troops, while at the same time reinforcing existing combat units. Similarly, if the enemy attacks a weak portion of the front line or a poorly defended locality far from base, men and material can be packed into aircraft and flown to the trouble spot quickly. Aircraft give a new and significant amount of mobility and flexibility to the ground forces.

There is evidence to suggest that these capabilities were recognized as early as the First World War. In the campaign against the Turks in Mesopotamia, for example, when British troops were besieged in the fortress of Kut-el-Amara between December 1915 and their surrender in April 1916, the Royal Flying Corps attempted supply drops to the starving garrison. Their efforts were crude by modern standards, entailing a low-level swoop over the fortress so that the observer could push sacks of food, medical supplies and other essential material over the side of the aircraft. The methods were a little short on success as no one had yet thought of attaching parachutes to break the fall. Many supplies were destroyed on impact, but at least the basic idea was there: it was to be remembered and built upon during the inter-war period.

The other element of air transport – the movement of troops to battle areas – was not attempted during the First World War, but experiments began quite soon after the end of that conflict. During the early 1920s, in an effort to preserve the independence of the Royal Air Force by making it as indispensable as possible, Trenchard and the air chiefs managed to station squadrons in the main trouble spots of the Empire to aid the ground forces in keeping the peace. At first this consisted of bombing isolated villages belonging to recalcitrant tribes in places like Iraq or the northern frontiers of India – areas inaccessible to the military without lengthy forced marches – but by about 1923 the idea of actually flying troops out to trouble spots seems to have occurred. Standards of comfort must have been abysmal in aircraft designed for other tasks, but the precedent was established. It was reinforced in December 1928 when the Royal Air Force successfully evacuated 586 British civilians from Kabul in Afghanistan, then in the throes of a bitter civil war, and thereafter the idea became widely accepted.

As with most air power roles, the opportunity to develop these ideas along the lines already laid down came with the Second World War. For geographical reasons, most examples that could be cited tended to be in difficult areas, where normal ground or sea movement was curtailed by problems of distance or physical barriers, and in this context the Allied campaigns in Burma and southern China between 1942 and 1945 perhaps offer the best illustrations. After the British forces had retreated through Burma to the Indian border in 1942, the problem of supply was immense. With the loss of Rangoon, all war material and reinforcements had to be brought to the front line from Calcutta and central India – a journey which could take up to two months overland – and the supply route to Chiang Kai-shek's Nationalist Chinese forces had been cut entirely by the advancing Japanese. If the British were to be sustained on the Imphal plain and the Chinese (dependent as they were for most of their arms and military equipment upon the Americans) kept in the war at all, some alternative method of supply was desperately needed. It was provided by aircraft.

Between late 1942 and early 1945 American and British pilots, flying C-47 Dakota transports, completed endless supply missions from India "over the hump" of the Himalayan foothills to southern China, bolstering the efforts of Chiang Kai-shek and, between June and November 1944, sustaining the B-29 strategic bombers in their campaign against the Japanese homeland. At the same time the British forces around Imphal and

Kohima were re-inforced and re-equipped; a process which reached new heights of urgency in early 1944 when the Japanese, in one of their last land offensives, laid siege to both localities. Indeed, as the sieges began to take effect, the entire 5th Indian Infantry Division, complete with its mules and essential fighting equipment, was air-lifted from Arakan on the eastern coast of Burma into Imphal itself; a feat which, at the time, constituted the largest air-movement of combat troops ever attempted. The arrival of these troops at Imphal is regarded by many as the turning point of the battle. Furthermore, while all this was going on, Brigadier Orde Wingate's Chindit patrols were operating behind Japanese lines, having been lifted in by air and depending solely upon re-supply by Dakotas for their survival.

This does not mean, of course, that all air movement and transport was successful. German efforts to supply the beleaguered garrison of Stalingrad on the Eastern Front in late 1942, for example, failed because of a shortage of suitable aircraft and a spirited defence of air space by Russian fighters, while similar efforts by the Royal Air Force over Arnhem in September 1944 made little difference to an already desperate situation. The lessons to be drawn would appear to be two-fold. Firstly, transport aircraft tend, almost by definition, to be slow moving and so require protection from both air interception and ground defences – considerations which imply that they can be used successfully only if you enjoy air superiority, at least on a local level – and that a substantial fleet of transports is essential if large numbers of troops are to be moved or supplied. If these

two prerequisites are satisfied, air transport will probably work; if one or both are unobtainable, it will more than likely fail.

Post-war examples re-inforce this theory. In late 1953, when the French were fighting desperately against the Viet Minh guerillas in northern Indo-China (now Vietnam), they established an isolated fortified base at Dien Bien Phu in an effort to draw the enemy, under General Giap, away from northern Laos. For a time all appeared to go well, with the French parachutists receiving regular supplies and reinforcements by air, using an airstrip carved out of the valley floor but, at this stage, opposition was slight. Then, in March 1954, the Viet Minh attacked, having approached Dien Bien Phu secretly. They managed to take the surrounding hills, unfortified by the French who thought that air superiority would make the fortress impregnable, and even brought up anti-aircraft guns from the Chinese border. Once these were established Dien Bien Phu was cut off, aircraft could not use an air-strip overlooked from all sides and ground forces could not approach the fortress through miles of dense and hostile jungle. The siege lasted fifty-six days, during which the French made repeated efforts to keep the garrison supplied by air-drops, but with a shortage of aircraft and the heavy Viet Minh anti-air defence, smaller and smaller amounts of essential equipment got through. In the end, supply drops became harder to deliver accurately to the striking perimeter and the garrison was forced to surrender. As had been the case at Stalingrad twelve years before, air transport had

An American McDonnell Douglas YC-15 jet transport makes a low pass during a flight demonstration. The YC-15 is capable of carrying 150 fully-equipped men or 62,000lb of equipment.

failed because of a shortage of aircraft and a successful defence of air space by a determined enemy.

At the other end of the scale, however, successes still occur. During the Arab-Israeli War of October 1973, for example, both the Americans and Russians, in possession of large transport fleets and acting with freedom from ground or air opposition, were able to deliver vast quantities of supplies into the war zone for the Israelis and Arabs. Air transport is therefore still a viable proposition if the conditions are right, and the fact that NATO strategy in the event of a Warsaw Pact attack depends to a certain extent upon the movement of reserves by air from America and Britain to the Central Front or flanks would imply that many expect those conditions to be easily found. How viable this is remains to be seen, for the recent decision to phase out the Royal Air Force Transport Command must undermine one of its basic foundations. However, this cannot alter the fact that the aircraft has given to the supply and movement processes a unique degree of flexibility and mobility.

The same general conclusion applies to airborne landings, for although they have had a shorter history, their impact upon the tactics of war has been considerable. The reasons are fairly obvious. If you are on the offensive and able to put in a powerful assault behind the enemy lines, this will clearly have an unsettling – even demoralizing – effect. Whatever the target for such an assault, the enemy will be forced to look two ways at once, withdrawing units from his front line or committing important reserves to deal with the new situation, and this will inevitably weaken his capacity to withstand the main frontal attack. If, in addition, you have directed the airborne assault against specific tactical strong-points or positions, the main attack will be further aided by the destruction of fortresses, airfields or concentration areas or by the taking and holding of bridges or road systems. Even on the defensive, there are advantages. An airborne landing behind the advancing enemy columns can disrupt their supply lines and communications, while weakening their strength as elements are forced to move back to counter the unexpected attack. In such cases there is, of course, little chance of the airborne troops being relieved as the main force will probably be retreating away from them, but the idea has been put into practice sufficiently often, particularly by the French in Indo-China (1946–54), to merit some consideration.

Airborne landings as such were not put into effect

until 1940, but in the years before a number of experiments had been effected which prepared the way. As early as 1918 the theorist Billy Mitchell, convinced to the point of extremism that air power could achieve victory, suggested training the 1st American Infantry Division in the art of parachuting and then dropping them from converted Handley-Page 1500s behind the enemy line to capture the city of Metz. The war ended before he could convince anyone in high command that his scheme was even worth contemplating, and it was not until 1927 that military parachuting was attempted. In that year eight Italian soldiers jumped as a team in full battle kit, and this may be regarded as the first successful human airdrop for purely military purposes. The Italians did not take their experiments very much further, however, leaving the large-scale development to Russia and Germany for the rest of the inter-war period. Initially, during the late 1920s and early 1930s, these two countries followed basically similar lines, chiefly because German soldiers and airmen, restricted by the terms of the Versailles Treaty to a very passive military role, conducted clandestine training in Russia. The experiments seem to have concentrated upon parachuting, for by the mid 1930s both countries possessed substantial airborne arms. The Germans had to wait until their invasion of Austria in 1938 before displaying their capability *en masse*, but the Russians were impressing foreign observers with parachute displays as early as the military manoeuvre of 1936 when, in a mock battle around Moscow, a total of 5200 fully-armed men descended from the skies. Meanwhile the

Germans had added another aspect to airborne landings through their experiments with gliders, begun as a secret method of training conventional pilots in the basic elements of flying. By the mid 1930s this was recognized as an important means of dispatching troops and equipment into battle behind the enemy lines.

With such equipment and experience available, it is little wonder that the Germans laid great stress upon their airborne potential as soon as the Second World War began. Their first – and many would argue, most successful – operation took place in May 1940, during the invasion of France and the Low Countries. When planning the overall campaign the Germans had originally thought along the lines of a repetition of 1914 – the strong right hook through the Low Countries aimed at Paris – but after a copy of the written orders had inadvertently fallen into Allied hands, the *blitzkrieg* practitioners, led by von Manstein, managed to persuade Hitler to permit an armoured thrust through the relatively undefended Ardennes region. This pre-supposed that the Allies would have advanced into Belgium to protect that area, so leaving the route to the Channel coast open, and for this reason an attack had still to be made upon the Low Countries to force such a commitment and to act as the northern part of a vast "nutcracker" operation. Field Marshal von Bock's Army Group "B" was detailed for this northern attack, with the Belgian fortress of Eben Emael, covering the approaches to the Meuse river and Albert Canal just south of Maastricht, as a primary objective. Designed to withstand all the most likely conventional attacks, the

A German Messerschmitt Gigant, Giant, the biggest operational transport aircraft of the war. The Gigant was slow and unwieldy and was effective only as long as the Germans had air superiority.

fortress was a potentially dangerous block, not only to von Bock's advance but also to the Ardennes assault which needed flank protection. A frontal attack would be extremely costly and would certainly fail but the new found flexibility and surprise of an airborne landing seemed to offer a solution. So before daylight on May 10 1940, a glider borne force of specially trained sappers landed on top of the fortress and began a systematic destruction of casements and turrets. At the same time, other small glider detachments seized bridges over the Albert Canal and one over the river at Maastricht. On May 11 the Belgian garrison of Eben Emael – over 1000 strong – surrendered. The airborne troops were relieved by ground units within twenty-four hours, before the Allies could react, and von Bock's forces advanced against little opposition. The potential of airborne landings was fully established.

Not all airborne assaults have been this successful, for the practical problems are immense. In the first place it is unrealistic to expect major victories from air-landed troops – on their own they are just not strong enough to decide a campaign. Because of their dependence upon aircraft they are not heavily armed, lacking both armour and heavy artillery, while the restrictions of re-supply mean that they can hold out for little more than forty-eight hours. Add to these factors the problems of weather, terrain, communications and target selection, and it is obvious that the planning and execution of airborne landings is a delicate business, becoming progressively more delicate the larger the landing to be effected. Both the Axis and

Allied powers discovered this to their cost during the Second World War.

In the case of the German attack upon Crete in May 1941, it was far too ambitious to be completely successful. The airborne troops were to take the entire island virtually on their own, and were then to use it as a stepping-stone for further attack upon Cyprus and even Alexandria. General Student, the German airborne commander, had nearly 23,000 men at his disposal – the bulk of Germany's airborne potential – but a lack of JU-52 transport aircraft in which to carry them. A proportion could be taken by glider, and a small number by sea, but if concentration of force was to be achieved, at least one of the three airfields on the island at Maleme, Retimo and Hearaklion had to be taken to allow men to be landed in conventional aircraft. Even then, the initial assault force of 10,000 parachutists had to be divided into three waves as the JU-52s in Greece could only lift a third of the force at any one time. The result was a dangerous diversification of effort, with very costly attacks at different times against each of the airfields. It was only the demoralized state of the Allied garrison that led to eventual German success. After ten days of fighting (May 20-30 1941) the British retreated to the south of the island and were evacuated to North Africa, but the cost to the airborne forces was enormous.

One in four of the German parachutists had been killed, entire battalions had been wiped out; JU-52s had been shot down in alarming numbers and any thought of further assaults in the area had to be discarded. It was a Pyrrhic victory, sounding the death-knell of a German airborne force which had been asked to do too much.

Almost exactly the same happened to the British 1st Airborne Division at Arnhem in September 1944. Their assault on the Dutch town was part of an elaborate airborne plan – code-named Operation *Market Garden* – in which a series of vital bridges at Eindhoven, Veghel, Grave, Nijmegen and Arnhem would be taken and held while the British Second and U.S. First Armies advanced in a rapier-like thrust for northern Holland and, from there, the industrial heartland of Germany. On paper the plan was ambitious but the potential gains were immense, for without the bridges the waterways of Holland could hold up the advance for weeks. In the event, the bulk of the operation was a success, with the British Guards Armoured Division punching through on the ground to link up with the U.S. 101st and 82nd Airborne Divisions at Eindhoven and Nijmegen respectively, but the forces at Arnhem were just too far away. In addition, the 1st Airborne had been dropped too far away from the objective and, although a small group did take and hold the bridge for a short time against tremendous odds, the rest of the force was trapped in fierce fighting which made any attempt at breakout towards the relieving forces impossible to coordinate. It also complicated the process of re-supply as there was no one drop-zone which could serve the whole division, and even when a Polish parachute brigade was put in as reinforcement, the problems remained. They were not eased by the unexpected vehemence of German opposition – the 9th and 10th SS Panzer Divisions had unfortunately chosen the Arnhem area in which to refit after the D-Day battles and so were on hand to counter the element of surprise – nor by a general lack of good communications due to faulty wireless equipment. After nine days of bitter fighting, the 1st Airborne was ordered to withdraw. Of approximately 9000 men dropped since September 17, only about 2400 made their way out on the 25th: once again the airborne units had been asked to do too much.

These two examples should not, of course, be taken to prove that airborne landings during World War II were dogged by failure: on the contrary, there were many successful operations, such as the invasion of Sicily in July 1943, the Normandy landings of June 1944 and the crossing of the Rhine in March 1945, but in all these cases the airborne troops were only expected to take specific tactical objectives which would be consolidated and held by rapidly advancing ground forces. The lesson seems to be that the smaller the committed force and, more important, the less ambitious the objectives, the greater the chance of success. Airborne landings are in essence limited tactical operations; to expect more is to expect too much.

Looking at the situation since 1945, this lesson seems to have been absorbed by those countries that can still afford the luxury of an airborne capability with all its attendant specialist training and equipment. With the possible exception of Dien Bien Phu in 1953/4, most post-war airborne assaults have been tactical affairs, opening the way in fairly unambitious terms for a ground or seaborne attack. The Anglo-French expedition to Suez in November 1956, for example, envisaged parachute drops which were merely a prelude to a seaborne invasion, and although super power pressure forced an end to the operation before it had been completed, this general pattern of events was certainly being followed. Similarly in July 1974 the Turks used their airborne forces to take the high ground in the Kyrenia Mountains of Cyprus which overlooked their landing beaches, and then relieved them quickly before advancing towards Nicosia. Small operations therefore seem to be the key to success, and the trend today in many countries, at least in the West, is to cut down the size of specially trained, expensive airborne units, replacing them with heli-borne forces which seem to offer a new potential, particularly in the difficult area of counter-insurgency. After all, helicopters are relatively cheap, the troops which use them do not need to be trained in completely new skills, and operations involving them can achieve the important element of surprise which slow-moving transport aircraft cannot match. In addition, they are not so dependent upon air superiority, being able to fly below radar cover and at speeds which make their destruction by ground units significantly more difficult. Two examples from the 1973 Arab-Israeli War illustrate the point: on October 6 a Syrian heli-borne force was able to take the important Israeli fortress on top of Mount Hermon with relative ease. On the Israeli side, as the war progressed and the new SAMs and ZSUs threatened to destroy escorting fighters or ground-

attack aircraft, it was reported that Israeli parachute troops refused to jump from slow-moving vulnerable transport aircraft. Technology seems to have destroyed many of the advantages associated with the parachute and glider, although it is interesting to note that the Warsaw Pact still maintains seven regular airborne divisions, with full reserve backing. Clearly, if you can afford to maintain such troops, are virtually guaranteed of air superiority and are planning a swift offensive to link up with troops dropped behind the enemy lines, the airborne potential may still be a viable proposition. Such circumstances are now so rare, however, that few countries really contemplate their regular occurance.

It might be tempting to conclude (reviewing the tactics covered so far) that the aircraft has contributed almost solely to the support of forces on land. This impression is false, however, for, although the processes of transportation, airborne landings and, to a certain extent, strike support are inextricably linked to land operations, the impact of the aircraft has been just as dramatic so far as naval warfare is concerned.

When the war potential of aircraft was first recognized just before the First World War, naval leaders were, if anything, more enthusiastic than their military counterparts. In Britain, for example, the Admiralty encouraged naval officers to learn the new art of flying, and when the Royal Flying Corps (RFC) was formed as a part of the Royal Engineers in May 1912 it included a Naval Wing, initially designed to provide the Navy with the same sort of basic reconnaissance that the Military Wing would give to the Army. The Royal Engineers were a military formation under the control of the War

Office and the inter-service cooperation implied by the inclusion of naval personnel within its ranks could not be expected to last. As a result, by 1914, a separate Royal Naval Air Service (RNAS) had come into existence under Admiralty control. Its duties were unclear, and for a time it merely duplicated the evolving roles of the RFC, but as the First World War progressed it acted as a centre for experimentation and new ideas. When Zeppelin airships attacked naval installations in England as early as 1914, for example, it was RNAS aircraft which were first used in a bombing counter-offensive, hitting Zeppelin sheds as far afield as Cologne and Dusseldorf before the war was six months old. Similarly in 1915, they were the first to be used in air defence when the Navy was given responsibility for trying to shoot down the airships as they raided English towns.

But these were roles which could be – and were – taken over by the other services, and it was not until 1917 that purely naval needs were identified and met. In an age when the fleet was the most important manifestation of naval power, the advantages of aircraft at sea with the capital ships, warning of enemy vessels approaching and tracking submarines, were quickly appreciated. At first, of course, continuous air cover was restricted to areas of sea within range of land, as the aircraft were dependent upon their airfields, and even when experiments were extended to the idea of seaplanes, the necessity of calm water conditions for take-off and landing precluded their presence in many of the important naval areas. But in 1917 the idea of mobile, sea-going air bases was successfully tried,

when a Sopwith Camel fighter of the RNAS took off from and landed upon H.M.S. *Argus*, a converted merchant ship. The aircraft carrier had been born, although it was not to be tried in action before the end of the First World War.

Unlike many other aspects of air power, however, this particular innovation was not ignored during the inter-war period, and although there was no evidence to support the efficacy of the aircraft carrier in a war situation, the major naval powers could not afford to do without it. Consequently, in a period when genuine efforts were being made to limit the size of world navies, with countries scrapping perfectly usable vessels as late as the 1930s, a minor arms race took place, principally among America, Britain and Japan, in the building of aircraft carriers. The reasons are understandable, for all three powers were concerned, or aimed to be concerned, with spreading or maintaining their influence over wide areas of ocean – Britain through the protection of imperial sea-lanes, America and Japan through their growing rivalry in the Pacific. In such circumstances, the flexibility and mobility of aircraft staying with the fleet at all times offered significant advantages, not least in the protection of the fleet itself. By the late 1930s, all three powers had considerable aircraft-carrier potential, the results of which were to be seen during the Second World War.

This was not the only air-power role to affect the naval side of warfare during the inter-war period. For if aircraft could act as early-warning devices and submarine-trackers, there was no reason why they should not extend their duties to include strike support, destroying enemy vessels before they even came in sight of the main fleet. Mitchell, as we have seen, was an ardent believer in the vulnerability of capital ships to air attack but, despite his graphic illustration of the potential when his aircraft sank the *Ostfriesland* in 1921, few believed the threat to be a real one. Never-

The helicopter in Vietnam. The Americans had vast numbers which were used for liaison, ground attack, troop carrying and evacuating wounded. Helicopters enabled them to penetrate remote jungle areas and reinforce troops under attack by the Viet Cong.

theless, even at this early stage it was possible to define fairly clearly the potentialities of naval aircraft, dividing them basically into offensive and defensive roles. On the offensive, the main advantage was the ability of aircraft to attack and destroy enemy shipping, so weakening his overall strength; on the defensive to search out enemy vessels, warn of their approach and protect the fleet when they, or their attendant aircraft, attacked.

Aircraft contributed significantly in all areas of sea conflict throughout the Second World War. So far as its offensive capabilities were concerned, there is even evidence to suggest that the aircraft changed the course of naval history by assisting in destroying the pre-eminence of the battleship, basically by following the ideas put forward by Mitchell in the early 1920s. As early as November 11 1940, when British Swordfish torpedo bombers from H.M.S. *Illustrious* damaged or destroyed a total of three Italian battleships in Toranto harbour, the vulnerability of capital ships to air attack, doubted by so many before the war began, was effectively proved. Not that this convinced the sceptics entirely. Many naval commanders still dismissed the idea of air attack as little more than an irritant, to be dealt with by anti-aircraft guns which were better organized than those of the Italians, but the evidence gradually piled up against them. In May 1941, for example, it was another Swordfish attack which crippled the German battleship *Bismarck*, slowing her down to the extent that she could be surrounded and destroyed by surface vessels. And seven months later, on 7 December 1941, the surprise attack upon Pearl Harbor

by Japanese aircraft, which destroyed or severely damaged some eight American battleships, should have left no doubts at all. Yet within three days of Pearl Harbor, the British battleship *Prince of Wales*, together with the battle-cruiser *Repulse*, was sunk by Japanese air attack off the eastern coast of Malaya. No naval commander could now venture out to sea, nor indeed remain in harbour, without anxiously scanning the skies for enemy aircraft.

It did not take very long to realize, however, that an effective form of naval protection against air attack was to provide constant air cover for the fleet, and this quite naturally brought the aircraft carrier firmly to the fore. Nowhere was this more apparent than in the massive sea areas of the Pacific, where both contending powers, America and Japan, began the war with large numbers of such vessels. Their existence gave the

major battles of the campaign a unique character, with rival fleets fighting through their aircraft rather than their surface vessels. The aim almost became one of gaining air supremacy, with the main targets invariably the enemy's aircraft carriers. The side which managed to destroy the most aircraft or their support vessels tended to force the other to withdraw and so win the battle. The first intimation of this new style of warfare came in May 1942 in the Battle of the Coral Sea, when each side tried to knock out the other's aircraft carriers by air attack. In the event, both suffered losses and the outcome was uncertain, but the Americans kept a slight advantage by managing to repair the carrier *Lexington* before the Japanese could recover. As a result, in the following month at Midway, American air strength was such that it led to the destruction of four Japanese fleet carriers and forced

Air power at sea, SBD Dauntless dive-bombers on the deck of the USS *Lexington*. They have returned from sinking the Japanese light carrier *Shoho*. A day after this picture was taken the *Lexington* herself fell victim to Japanese carrier-based air attacks.

the enemy to stop its wide-ranging naval actions. From then on Japanese battleships and cruisers had to keep to areas which could be covered by land-based aircraft, leaving the Americans with virtual control of the central Pacific. When the land-based potential was destroyed as well, chiefly at the Battle of the Philippine Sea in June 1944, Japanese naval power was, to all intents and purposes, at an end and American victory was in sight.

An interesting characteristic of the Pacific naval battles, particularly Coral Sea and Midway, was that the actual fleets rarely came into visual contact, sometimes steaming away from each other at distances up to 200 miles apart, leaving the aircraft to do the fighting. In many ways this was indicative of the effect that air power had on naval affairs as a whole, for it was also apparent in the Battle of the Atlantic, even though the aircraft was carrying out its defensive role for much of the time. When the German U-boat campaign, coupled with her surface potential and land-based air capability, threatened to cut the vital British life-line with her Empire, and after the Lend-Lease Act of March 1941, America as well, some form of air cover for the convoys was clearly essential. At first this was provided by long-range Coastal Command aircraft such as the Short Sunderland or land-based Liberator, flying from bases in Northern Ireland, Scotland and even Iceland, but they lacked the range to escort vessels more than about a third of the way across the Atlantic. When America entered the war, she too contributed aircraft from her side of the ocean, but this still left a gap in the centre, within which the convoys, devoid of reconnaissance, submarine early-warning and basic air protection, suffered their most grievous losses. It was not until special escort-carriers, equipped with fighter-bombers, were introduced in 1942 that the "air-gap" was closed. Similar techniques were used in both the Mediterranean and the Pacific, contributing to victories which established the aircraft as an essential defensive as well as offensive aid to naval warfare.

There can be little doubt that these roles remain important, although the post-war period has seen something of a decline in naval air potential. Britain is usually put forward as an example, for naval support has suffered considerably as a result of cuts in defence spending. To a certain extent this is understandable and is probably an inevitable outcome of the withdrawal from imperial commitments. At the same time,

vastly improved aircraft ranges and in-flight refuelling facilities have enabled most sea areas to be adequately patrolled from shore bases alone, and when this is added to the expense factor, the decision to phase out aircraft carriers – the most obvious manifestations of naval air potential – is easily comprehensible. At the moment one such vessel, H.M.S. *Ark Royal*, still remains in Britain, but it is destined for the scrapyard by 1980: a fact which leads many commentators to write off the ability of the British to protect their navy from air attack or to contribute to its strike potential is by no means devoid of its air cover.

This, however, ignores the impact of new techniques, for despite the disappearance of floating airfields which were always highly vulnerable targets, the British Navy

role, the development of Thru'-Deck cruisers, designed to do the jobs of carrier and fighting ship combined, maintain the strike potential of the fleet at sea, particularly when equipped with attack helicopters or VTOL (vertical take-off and landing) aircraft such as the Sea Harrier. For the defensive, long-range reconnaissance aircraft such as the Nimrod can act very effectively as the early warning "eyes" of the fleet, while specially equipped helicopters like the Sea King can track submarines and warn of an enemy approach far more effectively than Second World War carrier-based aircraft. The trend, as elsewhere, is towards multi-role equipment, whereby technology can make possible an increasing flexibility of both aircraft and ships by precluding the need to design them for specific roles.

Admittedly the aircraft carrier is far from dead – in areas such as Vietnam or the Eastern Mediterranean, the Americans have still found it a useful mobile support base, delivery platform and command centre – but it is being replaced in many navies by new types of vessels and aircraft with equal, if not greater, capability. It is perhaps no coincidence that the Soviet Navy, during its massive expansion programme of recent years, has not included conventional carriers in its equipment. With vessels like the Kiev – the nearest Soviet equivalent to the Thru'-Deck cruiser – and S/VTOL (short/vertical take-off and landing) aircraft such as the "Forger", there is no need. The techniques and equipment may have changed, but the importance of naval air support remains.

Maintenance
of air space

The final role to be examined – summed up by the phrase "the maintenance of air space" – is not easy to define. Perhaps the simplest way to understand it is in a peacetime context, when the air immediately above a country is internationally recognized as belonging to that country. Thus, if unauthorized aircraft fly through such air, they may be accused of violating the country's air space and run the risk of arrest or even destruction. In a war situation this concept obviously remains valid and is extended to include the air space above the country's armed forces, wherever they may be operating. As all air-power roles whether strategic or tactical, depend to a greater or lesser extent upon the ability of aircraft to move freely, the concept is clearly of paramount importance. Air warfare comes to depend upon the ability to defend or maintain air space while destroying that of the enemy. In other words, the aim is to gain air supremacy – a conquest of enemy air space which may be as effective in defeating him as a conquest of his territories on the ground.

Recognition of the possibilities along these lines undoubtedly came during the First World War. On the Western Front, for example, as soon as aircraft

began to be accepted as aggressive instruments of war, the maintenance of air space over the trench system became essential for secrecy in the planning of offensives and the protection of ground units from air attack. The evolution of the interceptor fighter, designed to carry out this task by destroying enemy reconnaissance and strike aircraft, has already been mentioned, together with the resultant "dog fights" between attacking and defending machines. As the war progressed, however, the Germans appear – yet again – to have been the first to develop the process to the extent of pursuing complete air supremacy, initially through the evolution of fighter "Circuses" (squadrons mobilized from place to place) which attempted to destroy enemy machines in the sky by totally swamping a particular area, and later by means of sustained attacks upon airfields and support services immediately behind the front line. Indeed, by 1917 the Royal Flying Corps was suffering so many losses, not only of aircraft but also of pilots, that German air supremacy was almost achieved. Fortunately for the Allies, a number of events, including the entry of America into the war and, perhaps no less importantly, the death of German

The air battles over the Western Front produced a few men more adept than most as pilots and tacticians; as they ran up a total of 'downed' enemy aircraft they joined that envied and short-lived group known as 'aces'. Two such, US Lt Frank Luke, Jnr left and Capt William Bishop, RFC below pose for pictures which would be treasured by an adoring public at home.

"Circus" leaders like Baron von Richthofen, combined to stop the rot, so that by 1918 it was the turn of the enemy the appreciate the necessity of maintaining air space as his armies came under unopposed air attack. By the end of the war the lesson had been learnt by both sides.

Meanwhile of course, with the Zeppelin and Gotha assaults on Britain, the maintenance of air space on the strategic level had become a matter of national security for one of the contending powers. This led to an increase in the anti-aircraft and fighter defences around the major English cities – which at least implied the possibility of counter-measures but seemed to suggest, through a conspicuous lack of success in 1917 and 1918, that air space was indefensible on a large scale.

This was perhaps an understandable point of view in the relatively unsophisticated days of the 1920s, but as the inter-war period progressed, technology once more swung firmly in favour of the defending side. On the one hand interceptor-fighter design was greatly improved as a spin-off from the air races and air-speed record attempts of the 1930s. By the end of that decade the old biplanes which had experienced problems achieving the height and speed necessary for the destruction of incoming aircraft, had been largely replaced by sleek, fast, more heavily armed monoplanes like the Supermarine Spitfire and Messerschmitt Bf–109 which could hold their own against almost anything else that flew. At the same time, radar made its first appearance, giving to the defending country an instant ability to track attacking aircraft. This in turn gave time for the defending fighters to take up advantageous stations from which they could attack and destroy the hostile machines with the essential element of surprise on their side. These two improvements combined to undermine the belief that domestic air space was impossible to maintain in a war situation, as the Battle of Britain in 1940 effectively displayed.

After the fall of France in the summer of 1940 it seemed natural to expect the next stage of German conquest to be the islands of Britain, for if they remained a centre of opposition the entire western flank of Hitler's empire would be vulnerable. As a consequence, a German invasion of Britain appeared inevitable, particularly when the Royal Air Force reported a significant concentration of barges in the Channel ports of France and the Low Countries and German troops were known to be practising embarkation and disembarkation drills. But from the German side the invasion was not likely to stand much chance of success so long as air space above the invading forces was not secure, and as the majority of the Royal Air Force Fighter Command had survived the Dunkirk evacuation intact, the undefended barges were sure to come under air attack as they crossed the Channel. The Royal Air Force had therefore to be destroyed as an essential tactical preliminary to the entire operation: British air space, at least over the areas of the Channel and South coast, had to be effectively conquered.

This was clearly a task for the Luftwaffe, and the tactics employed appear to have centred initially, in August 1940, upon the idea of putting in bombing raids against targets which the Royal Air Force would be forced to defend, so bringing the Spitfires and Hurricanes into the open for piecemeal destruction by the German fighters. Victory would result, it was argued, simply because the Luftwaffe was numerically

P38J LIGHTNING

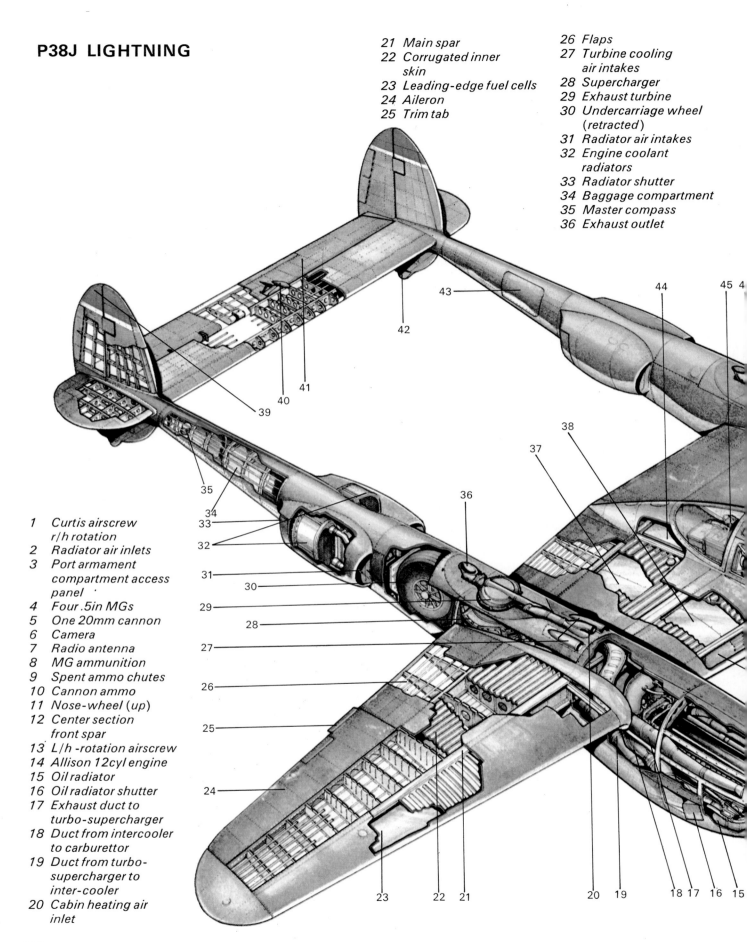

21 Main spar
22 Corrugated inner skin
23 Leading-edge fuel cells
24 Aileron
25 Trim tab
26 Flaps
27 Turbine cooling air intakes
28 Supercharger
29 Exhaust turbine
30 Undercarriage wheel (retracted)
31 Radiator air intakes
32 Engine coolant radiators
33 Radiator shutter
34 Baggage compartment
35 Master compass
36 Exhaust outlet

1 Curtis airscrew r/h rotation
2 Radiator air inlets
3 Port armament compartment access panel
4 Four .5in MGs
5 One 20mm cannon
6 Camera
7 Radio antenna
8 MG ammunition
9 Spent ammo chutes
10 Cannon ammo
11 Nose-wheel (up)
12 Center section front spar
13 L/h -rotation airscrew
14 Allison 12cyl engine
15 Oil radiator
16 Oil radiator shutter
17 Exhaust duct to turbo-supercharger
18 Duct from intercooler to carburettor
19 Duct from turbo-supercharger to inter-cooler
20 Cabin heating air inlet

37 Starboard fuel
   cell
38 Starboard reserve
   fuel cell
39 Starboard rudder
40 Elevator mass
   balance (upper)
41 Elevator
42 Tail skid
43 Battery compartment
44 Fuel surge tank
45 Radio equipment
46 Armor
47 Pilot's seat

48 Rear-view mirror
49 Reflector sight
50 Control column
51 Instrument panel
52 Rudder pedals

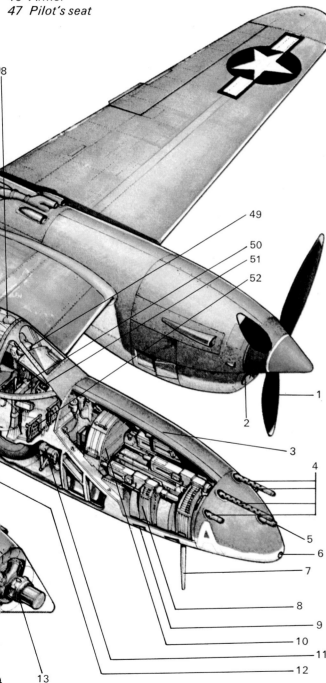

stronger and therefore capable of swamping the enemy – an interesting reversion to the "Circus" tactics of 1917. But things had changed dramatically since the First World War and, although the early raids against Channel convoys, port installations, radar stations and airfields did bring the Royal Air Force to battle, the Luftwaffe commanders had obviously underestimated the two defensive improvements of the inter-war years. The Spitfires and Hurricanes, despite their numerical inferiority, proved more than a match for the majority of Luftwaffe aircraft, forcing a complete withdrawal from the battle of the JU87 Stuka dive-bomber, which suffered crippling casualties in August alone. At the same time, although a number of radar stations on the south coast of England were attacked, the Germans do not seem to have regarded them as important, for enough were left intact for them to continue their essential early warning process, ordering the defending fighters into the sky in time to intercept the enemy raids and so achieve surprise. By mid-September 1940 the Luftwaffe was losing so many aircraft in British air space – a process which meant that any surviving crews automatically ended up as prisoners-of-war – that a change in tactics had to be made.

The ensuing alteration was of integral importance to the outcome of the Battle of Britain, for as the month of September drew to a close the Luftwaffe switched its aim away from the destruction of the Royal Air Force to a strategic bombing offensive against major British cities. As with all such offensives, it was hoped that the enemy's industrial base would be destroyed and the morale of the people undermined. In reality, all that it did was to give the RAF fighters and their support services a vital breathing space, during which their continuing hold over domestic air space was consolidated. The Luftwaffe attempted to by-pass the situation by bombing at night, but it soon became apparent that they had lost the battle. Their initial tactical aim, despite its feasibility, had not been achieved, forcing them into a long-term process of strategic bombing which did nothing to prepare the way for the invading forces. By late 1940 it was obvious that Hitler had lost all interest in Britain now that her defeat could not be obtained by a lightning stroke and, after his embroilment in Russia the following June, all thought of invasion entirely disappeared.

But if the pendulum of technological change had swung in favour of the British in 1940, it was clearly against them when they and their American allies tried

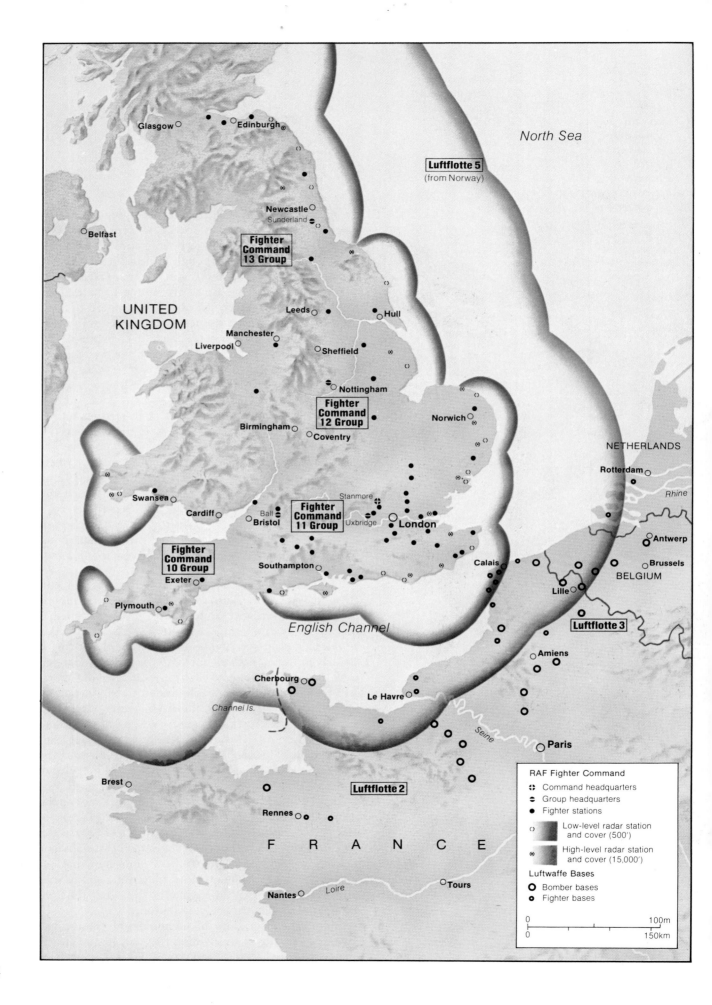

North Sea

Luftflotte 5
(from Norway)

Glasgow
Edinburgh

Belfast

Newcastle
Sunderland

Fighter Command 13 Group

UNITED KINGDOM

Leeds
Hull

Manchester
Liverpool
Sheffield

Nottingham

Birmingham
Coventry

Fighter Command 12 Group

Norwich

NETHERLANDS

Rotterdam

Rhine

Swansea

Cardiff

Stanmore

Ball
Bristol

Fighter Command 11 Group

Uxbridge

London

Antwerp

Brussels

BELGIUM

Lille

Fighter Command 10 Group

Exeter

Plymouth

Southampton

Calais

Luftflotte 3

English Channel

Amiens

Cherbourg

Channel Is.

Le Havre

Seine

Paris

Brest

Luftflotte 2

Rennes

F R A N C E

Nantes

Loire

Tours

RAF Fighter Command
- ⊕ Command headquarters
- ⊖ Group headquarters
- ● Fighter stations
- ◗ Low-level radar station and cover (500')
- ⊗ High-level radar station and cover (15,000')

Luftwaffe Bases
- ○ Bomber bases
- ◉ Fighter bases

0   100m
0   150km

A Messerschmitt 262 jet fighter caught in the camera guns of a diving Allied Mustang. The 262 was the last attempt to win control of German air space. Left: The Battle of Britain — without control of British air space the German navy and army would not have survived an assault on the British Isles. The margin of success and failure was very fine and the British 'victory' reflects the German decision to turn east and attack Russia.

from the front, sides and rear, and medium bombers even dropped fragmentation bombs from above. The American formations broke under the sheer weight of attack and the bombers were picked off one by one as the interceptors or anti-aircraft guns concentrated upon each in turn. Similarly, during the Royal Air Force night-time raids, radar was used to pinpoint the bomber stream and special night-fighters were guided into its midst, locating individual aircraft by means of air-radar and then attacking suddenly and invariably effectively. As late as March 1944, during a raid on Nuremberg, these tactics were working well enough for the Germans to destroy ninety-seven Lancasters and Halifaxes in one night. In such circumstances the defending power still seemed to hold much of the initiative.

The American decision to concentrate upon the total destruction of the Luftwaffe after late 1943 was clearly the turning point in Allied efforts to conquer German air space, although it is interesting to note that the basic tactics involved were very similar to those used by the Germans in 1917 and 1940. During the months when strategic bombing was possible in 1944, the Americans put in raids against targets the enemy was forced to defend, and when his interceptors arrived on the scene the P51 escort-fighters proved their worth by knocking them out of the sky. By the time of the D-Day invasion air space over the occupied countries of Western Europe was firmly in Allied hands, and by late 1944 the Luftwaffe had virtually ceased to exist. There can, of course, be little doubt that factors such as improved Allied offensive techniques, a growing lack of the vital materials needed to sustain the Luftwaffe, and the steady Allied advances on the ground all contributed to this destruction of German air superiority. However, the appearance and re-appearance of massed formations of Allied bombers and their escort-fighters day after day literally swamped the defensive capability of the Luftwaffe.

Events since 1945 reinforce this general conclusion, particularly in the context of the Arab-Israeli Wars. The Israelis, for instance, have come to depend for success upon the concept of mobile campaigns, not unlike the Second World War *blitzkrieg* idea, and for this they need to maintain complete air supremacy, at least immediately above and in front of their advancing ground forces. In the 1967 War this was achieved by means of the pre-emptive strike when, on the morning of June 5, the Israeli air force struck without warning at

to conquer German air space during the strategic bombing offensive upon the enemy homeland. We have already seen what happened when the Allied bombers tried to destroy German industrial targets: the British suffered losses up to 50 per cent of the committed force as early as 1939, while the Americans experienced the full effect of interceptor fighters and anti-aircraft defences during their raids on Schweinfurt in 1943. Indeed, by the latter date the Germans had developed their air-defence systems almost to perfection, using a combination of ground and air radar, fighter-control stations, good interceptor aircraft and effective anti-aircraft guns. In addition, their tactics were usually more than adequate: during the Schweinfurt raids, for example, radar and visual sightings guided the interceptors on to the B-17 "box" formations, whereupon the Americans were hit from every conceivable angle by almost anything that could fly. Messerschmitt 109 and 110 and Focke Wulf 190 fighters attacked the boxes

235

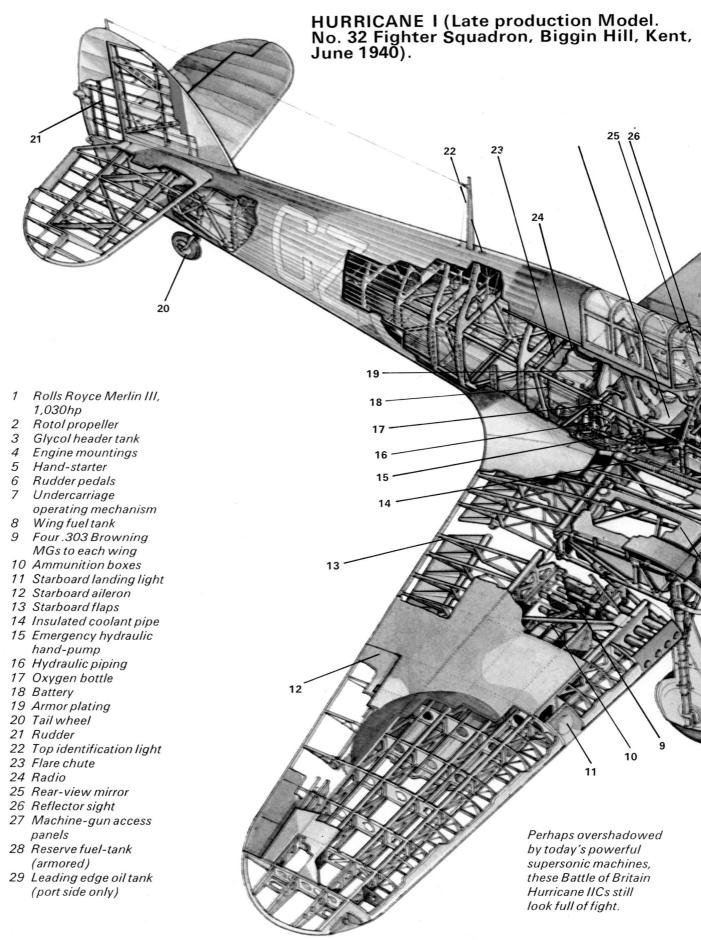

HURRICANE I (Late production Model. No. 32 Fighter Squadron, Biggin Hill, Kent, June 1940).

1 Rolls Royce Merlin III, 1,030hp
2 Rotol propeller
3 Glycol header tank
4 Engine mountings
5 Hand-starter
6 Rudder pedals
7 Undercarriage operating mechanism
8 Wing fuel tank
9 Four .303 Browning MGs to each wing
10 Ammunition boxes
11 Starboard landing light
12 Starboard aileron
13 Starboard flaps
14 Insulated coolant pipe
15 Emergency hydraulic hand-pump
16 Hydraulic piping
17 Oxygen bottle
18 Battery
19 Armor plating
20 Tail wheel
21 Rudder
22 Top identification light
23 Flare chute
24 Radio
25 Rear-view mirror
26 Reflector sight
27 Machine-gun access panels
28 Reserve fuel-tank (armored)
29 Leading edge oil tank (port side only)

Perhaps overshadowed by today's powerful supersonic machines, these Battle of Britain Hurricane IICs still look full of fight.

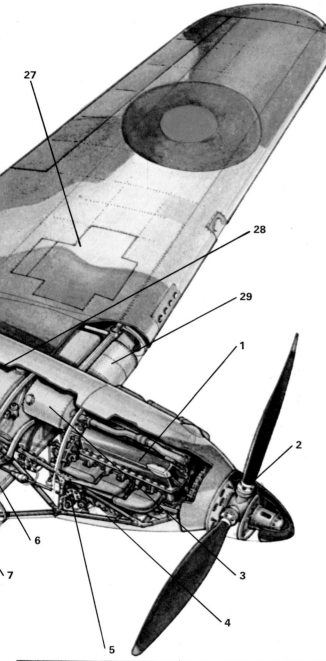

airfields in Egypt, Syria and Jordan. The Arab aircraft were dispersed in neat rows while their pilots and ground crews were at breakfast, and in less than three hours Egypt lost some 300 machines while the air forces of the other two states were entirely wiped out. This was the ultimate in the "swamping" technique of offensive air conquest, and led quite naturally to Israeli ground success as the armour and infantry units advanced into Sinai, Golan and Jerusalem unopposed by air attack. Arab air space had been conquered before the war had really begun.

Such brazen disregard for the niceties of war could hardly be repeated, however, and as soon as the Arab states recovered they began to improve their defensive positions for the future. With Russian aid, special hardened hangars were built to protect each of the replacement Mig fighters, and a completely new generation of anti-aircraft weapons was procured. In addition, when the next round of war broke out in October 1973, the Arabs made sure that they would escape another pre-emptive strike by attacking first, and when the Israeli Phantoms and Skyhawks tried to recover the initiative they encountered a solid wall of surface-to-air missiles and sophisticated anti-aircraft guns. The old SAM2s and 3s, which had proved little more than an irritant in 1967, had been replaced by mobile SAM6s and manportable SAM7s, while the radar-controlled ZSU-23-4s added a whole new dimension to effective air defence. Admittedly, the Israeli pilots did counter these measures to a certain extent, chiefly through Electronic Counter Measures (ECM) and a basic change in tactics which involved low-level attacks under the radar cover, but they lost valuable aircraft in the process and the idea of wide-ranging mobile ground offensives seemed extremely costly. The pendulum appeared still to be on the side of the defending power.

It is difficult to say to what extent this affects the situation today, particularly if we consider the Central Front in Europe should a war occur between NATO and the Warsaw Pact. So far as NATO, as the defending power, is concerned, technology appears to be acting in her favour, and with weapons systems such as Rapier, Blowpipe and Dragon available, Warsaw Pact air attacks upon the ground forces are likely to be opposed fairly effectively. But air warfare is a two-way business, and while the NATO forces are being protected in this manner, their air elements will be looking for opportunities to attack the enemy advance.

Right: An RAF Hawker Siddeley Harrier fires a salvo of air-to-ground rockets. The Harrier is also used by the US Marine Corps. Its vertical take-off capability allows it to be deployed close to the forward edge of the battle area.

Below: An American F86A Saber fires rockets at a ground target during the Korean War.

As the Warsaw Pact is equipped with many of the weapons used to effectively by the Arabs in 1973, and has of course improved them since that time, their air space too is going to be difficult to infiltrate. Air supremacy will have to be achieved by one side or the other if ground forces are to be effective, and the end result may be a return to the "swamping" technique, with either the pre-emptive strike or sheer numerical superiority tilting the balance. Since technology began to affect air warfare in the 1930s, these are the only measures which seem to have successfully countered the continuing defensive advantage in the maintenance of air space.

Conclusion

In order to sum up, a few general points only need to be made: firstly, it is apparent that the aircraft has never won a war alone using purely conventional weapons, despite the claims of the inter-war air theorists. The problems of mounting and executing a

The weapons of deterrence: Below: A USAAF fighter fires a Genie air-to-air missile, the Geni a range of up to six miles. Left: With a range of n 3000 miles, a Poseidon nuclear missile at the mo of launch from a submerged submarine.

successful bombing campaign on a strategic leve immense, and unless the weapons to be usec instantly devastating, the defending country invariably be able to hold out for a substantial p of time. Nuclear weapons are powerful enoug provide this instant devastation, but their use wou self-defeating in an age of mutual assured destruc For this reason, it is probable that a war involving full-scale commitment will never occur. Such an a ment, however, does call into serious question strategic viability of air power, for although ce aspects of transport and reconnaissance could, select number of cases, be termed strategic in they are nowhere near important enough to justify ideas of Douhet or Mitchell. The first overall clusions would therefore seem to be that the air has never really discovered an effective place in strategy of war.

But this should not be taken to mean that the im of air power has been small, for as the second gen point it is equally apparent that in the various tacr roles examined above, the aircraft has added a c pletely new and effective dimension to the face modern battle. In the sphere of reconnaissance ob vation, it has enabled commanders to see "the ot side of the hill" with unprecedented clarity; in tha tactical strike support interdiction the teeth of grou forces have been considerably sharpened; in the ar of transport, airborne landings, naval support and maintenance of air space, increased flexibility, mobil offensive and defensive powers have contributed t string of remarkable success. Technology may ca the importance of these roles to fluctuate from time time, but the tactical potential of air power remai The pre-eminence of these tactical roles has be officially recognized, and a quote from Sir Andr Humphrey, Chief of the British Defence Staff, appe to sum up the contribution of modern air power ve well indeed. Writing in 1976, he says. "Control of t air in war involves not only the guaranteeing of fr movement for our own troops and supplies, but al freedom to use the air space that matters to us f defence, offense, and reconnaissance while at the san time denying it to the enemy."

And to control the air, aircraft bring certa characteristics which are not shared by land or s forces – the ability to carry weapons over long rang at great speed, the ability to concentrate rapidly lar forces over a distant point, the ability to switch targe and to surprise and déceive – in a word, flexibility.

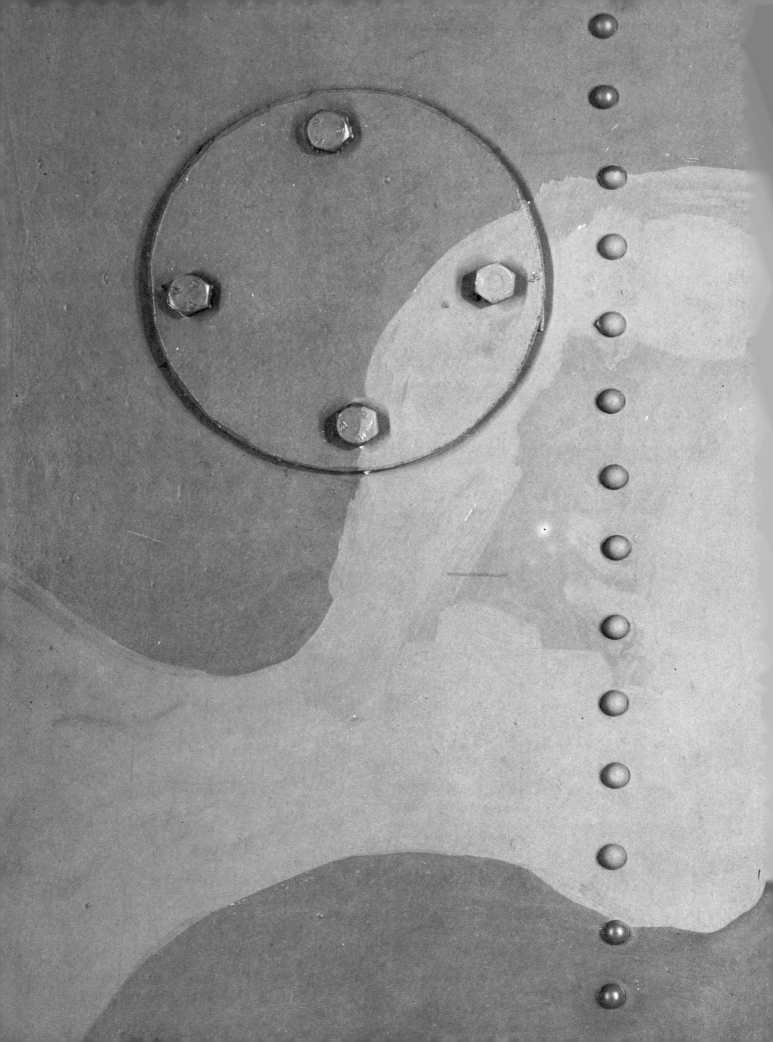